1001
Ideas to Create Retail Excitement

Prentice Hall Press

1001
Ideas to Create Retail Excitement

∎∎∎

EDGAR A. FALK

PRENTICE HALL

PRENTICE HALL
Published by the Penguin Group
Penguin Group (USA) Inc., 375 Hudson Street, New York, New York 10014, U.S.A.
Penguin Books Ltd, 80 Strand, London WC2R 0RL, England
Penguin Books Australia Ltd, 250 Camberwell Road, Camberwell,
    Victoria 3124, Australia
Penguin Books Canada Ltd, 10 Alcorn Avenue,
    Toronto, Ontario, Canada M4V 3B2
Penguin Books India (P) Ltd, 11 Community Centre, Panchsheel Park,
    New Delhi—110 017, India
Penguin Books (N.Z.) Ltd, Cnr Rosedale and Airborne Roads, Albany,
    Auckland, New Zealand
Penguin Books (South Africa) (Pty) Ltd, 24 Sturdee Avenue,
    Rosebank, Johannesburg 2196, South Africa

Penguin Books Ltd, Registered Offices:
80 Strand, London WC2R 0RL, England

First published in the United States of America by Prentice Hall, Inc. 1994
This revised edition published 2003

10   9   8   7   6   5   4   3   2   1

Copyright © Penguin Group (USA) Inc., 1994, 2003
All rights reserved

Publisher's Note
This publication is designed to provide accurate and authoritative information in regard to the subject matter covered. It is sold with the understanding that the publisher is not engaged in rendering legal, accounting or other professional services. If you require legal advice or other expert assistance, you should seek the services of a competent professional.

LIBRARY OF CONGRESS CATALOGING-IN-PUBLICATION DATA

Falk, Edgar A.
    1001 ideas to create retail excitement / Edgar A. Falk.—[Rev. ed.]
        p.   cm.
    Rev. ed. of: 1,001 ideas to create retail excitement. c1994.
    Includes index.
    ISBN 0-7352-0343-1
    1. Retail trade.   2. Sales promotion.   3. Marketing.   I. Title: One thousand one ideas to
create retail excitement.   II. Falk, Edgar A. 1,001 ideas to create retail excitement.   III. Title.

    HF5429.F242   2003
    658.8'2—dc21   2003050680

Printed in the United States of America   ∞
Designed by Katy Riegel

*This book is dedicated to Tina,
my nieces Julie, Karen, and Susan,
and my nephew Gary.*

Acknowledgments

A book on retailing cannot be written without acknowledging the millions of men and women who have dedicated their lives to the profession. We come in contact with them day-in and day-out and learn so much from these daily visits to their stores and shops. Much of what we have written has been inspired by what we have observed over the past thirty-five years as we have traveled and shopped throughout the United States. While we are based in New York City, the so-called retail hub of America, we have met some of the sharpest and most knowledgeable retailers in some of the smallest cities and towns in the country. We thank them for the knowledge they imparted to us.

We also want to thank the many trade associations, government agencies, and retail resources for their time and input. We are particularly grateful to the trade associations for the support they gave to the original edition. And to our readers, we want to thank you, too, for your support of the original edition, and we hope you find this revised edition equally helpful.

Contents

Preface: Meeting the Marketing Challenges of the Twenty-first Century

THE FIRST EDITION OF *1001 Ideas to Create Retail Excitement* helped tens of thousands of independent retailers meet the marketing challenges of the 1990s. But the 1990s are history and the smaller retailers today face the even greater challenges of the twenty-first century.

This revised edition of *1001 Ideas to Create Retail Excitement* explores these new challenges and the steps retailers must take to meet them. Seven new chapters have been added as well as many additional marketing techniques, ideas, and opportunities for retailers and restaurateurs.

This new edition provides insight into changes that can be expected to take place in the United States over the next decade that will impact retail. It outlines the steps the independent retailer must take to stay on top of these changes and convert them into opportunities for growth.

- It shows you how to become more aggressive, competitive, and promotion-minded in marketing your store.
- It shows how to make your place of business a more exciting and interesting place—a place people will not only want to visit but will go out of their way to visit more frequently.
- It provides you with an extensive menu of ideas and suggestions that

will enable you to develop an effective marketing program and create
the retail excitement to make your store that desired customer destination:

- Ideas on how to develop information and statistical data about your
  customers and potential customers so that you will have a better un-
  derstanding of who they are and how to reach them
- Ideas for successfully building local traffic through the Internet
- Ideas on seasonal and holiday promotions
- Ideas for sales and special events
- Ideas for building repeat business and incremental sales
- Ideas for cross promoting with other stores
- Ideas for developing community involvement programs
- Ideas for getting publicity in local media
- Ideas for working with fellow smaller retailers to promote joint in-
  terests to assure the future of independent-owned store retailing in
  your community
- Ideas for the retailer challenged by chain competition

How many of these ideas a retailer will use will vary from store to
store. It will depend upon your objectives, your budget, your staff, your
merchandise, your pricing, and your customers. Only you—being on the
scene—are in the position to develop the necessary data, evaluate the situation, and make the final decision on how to market your store or
restaurant. And only you can decide which of the many ideas will help
you fulfill your objectives and have the greatest amount of impact upon
your customers and potential customers.

Retail marketing is an idea-driven industry, and there is no such
thing as "too many ideas" in the business. Undoubtedly, your creative
juices will start flowing as you read *1001 Ideas to Create Retail Excitement,* and you will come up with additional ideas, or modify an idea to
better suit your specific needs. Some readers of our original edition used
the book as a takeoff point to brainstorm additional promotions, sales,
and special events with their managers and sales staff.

We encourage you to do that. It's one way to make your staff more
promotion-minded and give them a greater feeling of participation in
marketing the store. And you will be amazed to find that some of the
greatest ideas will come from the people you least expect.

To get the most out of this book, we ask that you recognize that the days
of just opening the doors and waiting for the customers to shop the store

are long gone. To be a successful retailer today, you must become a well-rounded expert in all phases of the business. You must know what you are doing at all times and leave nothing to chance.

- You must know who your audience is.
- You must know what your audience wants.
- You must know how to reach your audience.
- You must know how to broaden the base of that audience.
- You must know how to get that audience to shop more often.
- You must know how to get that audience to spend more money each time it shops.

You must know how to create excitement at retail!
Good luck!

Edgar A. Falk
edgarafalk@earthlink.net

1

■■■

The Changing Face of Retail . . .
and You Are in the Driver's Seat

*In business as in life, so many things that we do not have control
over occur and create situations which change the level of the playing field . . . but that doesn't mean you can't climb the hill and
plant the flag on top.*

NEVER HAS A nation undergone such dramatic changes in virtually every aspect of life as the United States since the end of World War
II, and probably no area of business has felt and continues to feel the impact of these changes as much as retail.

The massive increase in automobile ownership; the development of
major highway systems; the growth of suburbia; the birth of television,
the computer, and other technologies; the introduction of credit cards; a
better educated and more health-conscious consumer population; sharp
increases in both imported products and the foreign-born population;
baby boomers and longer life spans; more leisure time and changing
lifestyles; and an unprecedented rise in the standard of living have im-
pacted on virtually every aspect of how we do business.

As a result, since the the mid-1940s, the entire face of retail has
changed and continues to evolve. There is a continuous cycle of new
product introductions and categories created as a result of unbelievable
technological advances, an ongoing development of creative marketing
techniques to bring these products to the consumer's attention, and the
launch of new methods and outlets for selling through to the consumer.

We have grown from a nation of primarily mom and pop stores with
a limited number of department and variety stores, the Sears Roebuck

catalog, and the Fuller Brush man to a retail universe, which includes massive shopping centers and malls, discount stores, specialized catalog houses, large chains, specialty retailers, superstores, outlet centers, direct mail, cable television shopping channels, telemarketing, and now the Internet.

And as this change evolved, we saw many traditional forms of retail disappear or greatly decrease in volume and importance, including downtown shopping areas, door-to-door salesmen, and long-established department stores and chains. Scores of independent retailers also failed to make the cut.

We also saw significant fallout among many of the "new" retailers because they could not live up to expectations. Lack of consumer response, bad customer service, poor profit pictures, pricing policies, poor locations, oversaturation, underfinancing, wrong product mixes, bad marketing concepts, and rigid competition forced shopping centers and malls, telemarketers, e-commerce start-ups, mass discounters, specialty retailers, superstores, and even the so-called category killers, out of business.

In spite of all this turmoil there were many survivors in the small retailer category. Those independent retailers who had an understanding of what was going on and adjusted their operations to take advantage of new opportunities that developed as a result of these changes and trends not only survived but thrived. Those who conducted "business as usual," unfortunately, did not. Being able to meet these challenges of change has made the difference between success and failure at retail, and it will continue to do so during the twenty-first century.

To the small independent store owner, retail should not be as complex a business as it is to its large publicly owned competitors. It is really a business based on common sense. A key to the success of the small independent retailer is never to lose sight of the fact that your number one goal is to please your customers. Do that and you will be successful and make money.

Pleasing your customers requires a thorough understanding of your advantages as well as the development of a strategy that enables you to maximize these advantages.

You have many advantages because you are small. As a small independent retailer, you are in complete control of your destiny, an enviable position to be in since it gives you a significant edge over the so-called big guys of retailing.

- You are on the scene, know everything that is going on in the store, and make all of the decisions. The management of no national chain has its hand on the pulse of the action like you do. It must depend upon reports from the field, spread sheets, and infrequent management visits, all of which may not provide a totally accurate or objective picture of what's going on.

- Your allegiance is to your customers since they are going to provide you with your profits, while the management of the large national retailers you are competing against all too often are concentrating on pleasing their shareholders and the security analysts whose forecasts and judgments usually influence the value of the company stock as well as its management's job security. Often, large retailers must respond to demands for faster expansion, increased profits, cutting sales and overhead costs, and other steps aimed at quickly increasing the value of the stock with results that may be counterproductive to the best interests of their customers.

- You know your customers and their needs, what products they will buy, the prices they'll pay, and the hours they like to shop. You are not going to pull a "Bradlees." When that now out-of-business chain opened up a unit in the heart of New York City it quickly sank deeply into red ink because, as its then president admitted, they had the wrong product lines for that location. The CEO at the time, Mark Cohen, was quoted as saying in the *New York Daily News,* "They don't want snow blowers or 80-pound bags of fertilizer or grass seed or lawn mowers. When we opened, that's what we were trying to sell New Yorkers."

- Rather than carrying out rigid policies dictated by a corporate headquarters twenty-three hundred miles away, you have total flexibility in addressing local marketing and promotional opportunities as well as developing personalized customer-service policies, based on the needs of your customers and local traditions. You can quickly make changes to take advantage of targets of opportunity as they pop up. You can immediately structure a promotion or a policy to counter a competitor's effort, make the decision to participate in a joint promotion with another local retailer, participate in a special advertising supplement, or enhance your standing as a good citizen by immediately responding to a local emergency. In a large northeastern city, when local police attempted to place wanted posters in stores in an area where a serial rapist had been operating, the managers of several chains turned them down for "national policy" reasons. It wasn't until local media exposed this information that the embarrassed headquarters' offices finally agreed to cooperate. Naturally, all the locally owned stores earned the appreciation of the community while the chains were panned in the media.

■ Most important, you are a known quantity to your customers because of your personal reputation and the image earned as a citizen of the community. You are not a hired gun, who is taking money out of the community. As a local retailer you are making a significant economic contribution to the community by keeping that money in the community.

So, you are in the driver's seat! Don't move over!

But all these advantages will add up to zilch if you don't use them to take the bold steps required to meet the challenges of change. Unfortunately, this is where too many independent retailers lose the game.

The reason? *The resistance to change and the fear of failure.* These are probably the two greatest inhibitors of not only retail success but also success in life.

Often people grow accustomed to one way of doing things and see no reason why they should not continue in the same way. There is a fear that if they make changes in the way they conduct their business, they may fail. They may not be making as much money as they had in the past or attracting as many customers as they would like, but they are afraid to risk their present profitability picture by trying something new and different. Instead of trying to build their business and increase their profits, they fear that any changes might backfire, and the profit picture will get even worse. Change is considered a bad gamble. Status quo is considered the safe way to go. Unfortunately, all too often it is the status quo that is the bad gamble. Time passes by the merchant who resists change.

Some people carry this resistance to change to an even greater extreme. These are the men and women who feel that by making changes, they are admitting they were wrong in the past and that this admission of weakness will impact negatively on the minds of their customers. While this thinking is totally illogical, there are retailers who actually think this way. They are letting their egos get in the way of progress and profits.

Other retailers feel that size is a restricting force. They feel they are too small to benefit from any changes. What they fail to recognize is that size is immaterial when it comes to retail success. Just about every successful large retailer around today started out with a small operation, some with just pushcarts. *It is not the size of the retailer in the competition, but rather the size of the competitiveness in the retailer.*

To meet the challenges of change, a retailer must be ready, willing, and able to make all necessary changes to keep his or her store competitive. He or she has to forget about the fear of failure. Failure will occur only if you do not take action to stay in the ball game. As President Franklin D. Roosevelt said in his first inaugural address, "The only thing we have to fear is fear itself."

The sign of a champion is the person who makes adjustments during competition so that he or she will keep the title. A retailer must do the same. He or she must closely follow the changes and trends taking place in retail both nationally and in the local environment, determine how these trends are, or will be, affecting his or her business, and what steps he or she must take to remain an important local player.

This is especially important in the twenty-first century where vying for the consumer dollar is going to become more sophisticated, more competitive, and more challenging.

2

---■■■---

You Can't Go It Alone

ONE THING YOU must recognize is that while you may be in business for yourself, it is imperative that in the twenty-first century you take a much broader and more active interest and role in dealing with some of the problems that threaten small retailers as a group.

This is going to require that you work with fellow independent retailers, including at times with your competitors, to develop strategies and programs that will insure a healthy pro–small retail environment in your city.

Unfortunately, this has been an area too many small retailers have overlooked and is one of the reasons why local governments have often bowed to the pressures of national chains and big boxes. These big national corporations have been able to steamroller all types of concessions from municipal and county governments primarily because smaller retailers have all too often not been properly organized and lacked clout with their own governments. It is not uncommon for the newcomers in town to get tax breaks, as well as improvements in traffic patterns and even new streets and access roads from highways. And some of those new traffic patterns may make it harder for your customers to reach your store.

By the time local retailers find out what is going on, it is often too late to fight off the well-financed public relations programs and lobbying efforts. Small retailers must become more organized and vocal as a group so that government will be more responsive to its voice and needs. And it is not that difficult to achieve.

The initial step should be to organize a small steering group of retailers to evaluate the work, purpose, and results of existing business-oriented organizations in the community. A key role of this group would be to determine the clout each of these organizations has over elected city and county officials. It is also important to study each organization's membership roll. If retailers represent a small percentage while developers represent large numbers, you can be pretty certain that it might not be an organization that will represent the best interest of small retailers.

If none of the existing groups have been very effective in representing the small retailer interests, it probably makes sense to consider establishing your own local association. Your problems and needs are unique so that a small retailers-only organization may be the only way you are going to be able to achieve the power needed to speak with a unified voice. A well-organized group will become a very persuasive force in advocating its positions and gain the support and respect of both the community and its elected officials. When you add up the combined customer base of all the small retailers in the city, it represents a very significant voting bloc, which can become a great asset to your cause.

What can such a small retailer association do?

■ Conduct an educational program aimed at the movers and shakers of the community as well as the customers of its member retailers. One main point to stress is the combined dollar impact small retailers have on the community, including cumulative figures on gross sales, taxes, payroll, and number of jobs represented, as well as the fact that the profits of each business stay in the area rather than get sent back to a headquarters city a thousand or so miles away. The small retailer banks locally; uses local attorneys and accountants; and purchases many of his office and business supplies in town, instead of ordering them from a headquarters location. And the small retailer is a good citizen involved in all types of community events and programs. This educational program can be accomplished through writing periodic newsletters and personal letters and socializing with the movers and shakers at various events, becoming involved in the various pet community projects of movers and shakers, writing op-ed pieces for local media, providing fact sheets and other information to the business editors of newspapers and magazines, and arranging appearances on local radio and television business and public affairs programs. Each retailer should be assigned to personally lobby and keep in touch with individual movers and shakers. At least twice a year, the group should schedule a luncheon or social event. An annual luncheon might be held early in the year and a cocktail party just before the holiday selling season kicks off in November. The contact with customers should include a semiannual or a quarterly newsletter distributed at the store, distribution of reprints of favorable articles from the local media, as well as occasional informal chats with customers while they are in the store, and informational material on Web sites.

■ Each retailer should get to know the elected officials from the areas in which his or her store, as well as home, are located. He or she can send letters to the legislators who represent the district in which the store is located, inviting them to drop in the next time they are near the store. Every retailer should attend community meetings and greet the elected officials, always mentioning the store's name and the association, and send a follow-up letter the following day with positive comments on some of the things the official said during the presentation. He or she should coordinate with fellow members to see that a copy of every news-letter is sent to each official, with a covering letter from one of the retailers who has developed a good rapport with the person. As the retailer gets to know the official a little better he or she should tell him or her some of the problems smaller retailers are having in the community. And as part of the legislator's constituency service, he or she can always pass along requests for help on problems the retailer may be having that are unique to his or her store. The association should sponsor a "Government Day" at least once a year, inviting all elected officials to a special luncheon in their honor.

■ The program aimed at local elected officials can become a little more complicated when it comes to actually influencing legislation. You will need someone familiar with local lobbying and campaign finance laws to advise you since regulations can vary from city to city. The association might want to establish a political action committee to handle member contributions to the various elected officials' campaign committees. In addition, a strong program of lobbying both the executive and legislative branches of the city and/or county governments should be initiated. The format would have to comply with local regulations. The goal of the program would be to deal actively with individual officials regarding potential legislation that impacts on small retailers' interests. It should include proposing legislation that will protect and benefit your interests as well as opposing legislation that will have a negative effect on your business. In addition to closely following the legislative process, it is also very important to be aware of proposed changes in ordinances and regulations that are often made after hearings by the various appointed boards and commissions within local government, as well as by the mayor through executive orders. There is usually a state retailers association that monitors the activity of the state legislature and governor's office as well as lobbies them on issues of importance to retailers. However, these associations represent all retailers—both large and small—so you will want to get to know the men and women who represent your area in the state legislature, too. Some of the state associations will also track pending legislation in cities, but they usually do not actually lobby the city governments. Instead, they make the members in that city aware of the pending law changes so they can do their own lobbying. This lobbying effort must be aggressive. Use as many retailers as possible and as often as possible to reach out to the legislators so that they recognize you are a powerful group of businesspeople who must be taken seriously.

■ When legislation is actually, or about to be, introduced, is when the association goes into overdrive. You have already provided a general education to the movers and shakers and customers. Now is the time to get these people to act. You want to encourage your customers to bombard the legislators with letters and calls supporting your stand; you want to get the movers and shakers to call the legislators (most will know them personally); and you want to get the local media to take an editorial stand on your behalf. You will also want to send letters, as taxpayers and residents, to your legislators. Depending on local lobbying laws, you might want to arrange group meetings with the officials; pack hearings and the legislative chamber when bills are being discussed; and even bring down droves of customers to support your cause at rallies outside the local city hall.

■ While the association might involve itself in nonpolitical and nongovernmental activities in the community, its primary reason for being should be to protect the interests of local small retailers. Association members will probably want to continue to be active in other business groups in the community so that they remain aware of what they are doing and make use of some of their services. And of course, those members of any local merchants associations would want to continue their involvement since these groups are basically organized for the purpose of marketing a shopping district.

- To enhance its overall image, once a year, the group should arrange a citywide "Small Retailer Day." It should include a supplement in the daily newspaper, with additional copies available at all stores; a proclamation from the mayor and/or county supervisor and a series of events aimed at focusing in on the importance of the small retailer to the community. The group might also want to get involved in an important high visibility community project such as a children's hospital or scholarship fund. The goal would be to become the "naming sponsor" of the project so that the community will always hear and see the words *small retailer* whenever the project is mentioned. And whenever they see those words people will recognize the importance of the small retailer to the community.

IMPROVING THE RETAIL NEIGHBORHOOD

The concern of every retailer should be the environment of the area in which his or her store is located. Its streets should be clean. There should be adequate parking and policing, well maintained residential and office buildings, good lighting at night, and a low crime rate. A retail district that offers this type of environment will attract large numbers of browsers and shoppers, and have a high occupancy rate of quality shops.

This just doesn't happen by itself. It takes planning, organization, money, and people to create a good shopping environment. Malls are relatively easy to create since developers start from scratch. Improving an existing shopping district within a city is a lot more complicated. There are two programs through which such improvement is being done throughout the United States.

Business Improvement Districts

Business Improvement Districts, commonly known as BIDs, are established by municipal governments to improve a specific area after its commercial property owners approve the concept and agree to pay an annual special assessment to finance its activities.

The BID members, as they are called, elect their own board of directors and appoint an executive director, who in turn hires a staff. As its name implies, the purpose of the BID is to improve the specific business district it covers. What it does and how it does it will vary from city to city and even from district to district in cities where there is more than one BID.

BID activities that have had positive impact include additional security and sanitation services, the installation of new lighting, new benches on sidewalks, distinctive street signage, retail promotions, special events, and guides. The list is endless.

In the northern California city of Fortuna, among other things, the BID administers a gift-certificate program for its retailers. It promotes the program among the area's larger employers, urging them to use the gift certificate as an alternative to cash gifts, or gift certificates they might ordinarily give for use at other retail destinations. It also promotes the Fortuna gift certificates to the general public as an option for gifts to friends and family during holidays and other times of the year.

In Massachusetts, the Springfield BID has a four-phase program: "Clean It Up" supplies additional maintenance seven days a week in the form of sidewalk sweeping and graffiti removal. "Spruce It Up" includes floral plantings, hanging baskets, theme banners, lighting, and the Springfield Guide program. "Liven It Up" includes producing a number of large scale events along with maintaining a Web site, event calendar, and toll-free telephone number. "Sell It!" involves its general marketing program, including a real estate availability database.

In New York City, the Madison Avenue BID arranged for more than sixty boutiques on the avenue to join forces with forty of its art galleries to produce "Where Fashion Meets Art," with each participating retailer exhibiting art from one of the galleries. Restaurants on the avenue also participated in the month-long event.

Main Street Program

A longer range, more comprehensive effort adopted by about fourteen hundred communities across the country is the Main Street Program, designed to reverse the economic decline of the central business districts in cities by focusing on their revitalization and economic development within the context of historic preservation.

Typically, interest in developing a Main Street program comes from business or property owners, city government, bankers, civic clubs, the chamber of commerce, historic preservationists, and other civic-minded groups within that city. Leaders from both the public and private sectors discuss goals, establish an independent nonprofit organization, raise money to hire a manager, and create committees and a board of directors to carry out the work. The program's participants examine the commercial district's needs and opportunities and develop a long-term, incremental strategy to strengthen the community's commercial activity and improve its buildings. Financing of the program comes from the local entities who have a stake in downtown: city government, merchants, business, and the public.

According to the National Trust for Historic Preservation's National Main Streets Center (**www.mainstreet.org**), in a period of more than twenty years, main street revitalization efforts have created 227,000 jobs and 56,000 businesses, and have saved 89,000 historic buildings all across the country. Communities involved in Main Street programs range from Blanchardville, Wisconsin (population 821), to San Diego, California (population 1.2 million).

Merchants Associations

Even without the formal structure of a BID or Main Street program, retailers from within an area in the city can get together to jointly promote it as a shopping destination. They usually form a merchants association and design a distinctive logo, which is usually displayed in windows of cooperating stores. The association may develop joint advertising supplements and fliers, run special holiday promotions, have street entertainers, publish a shopping guide featuring the cooperating stores, and even have a central telephone number or Web site where people can get information on the stores, their hours, special sales and promotions, etc. With permission from the local government, the association decorates the streets for appropriate holidays. Some implement some type of buyer rewards program. Costs for such a program are shared among the participating retailers.

A NATIONAL TRADE ASSOCIATION

Your work with fellow retailers should carry over to the national level, too. There is a national trade association for virtually every type of retail store and most do an excellent job in offering a variety of services to members. Check out the association that covers your type of store. It can prove to be an important support group for you and your business. What each association offers varies. In addition to keeping you informed of what is going on in your industry, and serving as an advocate on issues affecting it and retail in general, many offer valuable education programs, low-cost insurance, and other business services. The associations communicate news and ideas through newsletters and/or magazines as well as Web sites; hold annual meetings and workshops on different phases of the business; and sometimes sponsor trade shows. Some associations develop national promotions; some others package promotions that individual retailers can conduct in their communities. These associations provide a good opportunity for retailers to network and exchange ideas with their peers. In some cases, the association may be structured to have local or regional chapters.

Three examples of the types of unique services some associations offer:

■ The National Association of Resale & Thrift Shops (NARTS) may be small in size but it is big in membership services. In addition to the usual association benefits, it offers, for example, an "Ask a Mentor" free consulting service. Members volunteer to mentor peers in areas where they have expertise. The NARTS membership directory lists the volunteer mentors by their specialty, and members can call for help. All it costs the member is the price of the telephone call to the mentor. The members-only section of its Web site includes live chat rooms where members can network with one another. The association is a strong believer in reaching out to its members and in addition to its four-day annual meeting, conducts a series of workshops and two-day seminars each year in up to ten different cities. It also offers a rare, actual cash-value, property-coverage insurance program for items that its members sell on consignment. And to help develop sales for its members, the association has an online shopping guide where consumers can search for member stores by location and/or merchandise category.

■ The South Texas Association of Resale Shops is an example of an independent regional association complementing a national association with programs that target the specific needs of retailers within its area, in this case approximately fifty Houston area resale shop owners. While some retailers belong to NARTS, there is no official affiliation. A bimonthly newsletter provides promotional ideas, basic information on different aspects of running a resale shop, as well as news on local legislation and other government activities that can impact on a member's business. Regular meetings give members a chance to network with one another. Twice a year the association publishes a directory of member stores that gets wide distribution in the area. In addition, its Web site enables residents to locate resale shops by area within the city, as well as by product categories. And once each month, the *Houston Chronicle* runs the association's banner, under which member stores can advertise.

■ Education and promotion are specialized services offered by NAMM, the International Music Products Association. Its "NAMM University," since being launched in 1995, has provided more than four hundred one- and two-day courses in cities across the nation on subjects including music product sales, marketing, customer service, hiring employees, and merchandising. Total course and seminar attendance at the start of 2003 had exceeded fifty thousand. Members can take the courses at regional seminars, at trade shows, and online. In the marketing area, the association has created innovative programs aimed at generating enthusiasm for music making as a recreational pastime, which its members can conduct in their areas. They include programs for children, schools, teens, adults, and seniors. Their "Weekend Warriors" program for adults, for example, is aimed at putting nonactive musicians back on stage to relive their fantasies of super stardom, while its teen program, "The Music Edge.Com" is designed to turn teenage music fans into music players. The association has integrated its database of NAAM members into this teen site so that once a teen becomes interested in playing and purchasing a particular instrument, they can search for a member retailer near them. The association also provides its members with the results of its annual cost of doing business survey.

By going to the Web site of the association that covers your field of retailing, you will be able to get a full rundown of member services. It is possible to join some of the associations online.

3

—■■■—

Tracking the Trends
to Stay Ahead of the Pack

WHILE NO ONE anticipates the same degree of dramatic change that took place over the past fifty-odd years to repeat itself, we have already seen trends developing in the infancy of the new century that can have a significant impact on retailing. Retailers who do not want to be left behind should carefully monitor these trends and develop strategies for responding to and taking advantage of any opportunities they may present.

The Economy

Foremost is the economy. Good or bad, it will *always* be a trend every retailer must monitor.

Too many people had high expectations for the economic prosperity of the 1990s to continue at the same rate in the first decade of the new century. It was unrealistic. The big questions are how long it will take for the economy to turn around, and if it will rebound to the 1990s level. Even if it does rebound, there is the question of how quickly consumers will return to their previous spending patterns. Most people returning to the workforce after lengthy periods of unemployment will probably concentrate on first replenishing their savings. And when they do return, their purchases will probably be on the more modest side.

Both the failure of dot coms and corporate scandals have resulted in trillions of dollars in losses by American investors. Many very wealthy people have seen multimillion-dollar portfolios shrink to the point where they are no longer very wealthy. In addition, the impact on 401(k)s and other retirement plans has been devastating, wiping out the rosy retirement hopes of large numbers of people.

Those people hurt by the economy, or worried about its future, will undoubtedly opt for more modestly priced items, postpone optional and high ticket purchases, and wait for sales. It will be a challenge to keep them away from the discounters. Workers who invested in 401(k)s and other retirement plans, especially those who plan to retire over the next decade, will be among the most conservative spenders.

It is important to track the local economy and any changes in the purchasing patterns of your customers, making adjustments to satisfy their needs so that they will maintain their loyalty to you. It may be necessary to reduce your inventories on certain products or product lines as well as offer special pricing to your regular customers.

The Population

The Hispanic population is the fastest growing group in the country according to Census 2000. It increased by 57.9 percent between 1990 and 2000, while the total U.S. population grew by only 13.2 percent. Even more significant is that 35 percent of the Hispanic population was under 18 years of age compared to 25.7 percent of the total U.S. population. The median age of the total U.S. population is 35.3 while the Hispanic population's median age is 25.9.

Hispanics are very proud of their heritage and represent a good market for products that enable them to continue the traditions of their culture, including foods and beverages, as well as art and music items. Most other purchases are for mainstream products. Retailers interested in the Hispanic market should have Spanish-speaking sales help even if their customers speak and understand English. It is both a sign of respect and a way to let people of Hispanic heritage know that you welcome them as customers. The Hispanic market is an important market and one that becomes even more important each year.

With immigration to the United States from throughout the world continuing at a healthy pace, it is important to track new arrivals from abroad who settle in your area. If there is a significant number of people, especially from the same country or continent, consider developing a marketing plan to reach them. Determine their product needs and stock your store accordingly. Even have point-of-purchase displays in the relevant language. Commemorate meaningful events and holidays and have at least one salesperson who speaks their language. Reach out to an immigrant group through the churches they attend and through any social clubs to which they may belong. Also try to identify and become acquainted with leaders or others of influence within the group(s).

Of the 32.5 million foreign born Americans, 52 percent are from Latin America, 25.5 percent from Asia, and 14 percent from Europe.

Consumerism

Consumer protection continues to increase as an important issue. As a result of the positive publicity elected officials receive from it, you can expect that they will continue to push for both stronger consumer protection laws and their rigid enforcement.

Since Americans are well educated on the subject, all retailers who want to stay out of trouble and stay in business must be very careful about their consumer practices and policies. Be especially careful that you are aware of and pay strict attention to local consumer-protection laws.

Retailers should demonstrate that they, too, believe in consumer protection by initiating active customer-service programs that include policies for return of merchandise, dispute resolution, and rain checks on sale items. Heavily promote your consumerism policy in store as well as through your advertising, flyers, and publicity.

Health and Obesity

Where the concern expressed by the medical profession and the government about the high percentage of Americans who are overweight and obese will lead is anyone's guess, but it is bound to have impact on both stores selling food products and restaurants. Retailers and restaurateurs can take the initiative by placing emphasis on healthy foods and meals, sugarless/low-sugar and low-fat/fat-free products. Set up special low-calorie and/or sugar-free and/or fat-free sections in food stores. You might even offer special pricing on combinations of products: A low-calorie, low-sugar, fat-free ice cream soda package (fat-free/no sugar added ice cream and syrup, skim milk, and seltzer), etc.

Lay out restaurant menus with similar headings and list the calorie count of each dish. Also include sugar-free desserts. Publicize what you are doing. As the medical profession and government information programs progress, you will be in an enviable position to cash in on additional consumer response.

The Internet

Online sales continue to grow in double digit percentage figures, with the greatest growth during the Christmas shopping season. However, online sales still represent only a small portion of the total retail figure. Just how significant this growth will be is anyone's guess. One research firm is forecasting online sales will represent only 8 percent of all retail sales by 2007.

See chapter 18 for more information on online sales and some of the ways small retailers can become involved.

Telemarketing

Consumer complaints, as well as state and federal government restrictions, are greatly decreasing the importance of this form of retail. If you plan to do cold calling, be certain you are aware of any local and state restrictions. In states where a roster is kept of people who do not want to be contacted by telemarketers, hefty fines can be levied on those who call people on the list.

Threats from New Technology and Products

This area has to be closely watched not just for the development of new products that you will be able to offer your customers but also for new products and technologies that can have a negative impact on your business.

New technology that offers consumers a very large catalog of movies, which they can rent and view online or through their cable system, could threaten the future of the video rental store business as it is today. The introduction of shirt fabrics that do not wrinkle when washed could drive away significant business from laundry and dry cleaning stores.

If a manufacturer whose line you do not carry introduces an innovative product and only offers it to its existing customers, you could face a major challenge. Another challenge could occur if you carry an innovative product that turns out to be a dud. While the manufacturer may take a financial loss, your customers will pin the blame on you for selling it to them. It is a tough call to make, but you have to be totally convinced the product is quality and ready for market.

One way to keep up on this new technology and product development is to attend the appropriate trade show(s) where the types of products you sell are displayed. You will get a good idea of what's new and what's in the developmental stage, and have a chance to get a hands-on feel for the products. Companies usually have their designers and technical people on hand, as well as their sales and marketing staffs. Since virtually every manufacturer is on hand, you will get a chance to see what the entire industry is doing, not just the firms whose products you carry in your store. You should also keep up with your industry by reading the trade publications that cover it.

Shifts in Emphasis

Sometimes a trend requires a shift in emphasis in both your product lines and customer base.

For example, when hospital patient stays were greatly reduced, resulting in fewer visitors per patient, on-site gift shops found they had to reassess how they did business. Many, while still carrying traditional patient gifts, put greater emphasis on pleasing an audience they were largely ignoring—the hospital employees. New products were added with special appeal to hospital staff, enabling the gift shops to pick up some of the lost revenues.

The problem of hospital gift shops is one example of why it is important to track, in the very broadest sense, all types of actions that can affect how you do business. Increased food service facilities in a new office complex can take business away from the restaurant across the street, but the restaurant might be able to offset its losses by providing a white-glove catering service for company meetings within the complex.

Diversified Eating Habits

Through their dining out experiences, Americans have become familiar with dishes representing all nationalities from all parts of the world. Food stores can capitalize on this interest by offering the products needed to prepare these dishes at home, or frozen versions of these dishes.

In addition, there has been a significant increase in both the number of kosher products available at retail and in the number of different audiences who purchase them. Today, people of the Jewish faith account for less than half the dollar volume of kosher products. Muslims, who have similar dietary requirements as observant Jews; vegetarians; lactose-intolerant individuals; and people who perceive kosher products to be healthier, purer, and of higher quality than standard packaged foods account for more than 50 percent of sales.

With kosher food becoming a mainstream product, creating special kosher sections in food stores could result in even higher sales figures. And because people regard kosher foods as healthier and of higher quality, you might place the kosher section near your health food section. While restaurants cannot claim to be kosher unless they follow strict rules in preparing meals, they might promote the fact that they use kosher products, or list on the menu the dishes that contain kosher products.

Closeout Stores

Closeout store chains, offering manufacturers' overstocked products at discount, are increasing in number and, suprisingly, moving into many upscale neighborhoods, including Beverly Hills and the Upper East Side of New York City. Some offer individual discounts per product while others have a one-price policy. Wal-Mart has already taken note and has 99-cent sections within a store at several of its locations. This could be the start of a trend for retailers to set aside a section within the store for one-price good buys.

In-Store Food Service

Espresso bars, salad bars, cafes, juice bars, and pasta parlors are popping up throughout the retail scene. Clothing boutiques, office supply stores, and bookstores are among those with food service operations. In addition to being profit centers, they also bring customers into the store. While the wife shops, the husband can relax over his espresso. At another store, three women dig into their antipasti while eyeing the clothing racks off to the side. At the office supply store, people drop by on their way to work to pick up their coffee and bagel. Some of the food service is operated by local restaurants or caterers, and some by the store itself. While large department stores traditionally have restaurants, they are usually away from the merchandise. Smaller stores, many of which used to post NO FOOD AND DRINK PERMITTED signs, now have their facilities right near the clothing. It is another trend to watch.

The Fallout Continues

Financial problems continue to haunt well-known retailers. Montgomery Ward ended a 128-year run in 2000 and 108-store discounter Bradlees checked out in 2001 after more than forty years in business. Kmart, which filed under Chapter 11 in 2002 in what was the biggest retail bankruptcy in history, emerged from it in May 2003 with six hundred fewer stores and fifty-seven thousand fewer employees. And FAO Schwarz's parent company, FAO, filed for bankruptcy protection in January 2003 and is planning to close seventy stores, most of them in their Zany Brainy division. It is interesting that while discounters are growing, some of the stores in trouble were discounters.

It would be worth your while to go online and read some of the reasons given by these giants for their problems. Not only can you learn a lot from the success stories in the industry but you can also gain valuable insight into the problems that catch up with both large and small retailers. It will help make you a better and more responsive businessperson.

4

■ ■ ■

Gathering the Data to Help You Make Your Marketing Decisions

A RESOLUTION EVERY retailer should make during the twenty-first century is to put more time and effort into collecting and analyzing demographics and data on a wide variety of variables that will influence how a retailer markets his or her store. You cannot make sound business decisions without such data.

This includes:

- Information on your present and potential customer bases
- Information on your competitors
- Information on the local economy
- Information on the local business climate

Once collected and analyzed, the data will help you:

- Evaluate just about everything you are doing to market your store
- Give you a better handle on who your customers are and what they want
- Identify special opportunities and new customers you should pursue
- Track changes that could significantly affect your business.

To be totally effective, your research must be ongoing so that you can quickly detect and respond to changes in the retail environment, converting them into opportunities that will ensure survival and growth.

What information do you need?

Your Present and Potential Customer Base

You need to collect as many demographics as possible about the population living in your area including: age, sex, singles/marrieds, size of families, income, value of homes, interests, nationalities, languages spoken, education, etc. You should collect demographics not only from where most of your present customers live but also from other areas where you might want to extend your customer base. While some demographic information is already available from government and private sources, you should be prepared to conduct original research, too. The information from both existing and original research will help you better identify your current customers as well as your potential customers, tell you more about them, give you an idea of what they want and don't want, set store hours, and decide how to advertise and promote the store.

Your Competitors

Information about your competitors should include a marketing analysis of all who operate in your area (both large and small), with emphasis on those closest to your store. It should include their programs, merchandise, and policies so that you can compare them to yours. This information will enable you to identify your competitors' weak points and turn them to your advantage by making sure their weak points become your strong points. You will now have information to outsmart your competitors.

A listing of your competitors may be available through local business organizations or government documents, but you will have to analyze the information yourself. A checklist on what information you should develop appears later in this chapter.

The Local Economy

Keep your hand on the pulse of the local economy since it is bound to impact on sales and profitability. You want to always be aware of local employment and unemployment figures, announcements or rumors of impending layoffs or plant closings, labor unrest and possible strikes, population gains/losses/shifts, housing starts, consumer income, highway construction, large business firms coming to town, developers planning commercial and retail space including shopping centers, new store openings, rumors about chain store openings/closings, and any other economic patterns that are developing in the community. You will also want to compare local retail sales growth/decline figures with national figures as well as monitor the impact national chains are having on local retailers. You can gather most of this information through local newspapers (both daily and weekly), local business publications, local government agencies, and local business organizations as well as the rumor mill. You should use this information to determine its impact on your business so that you can develop steps to overcome any potential problems or to exploit any potential opportunities.

The Business Environment

Every merchant should be fully aware of the local business climate, including the attitude toward retailers by legislative bodies and elected officials. This should include knowledge of programs the state, city, or county have that assist small retailers; empowerment zones and other special business zones that offer incentives; and low-cost loans that may be backed by government issued bonds. Is there a department within the local government that assists retailers in obtaining permits, offers demographic data and other information, and helps resolve problems that arise with other agencies?

It is equally important to develop information on the various business organizations in the community, such as the chamber of commerce. Do they do an effective job in representing the local business community? How much clout do they have with elected officials at all levels of government? What services do they offer their membership? Can they be counted on to come to the aid of a retailer who has a problem in the community or with the local government? Being an active member of one or more of these local organizations enables a retailer to be aware of what is going on in the area, and to be on top of issues that may affect his or her business as well as the entire retail environment. It is also a good opportunity for networking with other businessmen and women, perhaps gain customers, and enhance your image as a businessperson in the community. Join the organization that has the most clout and can be of most assistance to your store.

OBTAINING YOUR DATA

Existing demographic and statistical information is readily available at no cost from the federal government and state and municipal government agencies, as well as local business organizations. Most federal government data can be obtained online.

U.S. Bureau of the Census

The Census Bureau is the primary source for all types of demographics and business data that will help you zero in on target audiences as well as provide valuable industry information. The material is free and available through its Web site: **www.census.gov.** There is also a shortcut Web site called American Factfinder for some of the data: **factfinder.census.gov.**

Of greatest interest to you should be the data accumulated and available on what are called *census tracts*. Counties and equivalent areas are subdivided into census tracts, each averaging about four thousand people. Data you will find for each census tract includes:

- the population by age, sex, and race
- marital status
- educational attainment
- school enrollment
- language spoken in the home
- ancestry
- occupation
- household income
- household size
- time leaving home to go to work
- means of transportation to work
- types of households
- veteran status
- other categories

Your first step would be to identify the areas where your present customers live as well as the areas where you might want to draw new customers. From census maps, you will be able to identify the tract numbers and boundaries for those areas and then obtain the information you want. You might also discover other areas within the city or county where you should be marketing your store. For the person planning to open a store, or expand his or her business, this research can assist in the site selection process.

The information will give you some insight into the people living in each tract, whether they are your target audience, what it would take to make them a target audience, and how you may best serve them. Should you open a half hour earlier in order to catch the majority on their way to work (i.e., a dry cleaner who runs a "drop it off on your way to work, pick it up on your way home" special)? If most of your customers take a bus to work, you might want to consider advertising on the bus shelters in the area. If there is a large number of children in the tract, toy stores or children's clothing stores would be interested. High family incomes might be a factor dictating pricing and product mix. And if you plan to do newspaper advertising, for example, you might want to check the circulation reach in specific tracts where you have an interest.

To find a map enabling you to identify the census tracts in your county, go to **www.census.gov,** CLICK Maps, then CLICK Map Products, scroll to Reference Maps, and CLICK Census Tract Outline Maps. CLICK on the appropriate state, then county. The maps are available on Adobe Acrobat PDF files.

To find the tract data, go to **factfinder.census.gov.** The most helpful information will be charts DP-1 in 2000 Summary File 1, DP-2, DP-3, and QT-P23 in Summary File 3.

On the home page, CLICK on 2000 Summary File 1. CLICK on it again when you get to the Data Sets Page. Then CLICK on Quick Tables. For selection method CLICK on List; for geographic type, CLICK on Census Tracts, then choose the appropriate state and county, then CLICK on All Census Tracts, and Show Table. You will then be able to scroll through Chart DP-1 for the profile of general demographic characteristics for each of the census tracts in that county.

For DP-2 and DP-3, CLICK on 2000 Summary File 3 on the home page and follow the same instructions as the previous paragraph except you will have to select the table you want before you get to Show Table. To obtain QT-P23, which gives means of transportation to work and time leaving home, you have to go back to the Data Sets Page and CLICK on List All Tables, then QT-P23.

Additional statistics down to the census tract level are available from research firms on a fee basis. See Independent Research Firms later in this chapter.

Other Census Bureau information, which might be helpful to you, would be to determine the number of retail establishments in the category similar to yours within your county or zip code. To find this data, go to the Census home page, CLICK on Economic Census. On the first page that pops up, CLICK on Latest Results 1998–2001, which is on the left-hand side of the page. On the next chart, CLICK on County Business Patterns." We suggest you do it by zip code. Then CLICK on *Retail,* and you will get information on the stores within that zip code in more than fifty categories. You will get the total number in each category as well as a breakdown by number of employees. If you CLICK on Compare for a category, you will receive the same information for that specific category in every zip code in the county.

This is one way to determine how much competition you have in your area of operation. From the number of employees in a store, you can get a feel for its size and volume of business.

Another type of information available from the Census Bureau is the annual *Statistical Abstract,* containing almost a thousand pages of statistics on virtually every subject on which the government keeps statistics. There is some data on retailing and consumer purchases, primarily on a national level. This information may help you detect national trends. To view the *Statistical Abstract* online, go to the Census Web site home page and CLICK on Statistical Abstract. It is on Adobe Acrobat PDF file.

In addition to the Census Web sites, there are numerous outlets locally where you can view reports, request printouts of tabulations, or otherwise obtain assistance on accessing, understanding, and using Census 2000 information. To access a list, go to the Census Bureau Web site, CLICK on Your Gateway to Census 2000, then CLICK on Local Sources for Census 2000, which is toward the bottom of the left-hand column.

Bureau of Labor Statistics

The Bureau, part of the Department of Labor, is the principal fact-finding agency of the federal government in the field of labor economics and statistics. It is the agency that develops the consumer price index and calculates the rate of inflation. Retailers will be most interested in its detailed study of individual consumer expenditures for approximately fifty different retail products. The information is available by age, family, education, race, housing tenure (urban, rural, home owner, renter), income category, occupation level, region, and twenty-eight current metropolitan statistical areas (MSA). Other than the regional and MSA breakdowns, the statistics are shown on a nationwide basis. A retailer might want to concentrate on the chart representing the metropolitan statistical area nearest his or her city, or a regional chart if not close to an MSA.

This information can assist you in establishing marketing goals. Online at **www.bls.gov,** CLICK on Consumer Expenditures on the home page, under the upper left-hand column headed Inflation & Consumer Spending. Then CLICK on Tables Created by BLS (Bureau of Labor Statistics), and you will find the various charts available. Scroll to the one Current Statistical Areas Tables as well as Current Region Tables.

Local Media

The advertising departments of local newspapers, radio and television stations, cable systems, city magazines, and companies selling outdoor and transit advertising are good sources for data.

While the data provided by each will probably emphasize the superiority of its product over competitive media, the general demographics used as the base for each study will probably provide you with legitimate statistics. Of help to you would be any research local media has developed on purchases made at your type of store, for your type of product lines, and seasonal and other purchasing patterns.

To obtain this material, contact the local media advertising departments and ask for their media kits. A salesman will probably want to call on you to persuade you to advertise. While advertising should be considered when developing your total marketing program for the year (see chapter 23), don't feel pressured by the salesman's visit. Explain you are in the preliminary phases of putting together your plan and are presently evaluating media data. The presentation should be a valuable learning experience itself.

State, City, and Regional Governments

State, city, and regional development and planning commissions often have extensive statistical data and other economic information about their areas. They use this data to attract new business to the area.

Contact these agencies to see what they have available. Local government finance administrations might also have data based on tax collections.

Banks, Real Estate Developers, Utilities, and Chambers of Commerce

Banks, real estate developers, chambers of commerce, utilities, and other business groups may also be good sources for statistical and economic data. Contact your bank, for example, to see what information and studies it may have available. Also contact your local utilities. Real estate developers may also have good data, but in order to obtain information from them you will probably have to show some interest in their services. Local chambers of commerce and other business groups may be able to supply economic research they have either conducted or collected from various sources. Of course, if you are located in a shopping mall, ask its management for any consumer research it has conducted.

Public Libraries

Libraries are depositories for all types of statistical data. An important potential source for information is your public and/or business library. Contact the local research librarian who will quickly tell you if the type of information you need is available. Some of it may even be available through the library's Web site.

Retailer Associations

Most retailer associations have industry statistical information, which they share with their members, including surveys of the category of stores they represent. Some of these national associations have state and local chapters and offer a broad variety of programs to assist the retailer. (See chapter 2)

Independent Research Firms

There are many independent research firms that have banks of data, which might be useful to you and which they sell online. One of them, ESRI Business Information Solutions (Web site **www.esribis.com**) offers retail market-potential reports, restaurant-potential reports, and retail expenditure profiles at census tract level for under $100. A complete listing of available reports, along with samples of what each contains is on its Web site.

Look at Demographics on your search engine for other research firms.

LOCALLY GENERATED RESEARCH

While basic demographic information is readily available at little or no cost, original research, to bring you and your customer closer together must be developed and conducted locally by people who can interpret its results. It may be possible for you to get some original research done at little or no cost.

Assistance from College Marketing Classes

There are several forms of assistance you might be able to get from local universities, especially schools of business. For example, see if you can arrange for a marketing professor to assign a group of graduate students to conduct research for you as a term project. While there will usually be no charge for this type of project, you might give the students a small honorarium.

Check also to see if any universities have internship programs. If they do, see if you can get one or more interns to help you develop and conduct your research program. A modest honorarium might be given to cover transportation and meals.

While students will do the work involved in term projects and internships, there is usually some supervision by the faculty. This will vary from school to school.

Hiring a Firm or Person to Do Research for You

There are firms that specialize in research in most major U.S. cities; they can be found in both print and online Yellow Pages under the heading Market Research and Analysis and on the Internet under Demographics. Some advertising agencies also have research capabilities.

It is best to deal with a firm that comes highly recommended. Ask other local businesses, business associations, advertising departments at local media, and local advertising agencies that farm out their research projects for recommendations.

In order to keep your research expenses down, consider teaming up with other local, noncompetitive retailers to commission a joint research project. This would probably be most effective if your project partners were located close to the store, sold merchandise in the same price range, and were interested in reaching out to customers from the same area.

You might also want to consider hiring a freelance research person to handle the project, such as a local marketing professor, someone working in research who is looking to moonlight, or even a retired researcher. Another possibility is to hire one or more highly recommended graduate students.

Conducting Your Own Research

While it will take planning, time, and staff, it is possible to conduct some of your own research. Some of the data you need can be extracted from store records; other data from passersby and in-store traffic counts. For store-conducted questionnaire surveys, it is recommended that even if you choose this option, you should use a freelancer or some other person experienced in the field to structure the projects, develop the questionnaire, and supervise your staff.

WHAT INFORMATION YOUR LOCAL RESEARCH SHOULD DEVELOP

There are three key audiences on which your local research should focus: people who already shop at your store, people who you would like to attract to the store, and people who have stopped shopping at the store.

From your present and past customers you can get data based on their experiences at your store. From your potential customers, you can get information on their perception of your store, what might be keeping them away, and what it might take to attract them.

People Who Are Already Customers

Statistical data on the entire community is readily available from census reports and other sources discussed earlier in this chapter. It is important to develop very specific data about your present customers, including their shopping patterns, attitudes toward your store, your staff, and your merchandise. The data you develop should provide you with a better understanding of your customers, enable you to improve your services to them, and result in both increased loyalty and sales. In addition, this information should provide you with a customer profile that will enable you to clearly identify sections of the city where you should prospect for new customers.

Specific information you want to develop:

- Demographics about your customers including age, income bracket, marital/family status, occupation, where they live (zip code, section, census tract), education, and language spoken. Rather than ask for the customer's address, just request name of street and intersection. You will be able to find the census tract and then make a ballpark estimate of some of the data by going to the census tract tables.
- Information about lifestyle interests.
- Frequency of visits to the store.
- Average purchase per visit.
- Days and times of the day they shop at your store.
- Why do they shop at your store? What are they seeking from you?
- What is it that they like most about your store?
- Evaluation of the quality, styling, and availability of your merchandise.
- Seasons and holidays that have the most influence on their buying patterns.
- Attitudes toward promotions, sales, special events.
- Do they already have specific items in mind to purchase when they enter the store?
- Items they buy on impulse.

- Reactions to salespeople: Are they helpful? Do they quickly resolve any problems? Are they knowledgeable about products?
- What do they like most about the store?
- What do they like least about the store? Anything else they dislike about the store?
- Other stores in the immediate area where they shop.
- Media they read, watch, or listen to.
- How do they learn about your specials, sales, etc.?
- Which media do they usually rely upon for retail advertisements?
- The influence advertising has on their shopping.
- How do they rate your customer service?

People You Would Like to Attract as Customers

You should also survey people who are not customers in order to determine how you can expand your base. Once you have specific demographics on your present customers, you should use it to identify the census tract areas in which people with similar demographics can be found. You could then concentrate some research in those areas to see how you might attract more customers from among your prime target audience.

Using census tract tables, you might also identify areas where a more upscale audience than your present customers live, and do some research to try to determine what it will take to attract these people to become customers.

In addition to the demographics, the information you want to develop from potential customers includes:

- Do they normally purchase the type of products you sell?
- Where do they currently shop for your lines of products?
- What do they look for when shopping for the type of products your store carries? Convenience? Pricing? Quality? Service?
- Have they ever heard of your store?
- What is their impression of it?
- Have they been in it? If not, have they looked at its windows?
- Why haven't they shopped at it?
- What would induce them to shop at your store?
- What are other stores in your immediate area where they currently shop?

- What seasons and holidays most influence their buying behavior?
- What role do promotions, sales, and special events play in attracting them to a store?
- What items do they purchase on impulse?
- What are their shopping times and other patterns?
- What amount do they usually spend per visit on your types of products?
- What media do they read, listen to, or watch?
- From what media do they receive their information about the type of products/styles you sell?
- What influence does advertising have on their shopping?
- Profile of age, income, education, occupation, lifestyles, where they live.

Customers You Have Lost

There is a third audience about which you should be concerned: customers who no longer shop at your store. You should survey them, preferably by telephone, in order to determine the problem(s). The key question you want answered, of course, is why the customer has stopped shopping at your store. If they do not volunteer the information at the top of your conversation, focus on asking them about your pricing, quality of products, selection of products, service, convenience (location, days, hours open, etc.), competition. A suggested questionnaire and telephone script appears toward the end of the chapter.

This information will be extremely important since it can help you spot problems that must be attended to immediately.

UNDERSTANDING RESEARCH FORMATS

There are several formats that can be used to solicit research data. Some *must* be conducted by professionals; others by individuals under the direction of a professional; still others by virtually anyone.

Here are some examples:

Questionnaire

Questionnaires are generally used to develop the major information you want concerning your customers' likes and dislikes, buying patterns, and personal demographics. If you have a customer mailing list, use it. The questionnaires can also be given to customers in the store to fill out on the premises, or to take home and return on their next visit. A questionnaire can also be used for a face-to-face interview. The customer should not be asked to identify him- or herself, and it would be preferable not to have a store employee doing the interview. However, try to get the customer to give you their street and nearest intersection. You can then identify their census tract and factor in its statistics.

The key to obtaining valid information is in the structuring of the survey. How questions are written will determine the objectivity of the responses. While questions concerning general demographic data are easy to write, questions concerning other information must be carefully written to avoid any form of suggestion or bias. That's why it is important to have someone with experience in the research field prepare the questionnaire.

Mini-questionnaires can be used to develop information about customer service and other single service items. They are easy to prepare—you can probably prepare them yourself—and can be filled out by customers while still in the store. Several examples of mini-questionnaires can be found later in this chapter.

You may also try one-question surveys. Give your sales staff "a question of the day or week" to ask customers in a conversational tone. Questions like: Is there any product or product line you would like to see added? Did you have difficulty finding what you were looking for? Is it easy finding your way around the store? Are our hours convenient for you (if not, ask what would be)? After the customer is out of sight, jot down the answer. This is a very informal means for gathering information. On slow days, the salespeople could engage in longer conversations and try to get a greater amount of information. Customers should not be aware that you are conducting a survey but rather think it is all part of your customer service program.

Focus Groups

Focus groups are group discussions aimed at eliciting information you seek. There might be ten to twelve people in the group with a trained moderator leading the discussion. Focus groups must be organized and led by professionals. They are usually conducted in a room with a concealed observation window from where you can view the entire discussion and see the facial reactions and body language of the participants as they discuss the subjects.

Panels

You might set up a panel of customers to serve as an "advisory board" for the store. Panels can be set up two ways: a mail panel or a discussion group. Every month or so, the members of the mail panel would be sent questionnaires aimed at developing whatever information you might seek, as well as trying to determine both problems and opportunities that might exist. For serving on the panel and responding to all the questionnaires during the year, the panelist might be given a gift in the $25 to $35 range, or a gift certificate. The discussion group panel could meet every two or three months to provide input during an informal discussion led by the store owner. You might do it at a buffet lunch, or just over coffee and pastries.

Telephone Interviews

It is also possible to conduct interviews over the telephone. Since it is difficult to keep a person on the telephone for a long period of time, usually less information can be gathered through this method than through written or in-person interviewing. Since it is possible to work from a script, telephone surveys are easy to conduct even by inexperienced interviewers. However, the interviewer should have a pleasant, conversational voice and not sound as though he or she is reading off a script. The person called should be aware they are being surveyed.

One type of telephone interview is to call customers who have made a recent purchase. The announced purpose of the call is to check to see if the customer is happy with the product. During the course of the conversation, the caller should ask a few questions to see if the customer has been happy with the service he or she is getting at the store. A sample script can be found at the end of this chapter.

Studying Purchasing Patterns

A great deal can be learned by studying the purchasing patterns of your customers. An easy way for doing this is through the development of a "Frequent Buyers Program." (See chapter 14.) A second technique is to have customers register for your (snail or e-mail) mailing list so that they can be informed of upcoming special sales, discounts, and various events. Give each customer a rewards savings card with an identification number and have your cash register programmed so that it can compile sales data. You might offer special discount rewards when the customer reaches a certain purchasing level, and also special rotating product discounts to customers with the card. Ask the customer for the card when making a purchase; thus you will be able to keep a running record of purchases, days and hours shopped, and other information from which you can develop all types of patterns and trends.

Counting Heads

From time to time, it is a good idea to station someone outside the store to take a count of passersby. You want to know the number of people by sex, estimated age (from under twenty-five to over sixty), whether they looked at your windows and whether they entered the store after looking at them, and whether they appeared to be casually walking or were headed to a specific location. You should take these counts at times when you have different windows—for example when you have a window with movement in it or when you have specials, bright colors, etc. One purpose is to determine if any one type of window has greater impact than another. This job can be done by a student or a part-time worker.

Day-to-Day Analysis of Sales

Every retailer should keep a day-to-day analysis of business. Included should be: sales broken down into one- or two-hour increments; number of customers entering the store during these same increments; sale or promotion taking place; weather; competitor activity (sales or promotions);

other events taking place that day (local college football game, special on television, etc.). A suggested work sheet appears later in this chapter.

GET TO KNOW YOUR COMPETITORS

Of major importance in your fact-finding efforts should be as complete an analysis as possible of your competitors' marketing operations. It should be conducted on an ongoing basis. You want to gather information that will help you identify both the strong and weak points of each competitor:

- The type, quality, and selection of merchandise your competitor sells as well as pricing policies.
- Store hours and amenities offered customers (free deliveries, free alterations, return policy, telephone ordering, frequent buyer's programs).
- Marketing program, including advertising, special promotions and events, and sales (type, time period, frequency, how promoted).
- Competitor's pricing against yours on your twenty-five best-selling items.
- An evaluation of competitor's sales force.

The techniques to use in studying your competitors include frequent shopping of their stores:

- Have a relative, friend, or professional shopper shop the stores. He or she should also try to get to know a salesperson at each store. By earning his or her confidence, he or she may learn about special upcoming sales and other information that might be helpful to your planning effort. To accomplish this your shopper(s) might have to purchase products from these competitors.
- Have your shopper get on the competitors' mailing lists and in any special sales programs or clubs. Naturally you will have to be discreet as to whose name is on the lists. Use one of your relatives who has a different family name.
- Monitor the media to determine the competition's advertising programs and estimated expenditures. Determine the patterns of their advertising (days, seasons, times of day if radio, cable or television) as well as their creative approach.

SAMPLE MINI-QUESTIONNAIRES

To Determine Best Methods to Reach Customers

We are interested in determining how we can best reach you with our specials and other information about our store. Would you please take a few minutes to answer the questionnaire and drop it in the box near the cash register. Thank you.

- What radio station do you most frequently listen to?

_____

- At what times do you usually listen? _____

- What newspapers do you read (dailies and weeklies)? _____

_____

- What sections of the newspapers do you usually read? _____

- What newspaper do you read Sundays? _____

- What sections? _____

- What television channel do you most frequently watch? _____

- Do you watch local news on television?

_____

- If you do, at what time and what channels? _____

- Do you watch cable television? _____

- What system do you have?

_____

- What channels do you watch on cable? _____

- Do you log onto any local Web sites run by local radio, television, newspaper, or other area organizations? _____

- If yes, which one(s)? _____

  _____

- Would you like to receive e-mails from us on sales, special events, and other specials? _____

- Would you like to receive a circular mailed to your home?

  _____

If you already advertise, ask the following questions:

- Do you recall seeing any of our advertising in any of the following media?

  Radio _____ Television _____

  Daily Newspaper _____

  Sunday Newspaper _____

  Weekly Newspaper _____ Cable TV _____

  Circular _____ On the Web _____

- Which would be your favorite way to hear from us? Please list in order:

  Radio _____

  Television _____

Daily Newspaper _____

Weekly Newspaper _____

Cable Television _____

E-mail _____

Circular in the mail _____

Optional: Name_____ Address _____

Telephone Number_____ E-mail _____

To Determine Customer Satisfaction

We are interested in learning if we are living up to your expectations during your visits to our store. We would appreciate a few minutes of your time to let us know how we are doing.

- How do you rate our sales help?

  Excellent _____

  Good _____

  Fair _____

  Poor _____

- Do you find that they are knowledgeable about our products?

  Yes _____

  No _____

  Sometimes _____

- Are you able to find exactly what you are looking for when you shop at our store?

    Yes _____

    No _____

    Sometimes _____

- What attracts you to shop at our store? (Check as many as applicable.)

    Convenience _____

    Pricing _____

    Selection _____

    Quality _____

    Service _____

- Now, please rate those factors you have checked above on a scale of 1 to 5, with 1 being the most important, and 5 the least important.

    Convenience _____

    Pricing _____

    Selection _____

    Quality _____

    Service _____

- How do you rate our prices?

    Above Average _____

Below Average _____

Average _____

- How do you rate the quality of our merchandise?

    Above Average _____

    Below Average _____

    Average _____

- How do you rate the selection of merchandise we usually have on

hand?

    Excellent _____

    Good _____

    Fair _____

    Poor _____

- Do you usually shop during our sales?

    Yes _____

    No _____

    Sometimes _____

- Do you usually shop during our special promotions or events?

    Yes _____

    No _____

    Sometimes _____

- Do you have any problems finding your sizes (if appropriate)?

    Yes _____

    No _____

    Sometimes _____

We would appreciate receiving any additional comments you have about our store, our sales help, our merchandise, or any other facet of our business. _____

_____

_____

Optional: If you would like to provide your name and address and/or telephone number, please do so in order that we may follow up on any complaints you may have.

    Name _____   Address _____

    Telephone Number _____

SAMPLE QUESTIONNAIRE TO SEND TO A FORMER CUSTOMER

We miss you!
We notice that you haven't visited with us for some time, and we wonder if you have found some serious problems with our service, merchandise, or some other phase of our business. Since you are important to us, we would appreciate it if you would take a few minutes of your time to fill out the attached questionnaire and return it in the stamped addressed envelope.

While it is not necessary to identify yourself in this questionnaire, I would like to discuss with you any problems you might have had with us. Please call me at (telephone number) anytime at your convenience.

John D. Owner

- Do you still have a need for the type of merchandise our store carries?

    Yes _____

    No _____

(If you checked "yes," please complete the rest of the questionnaire.)

- How did you find our prices?

    Above Average _____

    Below Average _____

    Average _____

- How did you find the quality of our merchandise?

    Above Average _____

    Below Average _____

    Average _____

- How did you rate the variety of our merchandise?

    Above Average _____

    Below Average _____

    Average _____

■ Was the merchandise you wanted usually available when you shopped at our store?

    Yes _____

    No _____

■ How would you rate our salespeople?

    Excellent _____

    Good _____

    Fair _____

    Poor _____

■ Were you satisfied with the service you received at the store?

    Yes _____

    No _____

■ If no, please explain the problem. _____

_____

_____

■ Please check off as many of the reasons as necessary to describe why you stopped shopping with us.

    Pricing _____

    Quality of Products _____

    Selection of Products _____

Sizes Not Available _____

Sales Help _____

Service _____

Location _____

Store Hours _____

■ If you have any other reasons, please list them. _____

_____

_____

_____

Optional: Name _____   Address _____

              Telephone Number _____

Thank you for filling out this questionnaire.

As a former customer we value your opinion highly, and we hope to learn from it how we may have failed to serve your shopping needs and what we can do to correct the problem.

SAMPLE TELEPHONE SCRIPTS

To Determine Customer Satisfaction

Here is a sample of a telephone script that might be used not only to determine customer satisfaction with a recent purchase but also to elicit other information. While telephone interviews can be formally structured with the interviewer asking questions and offering multiple choices of answers, this survey uses open-ended questions. The interviewer must take extensive notes during the conversation since the subjects will be expressing their views in their own words.

Hello, is this Ms. Arlene James?

This is Harvey Smith of The Downtown Store. I was just calling to see if you are happy with the blazer and skirt you purchased two weeks ago?

Have you worn it yet? Are you completely satisfied with its fit? Was the salesperson who assisted you helpful?

We're interested in your comments because we consider customer satisfaction our number one goal. I was wondering if I could ask you just a few questions?

- Can you usually find what you want when you are shopping with us?
- If we happen to be out of your size, does our salesperson offer to order your size?
- Do you feel we have a broad enough selection for you to choose from?
- What about our pricing: how do you find it?
- Are you satisfied with the quality of our merchandise?
- One last question. From your point of view, what can we do to improve our services for you?

Thank you very much for your time, Ms. James. And if you have any problems with the blazer, or anything else you ever purchase from us, please be sure to bring it back.

To a Former Customer

You may also interview a former customer by telephone. It may be advantageous to do a telephone interview instead of mailing a questionnaire since, in addition to getting the information in the customer's own words, you may be able to persuade him or her to return.

Hello, is this Ms. May Smith?

This is John D. Owner from John D's Shoe Store. We have noticed that you have not been in to see us for some time, and we were wondering if you were having any problems with our store.

(Note: You may get the answers to all of your questions as she responds to your opening line. If not, follow the script and ask the questions for which she may not have given you information.)

We value the opinions of our customers and would like to ask you a few questions to find out how we may have failed to serve your shopping needs.

- Has our pricing been a problem?
- Were you satisfied with the quality of our products?
- Do you feel we have enough of a variety of merchandise?
- Did we always have your shoe size in stock?
- If not, did the salesperson offer to place a special order for your size?
- How did you find our salespeople? Were they helpful and knowledgeable?
- Was there any one reason why you stopped shopping with us? (If the answer is "no," ask the next question.)
- Why then, may I ask, did you stop shopping at our store?

Thank you very much. We appreciate your time, and we'll do everything we can to correct the problems you discussed with me. I hope, perhaps, at some future date, you will try us again. (Note: Interviewer should use a conversational tone with the former customer, and if the answers are not clear try to get a firmer answer during the course of the conversation.)

SINGLE DAY BUSINESS ANALYSIS

Date _____ Day of the Week _____

HOUR	NUMBER OF CUSTOMERS	PRODUCTS SOLD	GROSS SALES
9 A.M.			
10 A.M.			
11 A.M.			
Noon			
1 P.M.			
2 P.M.			

3 P.M. _____

4 P.M. _____

5 P.M. _____

6 P.M. _____

7 P.M. _____

8 P.M. _____

9 P.M. _____

10 P.M. _____

TOTALS

Promotion/Sale _____

Other Competitive Events (Competitors' Sales, etc.) _____

_____

5

—■■■—

Developing a Marketing Strategy
and a New Age Sales Force

BASED ON THE data you have collected, including the comparison between your store and your competition, as well as the knowledge and experience you have acquired as a retailer, you are ready to develop a strategy designed to give you the competitive edge against all comers.

Your ultimate goal is to develop a broad base of loyal and satisfied customers who will not only regularly shop at your store but also tell friends, neighbors, and relatives about it and encourage them to shop there, too. You want your customers to understand who you are and why you are important to them.

How do you do it?

- By positioning your store as a highly successful, knowledgeable operation that provides a shopping environment beyond what your competitors offer
- By offering the merchandise, convenience, service, caring sales staff, and excitement that will make the shopping experience unforgettable to the consumer

Perception of Store

Consumer perception of your store can mean the difference between success and failure. Customers have to feel comfortable when they enter the store to shop and even more comfortable when they leave with their purchases, confident that they received quality products at a fair price. This comfort level is what converts a casual shopper into a regular customer, which in turn is what you want and need for a successful enterprise.

But you have to work to earn it. And once you earn it, you have to work even harder to maintain it. According to a study by George S. May International Company, a leading consulting firm to small businesses, customers have expectations and if they are not met, they will sense something is wrong. They'll forgive an occasional lapse but if it becomes a general trend, they'll start to shop elsewhere.

That's why the core of your marketing strategy must always be:

- Quality merchandise
- Fair pricing
- Convenient location
- Good customer service
- Knowledgeable sales force

SELECTING THE RIGHT PRODUCT LINE

Your research and experience will tell you what your customers want. Your challenge is not only to provide those products but also to bring in new products and additional product lines to appeal to your customers and result in incremental sales. It is important that product line expansion within the store be slow and appear as a natural extension of your core lines. Otherwise, your customers may perceive that you are drastically changing direction and begin thinking about shopping elsewhere. Make certain that you do have a good selection of quality products on hand at all times. And, if you sell clothing or shoes, a good selection in all sizes.

If you do not have a strong customer base, or are just starting a business, your approach to selecting your product lines may be different. You will have to define who you want to attract to the store as well as their needs. Combine that with your objectives for the type of store you want to operate. Initially, you will have to be careful not to overstock in case you have to change direction in your product lines.

A word of caution: In many instances, too many stores within a small radius are selling the same product lines. This is especially true in both men's and women's clothing, particularly sportswear. To gain a competitive advantage, your product line should be distinctive from that of your key competitors. Even if demand requires you sell some of the same products, the bulk of your line should differ from the other neighborhood stores.

SETTING A SOUND PRICING POLICY

Pricing is probably the trickiest part of retailing. Certainly it is not as simple as it may appear.

You want your customers to perceive they are paying a fair price for the products they purchase but *fair price* may have a different meaning to different people. The convenience of your location and hours, the quality of your products, the professionalism of your sales staff, the quality of the bag in which you place the product, and the ambiance of the store can strongly influence how your customers determine a fair price. If these factors are all positive influencers, a fair price will be perceived to be higher than if they are negative influencers.

You must examine and evaluate the advantages and disadvantages of the various pricing options:

- Are you going to hold the line and keep firm prices on your merchandise?
- Are you going to consistently place merchandise on the shelves at full price with the intention of quickly marking it down?
- Are you going to establish a policy of "everyday low prices"?
- Or are you going to follow a policy so many customers are used to: sales, sales, sales?

You must evaluate the advantages and disadvantages of each.

- An upscale store can often hold the line on its regular pricing, conducting just a couple of sales a year. The argument is that the image of the store will suffer if it becomes too promotion-oriented. However, up-scale customers like bargains, too.

■ A midprice retailer who provides superior customer service, quality products, and a pleasant store environment can also often hold the line, especially if he offers a frequent buyers club and a few promotions throughout the year.

■ Retailers who initially display merchandise at full price and then quickly mark it down are fooling themselves. It usually doesn't take long for consumers to become aware of the tactic. They just delay their purchases. It also kills the credibility of the store's pricing policy and may draw complaints from local consumer affairs agencies if they perceive the initial pricing to be bogus. This, of course, would result in negative publicity.

■ Under the everyday low pricing concept, products are introduced at a lower than usual price. Markdowns and sales, for the most part, are limited. Once you have effectively established awareness for this pricing policy among your customers and in the community, you can usually spend less money on promotions. A negative side of this concept is that people may perceive your merchandise to be of lower quality, even if it isn't. Also, many people like sales, and even though your prices may be lower, their perception may be that they are not getting a bargain because they do not see the prices being marked down.

■ The "sales . . . sales . . . sales markdown" policy remains very popular among consumers. Even large national department stores have been picking up on it. When you have sales on products that have already been on sale, and then add a discount price on top of that, you are seriously cutting into your profits. You are also sending a message that business is bad, and you are trying to unload an inventory of products that have not been selling. If this becomes a regular practice, your customers will be sitting on their hands waiting for the "sale on the sale plus additional discount" before they buy. It could put you out of business.

MAKING IT MORE CONVENIENT
TO SHOP THE STORE

Every retailer should reflect on the meaning of the words *convenience store*. It is usually a store that is convenient for its customers both in its location and hours of operation and in fulfilling their product needs.

In reality, all stores should think of themselves as convenience stores. That's not to imply that every store should be located around the corner from the majority of its customers and should be open around the clock. Rather the convenience of location and business hours should be realistically established in order to fulfill the needs of your present and potential customers. For example, if you are operating a shoe repair store and your research shows most of your customers leave for work at 8 A.M. and return at 6 P.M., you are not offering convenient service to them if your hours are 9 to 5. Nor are you offering convenient shopping hours if you are located in the downtown shopping area and close your doors at 5:30, just thirty minutes after people get out of work. And if demographics show that the largest segment of consumers most likely to be attracted to your business live on the north side of the city and you are located on the south side, you probably will not be getting as much business from them as you should.

Other convenience factors to consider include your store's location in relationship to public transportation, traffic flow, highways and highway exits, and public parking.

MAKING THE MOST OF YOUR SALES FORCE

It is time to evaluate how you presently use your sales force and explore new techniques to make it more efficient and important to your profit structure.

First and foremost must be your recognition that your salespeople are the store. They are the people your customers deal with and from whom they gain their impressions of the store. As such they are in a position to guarantee your success, or cause your failure.

Do they truly represent what you stand for? Are they working in the best interests of your investment? When you invest your money, you look for the best possible return. You should think along the same lines when you hire a sales force. Are they giving you the maximum return on your investment in the store and your investment in them?

Unfortunately, a big mistake retailers make is not placing enough importance on the salesperson's role, all too often accepting a mediocre performance. This won't fly in the twenty-first century. You have to look at your sales force the same way a football coach looks at his team: with an eye toward improving its quality, its loyalty, its productivity, its effectiveness, and its chemistry. And you yourself have to improve on the play book.

Hiring the Right People

Start off with whom you hire for your sales team.

A key trait in a salesperson is how he or she will relate to your customers and vice versa. The criteria will vary from store to store. While the sales person at an upscale store does not necessarily need to have the same socioeconomic or educational background as its customers, he or she should project an image of intelligence, refinement, culture, and interests to which a customer can relate, and show the same appreciation for the products as the customer. A store appealing to the under twenty-one age group should have salespeople who talk the same lingo and dress like its target audience. If you have a large senior citizen base, you are not going to want to hire a sales staff in their twenties. And if you have a large foreign-born customer base, you will want to hire people who speak the language(s) and are familiar with the customs and culture of the group(s).

It is also to your benefit to hire salespeople who live in the store's marketing area and are known in the community. You want people who are active in church groups, PTAs, business and civic clubs, lodges, Little League, veterans' groups, etc. You want people who are in a position to draw customers to the store.

The other qualities you should look for in candidates for your sales job are:

- People who have knowledge of the products they will sell, or the aptitude to learn about them quickly. A major customer complaint is lack of knowledge and ability to answer questions about products by sales staff.
- People who like to sell and take pride in closing a sale.
- People who are dependable and whom you can count on to show up for work every day.
- People who do not fear rejection or feel personally rejected when they fail to close a sale.
- People who are intelligent, who are quick learners, and who have the curiosity to expand their knowledge.

- People who have a pleasant and positive image, which mirrors that of the store.
- People who like people and easily relate to them.
- People who are neither impressed with their own importance nor overwhelmed by the importance of VIP customers.
- People who are helpful to customers as well as their fellow employees and management.
- People who are real team players.
- People who need a job and are willing to work hard to keep it.
- People who are ambitious and hope some day to have your job—or their own store.

There are, of course, other factors to take into consideration. These include appearance, speech, "chemistry," past employment history, and references. In addition to former employers, ask the candidate to supply the names of former customers whom you can call for a reference.

The most effective way to find good sales help is to recruit them yourself from among the salespeople you come across while shopping. Ask family and friends to "scout" for you and tell you about any good candidates they encounter. A second good source for recruits is from trusted employees. Offer them a finder's fee for anyone they recommend whom you hire, plus a bonus if the new salesperson remains with the store for at least a year.

Your New Play

As noted in the preface, the days of unlocking the door and waiting for customers to come in are long gone. You are in a new, more competitive century, and you have to be innovative and try new approaches to stay ahead of the competition.

When it comes to the sales force, your challenge is to figure out a way to motivate them so that they will be more effective and important to the bottom line.

Money is the most effective motivator. However, if a salesperson is paid on an hourly or weekly basis, what is the incentive for that person to go out of his or her way to close the sale? There really is none. He or she will be paid the same salary whether they aggressively sell a large dollar amount of products, or take it easy and handle a minimum number of customers each day. While an hourly or weekly wage may work in grocery, drug, hardware, produce, and variety stores, it will not work if you sell larger ticket items, or products that require salesperson assistance.

There are several solutions. One is to put the sales staff on commission; another is to pay a salary with a bonus on top of it.

However, while this will greatly motivate your salespeople to work harder in the store at helping customers and increasing sales, it will not necessarily bring in that much additional revenue or customers. As a matter of fact, you can end up with a happier, better paid sales force and fewer dollars of profit.

That's when you call in your new play. Use your salespeople to generate more traffic to the store. Since one of the qualities you should be looking for when hiring sales help is people who are active and well known in the community, design a play that makes use of their skills.

Set up your compensation program so that it pays bonuses for generating sales with a higher bonus rate paid for sales to new customers the salesperson brings into the store. The program evolves around a "Friend of (name of salesperson)" courtesy card entitling the "Friend" to special discounts and other promotional considerations. The sales force would use the cards to invite their friends, neighbors, acquaintances, and fellow members of religious, civic, veterans, and other community organizations, including PTAs, women's and garden clubs, to shop the store. The salesperson could also distribute the cards to waiters and waitresses when they eat out and even salespeople at noncompetitive stores where they shop. Each time the card is used, the sale is recorded so that bonus points are given to the salesperson and frequent buyer points to the customer. Friends would have to fill out a short registration form the first time they shop at the store.

You can develop a variety of support programs to assist the salesperson, including donating product for raffles and door prizes to the organizations of which he or she is a member, an e-mail newsletter to his or her "Friends," special shopping evenings with light refreshments exclusively for his or her "Friends," and even a "Night Out on the Town with (salesperson's name)" for "Friends" who reach a certain purchasing plateau.

Certain checks would need to be developed to assure that the salesperson is not just passing out the cards to customers who already come into the store.

Breaking in a New Salesperson

It is a good policy that once you hire a salesperson, you team him or her up with a senior person for a few days until the new person becomes familiar with the merchandise and the store's standard operating procedure. Have the new employee positioned close enough to the senior person so that he or she can overhear the conversations between salesperson and customer. It should give the new employee a feeling of how things are done at the store. Likewise, the senior employee should be close enough to overhear the conversation when the new salesperson is talking to a customer. At the end of each day the senior salesperson can offer any suggestions he or she might have. After a week or so, you should sit down with the new salesperson for a general chat, offering any tips you might have as well as words of encouragement.

Sales Training

An ongoing product training program should be a must for every store. It is the only way your staff will acquire the knowledge required to do a superior job on the sales floor.

How much time is devoted to product training will depend upon the complexity of the products you sell as well as the number of product lines. If you are selling consumer electronics, you probably need at least one hour each week and during new products season, you may have to raise it to two or even three hours a week. For other products, it might only require an hour every other week.

Ask manufacturers or their distributors to conduct the training or provide videotapes, lesson plans, and handbooks so that you can conduct it. A technique often used is to assign a different salesperson to conduct each class. In order to be effective, the salesperson will have to become an expert in the products he or she covers. As a result, later on whenever a fellow salesperson has a question about those products the "expert" on the sales floor can be consulted. Using this technique, each member of your staff is not only trained in every product but also becomes your "expert" in at least one of them. This is an excellent technique to motivate your sales force to learn, and at the same time to encourage teamwork.

A good technique to reinforce the on-the-job training for the sales force, and at the same time provide product information for customers, is to place special "talking points," or point-of-purchase materials (p-o-p), with the products on display. The salesperson can use this p-o-p material as a cue card for reference while talking to a customer.

Whenever a new product or product line comes in, immediately schedule a sales training session. This is especially important if it is a nationally well-advertised, highly technical product in the computer or home entertainment fields. Chances are that customers will have seen the manufacturer's advertisements and will have many questions about the product.

Sales Meetings

It is a good idea to hold sales meetings on a regular basis in order to review results since the previous meeting: which products are selling and which are not, consumer feedback, problems the salespeople are running into, and plans and promotions for the coming month. Also at each meeting, review one or more features of your customer-service program, emphasizing the important role it plays in supporting the sales staff's relationship with the customer. Successful sales meetings are those in which the sales force is encouraged to not only listen but also to actively participate in the discussions and offer their own ideas. You might also turn a sales meeting into a brainstorming session.

Keeping the Staff Motivated

As you are well aware, in motivating people, what works for one person may not work for the next. Some people will be motivated by a pat on the back; others have to be given a pep talk; most respond to money; still others are turned on by gifts and other nonmonetary rewards. You are the one who has to decide which route to take.

Even if you have a good compensation program, you may still want to offer special incentives to further motivate your staff from time to time. It might be to spur business on during down times. It might be to introduce a new product line or product. It might be to push closeouts. It might be to kick off your Christmas shopping season. It might be to rejuvenate your sales force if you detect they have been coasting. Or, if you do not have a regular bonus program, your incentive program might be an ongoing effort with prizes awarded monthly or even weekly.

You have several options in organizing a program. Each salesperson can be rewarded on an individual basis, can be teamed with a partner, or placed on a larger team. The latter two methods may be more effective because of the influence of peer pressure. And they are good team-building and chemistry-developing techniques.

It is important that any incentive program be carefully structured to avoid any claims of favoritism. It might involve points awarded per sale, per dollar total, or per specific product sold.

Also reward salespeople who go that extra yard for a customer: drove five miles in a heavy snow storm to deliver a birthday gift a customer ordered for a friend or helped fix a flat tire on a customer car in your lot, etc.

If any of your manufacturers are offering retail salesperson incentive programs, consider participating in them.

As a further incentive, you might invite customers to nominate a "Salesperson of the Month," as well as a "Salesperson of the Year" from among those who won the monthly awards. While your monthly awards might be a $100 bonus, a night on the town, or a weekend at a nearby resort, the annual award should be something more substantial like an extra week's vacation, $1000, airline tickets, etc.

A Word of Caution

It is important that the dress and appearance of all employees, as well as their handling of product, reflect the image you are trying to project to customers. People who are dealing with customers should be well groomed and dress accordingly. They should also handle the products with care. You don't want a salesperson handling a delicate sweater when she has two-inch nails, or a salesperson who carelessly squeezes a suit back onto a rack when it is apparent there isn't enough space.

Customers who see this type of action can soon be ex-customers.

6

■ ■ ■

Establishing a Winning
Customer Service Program

WHILE YOU MAY believe you are in business to make a good income, in reality you are in business to please your customers because that's the only way you are going to make that good income. Yet consumers constantly complain about the problems they run into when shopping. While most problems occur in the chains, small retailers are not totally exempt.

Customers consider service to be one of the most important parts of the retail experience. Good customer service will keep them coming back, while bad service experiences can mean the end of a relationship with the store. In addition, a store's reputation for providing good service can, through word-of-mouth advertising, attract a lot of new business.

Most important, good service means greater profits. Customers are usually willing to pay more for that extra service.

What are the tenets of good customer service?

- The awareness of everyone on the store's staff that only a satisfied customer will become a regular customer. Conversely, a regular customer can quickly become an ex-customer if his or her level of expectation and satisfaction is no longer met.

- The acknowledgment that customer service is *everyone's* responsibility. There cannot be a single weak link in the chain.
- The anticipation of the customer's needs and fulfilling those needs.
- The solution of potential problems before they have a chance to develop into serious problems.
- Good two-way communication with the customers. Listening to what they have to say, and implementing their suggestions.
- The recognition that the customer is always right and that you need the customer more than the customer needs you.

A copy of these tenets should be given to each employee, and a copy should be posted in a back room of the store so that employees are very aware of them and see them every day they are at work.

What are the elements of a good customer service program?

- First and foremost a helpful, knowledgeable professional sales staff. Customers want salespeople who will take an interest in them, know the product lines, and help them find products that fit their needs and desires. You want your customers to look upon your salespeople as problem solvers and counselors, men and women whose advice is impeccable.
- A warm feeling of welcome for your customers from the time they come through the front door till they leave with their packages. Customers should be thought of as guests and should always be greeted when they enter the store and always thanked when they leave, whether or not they make a purchase. If they present a credit, frequent buyer, or VIP membership card when they pay for their purchase, always thank them by name when you hand back the card.
- The realization by the owner that he or she sets the example. By actively participating in every aspect of the customer relations program, he or she is sending an important message to his or her employees that they had better buy into it.
- Space permitting, offer customers a hot drink in the winter or a cold drink in summer. And if it is a rainy or snowy day, have a place where customers can leave their umbrellas and perhaps even a rack to check their coats.
- Store hours and days that are convenient for the customers and not because they are convenient for management and staff. Also be flexible during holidays and other periods of the year.

■ A liberal product return and exchange policy. If possible the policy should be printed on the register receipt in order to avoid any misunderstanding. If not, the policy should be posted near the cash register and a copy of it stapled to the cash register receipt.

■ Quick and fair resolution of customer complaints. Many retailers find that the fastest, easiest, and least expensive way to resolve a problem is to ask the customer how he or she would like the store to handle it. Most of the time the customer's solution is the simplest and least demanding. If the store makes the first offer, all too often the customer turns toward negotiating a better offer.

■ An ample supply of products on hand when you are having a sale and a liberal rain check policy except, of course, on closeouts.

■ If you sell clothing or shoes, have a wide variety of sizes and the ability to special order quickly a size you might be out of when a customer requests it. Offer to deliver the product to the customer the day it comes in.

■ A note to first-time customers, thanking them for shopping at the store and inviting them to come by again. Always follow up with a telephone call when a customer makes a large purchase, especially a consumer electronics product or an appliance.

■ Prompt answering of incoming telephone calls with a pleasant greeting and never putting anyone on hold unless he or she volunteers to wait while you check something out. If you have to call back, ask the customer what time it would be convenient to call. Instruct your staff to smile when they are talking on the telephone. Believe it or not, it does help to project a friendlier tone of voice!

■ Free gift-wrapping for products over a certain price point as well as free or low-cost packaging and delivery for local and out-of-town shipments.

■ A child-friendly atmosphere. Reserve parking spaces closest to the front door for families with young children and expectant mothers. Space permitting, set aside an alcove where children can watch TV or play games while their parents shop. Offer a baby-sitting service while mothers shop the store, and have a baby changing station.

■ Personal amenities. Sew back buttons that have come loose or have come off. Provide replacement buttons for the clothing you sell. Stock a closet with supplies customers might need in an emergency: plastic rain hats, emery boards, nail polish, sewing kits, pins, diapers and Handi-

Wipes for children, etc. Have a shoe-buffing machine and a place for customers to retrieve e-mails. Carry customer's packages to their cars.

- Customer-appreciation activities including frequent buyer programs, reward savings cards, special previews and events, drawings for prizes, selecting customer of the month, birthday gifts, and special offers.

- Special assistance to customers who purchase electronic and technical products and need help in understanding and installing them. Hold in-store seminars on the installation and operation. Depending on price, offer free or low-cost installation of the more complicated products. Prepare a simplified "shortcuts" for operating and caring for products when the manufacturer's instructions are complicated.

- Hot line for customers to call when they have a question or problem. After hours, have an answering machine take the calls. Have someone monitor the machine every two hours so that calls can be promptly answered even when the store is closed. Customers will be very impressed with the store's efficiency.

- Two-way e-mail communications program with customers (see chapter 18).

- An improved communications program. The owner/managers/sales staff should engage customers in conversation during store visits, trying to gauge customer satisfaction and information on improving service. Send out periodic customer newsletters. Web site (see chapter 18).

- Enable customers to register their interest in specific products so the store can call them when the products come in.

- A husbands' corner at women's clothing stores so while the wife shops the store, he can relax, watch television, read a magazine, have a cup of coffee or tea. In smaller stores, this alcove might be combined with the childrens' corner.

- If packaged goods, beverages, and other dated products are sold, make certain that expired products are pulled from the shelves. Since some expiration dates are in codes that consumers can not decipher, it is good customer relations to make certain that shoppers don't take home an expired product and become a dissatisfied consumer.

- If you are in the service sector of retail, be very careful how you handle customers' personal property. A person who brings a $750 suit to a dry cleaner is not going to feel comfortable when the person waiting on him slides the suit across the counter and then throws it into a bin.

- If in the service sector, offer a pickup and delivery service.

- Conduct frequent surveys of customers to gauge satisfaction with their dealings with the store, and take immediate action to remedy weak spots in the program. On an ongoing basis seek out new elements to add to the customer relations program.

- Establish a customer advisory council to meet with you a few times a year. It not only demonstrates your recognition of the importance of the customer to the store but will also provide valuable input from the customer standpoint.

- An annual "Thank You" event, perhaps a picnic, for your customers. In addition to thanking them for their support, it gives you and your sales force an opportunity to get better acquainted with them.

- Have bilingual sales people, p-o-p materials, and circulars if you have a large base of customers whose native language is other than English.

- Institute a personal shopper service on a fee basis if it is appropriate for your store.

- Offer customers who purchase any piece of jewelry valued over a certain amount of money ($500 to $1000) an appraisal certificate, photograph, detailed description, and estimated retail replacement value.

- Heavily publicize in store, on your Web site, and in your e-mail newsletter information about any recalls of products you carry.

7

———■■■———

Looking Good from Your Front Windows to the Back of the Store

UNLIKE THE FAMILIAR saying, "Don't judge a book by its cover," people do judge a store by its "cover." The first impression a person is going to get of your store is from its windows, the front door, and the outdoor signage. Many a decision on whether or not to enter the store is going to be based on this first impression. Furthermore, if the potential customer does get by the cover and enters the store, he or she must feel comfortable inside, or chances are he or she will walk right out.

So it is very important that both the inside and outside of your store are kept as attractive as possible. Both should reflect a personality and image that appeals to your target audience.

Think of your store as you would of an impulse item. You want the passerby to be stopped in his or her tracks by your windows and signage, and drawn right through the front door. Then, once the customer opens the door, you want him or her to be further drawn to your merchandise.

START WITH YOUR SIDEWALK

The image of your store begins with your sidewalk. You want it to be head and shoulders above all the other sidewalks on the same street. If someone surveys the entire block from across the street, you want your entire package—sidewalk, store, and signage—to stand out from all the others.

If the zoning laws permit, think of ways to improve the pavement in front of the store. Perhaps a red brick sidewalk will give you the distinctive look you want. Or perhaps just a red brick path leading to the entrance. Or some other unique paving.

- If you have trees in front of the store, plant flowers in the tree bases. In addition, planting flowers in other appropriate places around the front of the store will create an attractive atmosphere.
- Consider installing decorative lights on the trees, turned on at sunset. Originally used around the Christmas holidays, lighted trees are becoming popular year-round in many business districts. They'll focus attention to your store front, especially if you have evening hours.
- If you have a wide sidewalk and zoning laws permit it, consider installing one or two benches near the curb, facing your windows. It is a nice amenity for the community, and anyone sitting on the benches will be looking right at your windows.
- Another popular amenity, one which will gain the appreciation of the growing number of pet owners, would be to have a dog water fountain somewhere in front of the store.
- Keep the sidewalk clean. It should be swept several times a day. A dirty sidewalk is easily noticed and is a turnoff.
- On snowy days, keep the sidewalk clear of snow, even if you have to do it several times an hour. It is a way of showing that you are a good citizen and care about your neighbors. The community will appreciate it, especially your customers.

. . . THEN THE SIGNS, AWNING, AND CANOPY

A great deal of thought should go into your decision on how to display the store's name as well as whether or not you will have a canopy or awning over your windows and/or doors.

To assist you in developing your outside look, hire a designer to look at the exterior as a package and advise you on color, types, and sizes of signs; type of canopy or awning to use; and type of window.

In reaching your conclusion, take several factors into consideration:

- Local zoning regulations. There may be restrictions regarding the type and/or size of signage you can use, especially if you are located in a historic district.
- The surrounding stores. Some uniformity in store signs on the same street is usually a good idea. Otherwise you can end up with a maze of signs, each trying to overwhelm the other. To achieve this uniformity, it may be necessary for you to compromise on the signage that you really want. This is one particular area in which your designer can be of great assistance.
- Your location. If your entrance is right on the corner, your signage will probably be different than if you are in the middle of the block. For a corner entrance, you might want an overhanging vertical sign attached to the corner of the building so that it is visible on both streets. If your store is visible on a highway, well-traveled road, or commuter rail line, you will probably want a lighted sign in order to attract attention to the store's name.
- Some stores use canvas canopies with no overhead covering. As a result, they do not protect passersby from inclement weather the way an awning does. When people take cover under an awning, they are a captive audience for your windows. You never know how many customers you will pick up that way. This rainy day added exposure you get can be very meaningful, especially if you are located right by a bus stop or some other heavily traveled area.
- A relatively new technique enables you to project the store's name or logo on the sidewalk at night. The logo or name can remain static or revolve.

. . . LOOK AT THE WINDOWS

The one place where you should not cut any corners is with your windows. They might be the most important part of the store because they set the scene for what the customer will find inside. When properly used, your windows are your least expensive and most effective form of advertising. *They bring customers into the store!*

Your initial step should be to decide on an overall philosophy of how you will use your windows, what you want them to say, and how you want them to deliver your message. There are many options available, and what you do and how you do it will depend largely upon your type of store and your marketing strategy.

A Minimum of Product Versus a Packed Window

Just how much product you put in a window will depend upon what you are trying to accomplish. Retailers who display a minimal amount of product are usually trying to project an upscale image. By delivering a limited message through their windows, they appear to be saying that they have an exclusive grouping of products for a select audience. Other stores will pack their windows with as much product as possible. Shoe stores do this to show the variety of styles; hardware stores show the variety of products they carry; drug stores display their many specials. Still other stores try to present a cross section of products they carry so that window shoppers get a sense of what is available inside.

A relatively small store with an all glass front might opt for an open look that exposes virtually the entire store and all of its products. By keeping the product display at the window just a few feet above ground level, and then staggering the height of other interior displays near the window, a passerby has a good view of just about everything in the store.

Yes or No on Price Tags

Should you place price tags on products in the window? Stores, which usually display prices, do it so that shoppers will know the price range of their products, and also be aware of specials and sale items.

There are various reasons for not featuring price tags in the window. Some retailers feel the absence of price tags lures shoppers into the store, creating an opportunity to close a sale, while a visible price tag might turn shoppers off and keep them from entering the store. Others feel that by not posting prices, they avoid getting involved in open price wars with competitors. Still other retailers look at not displaying price tags as a way to project an upscale image: People with limited budgets will feel they cannot afford to shop at the store and won't waste the time of the sales help, while wealthier people will perceive that the store is upscale with a rich clientele.

Movement in the Windows?

Movement adds excitement to your windows and attracts attention. It stops people on the street and draws them toward the window.

Some retailers feel that the use of turntables and other animated devices will focus attention on only that part of the window causing remaining products to be ignored. For the same reason, other retailers feel that you will accomplish your objectives if you feature the key products you are promoting in the moving display. The star products get the star treatment, and the others fill the supporting role.

There are also different theories about the effectiveness of zippers and electronic message boards. Again, some retailers feel they detract from what is displayed in the window, while others feel that they actually attract people to the window. The latter group's argument is that people stop to read the message and in doing so are exposed to the store window. The messages can direct the reader to specific products in the window or to a sale or promotion. Or messages can feature trivia information, to announce upcoming civic events, give high school sports results, or carry public service messages.

The use of video in the window can be a very effective way to promote certain products. It is a great way to present fashions being sold inside the store, to show product features on appliances, to demonstrate do-it-yourself projects. The videos have to show movement and the picture has to speak for itself since it is doubtful you will want to hook up audio outside the store. Many manufacturers have videos you can use in-store or in your windows.

Another form of movement is the use of live performers in the window. In the chapter on special events (chapter 10), you will find examples of how performers can appear in the window for the specific purpose of attracting a crowd and leading it into the store. Naturally, when you have live performers in the window, you will have less product exposure since people will be concentrating on the performance and not looking at what is on display.

Finding a Window Decorator

Once you have decided on the direction your window project will follow, your next step should be to find a decorator. If the budget permits, you should hire a professional window dresser. How do you find one?

Spend some time looking at store windows throughout the area. When you see a window you like, ask the owner for the name of the dresser. You might want to compile a list of three or four and interview each one. See if they agree with your objectives for your windows. Study their portfolios to get a more complete feeling for their work. Find out their work procedures. Do they provide you with a sketch of each window? Do they lean toward expensive props? Are they willing to repaint and reuse old props? How quickly do they work? How long will it take from concept to final execution? And most important, is the chemistry there? Will you be able to work with one another?

If you cannot afford to use a professional window dresser, you may be able to find help locally free of charge, or at a relatively low cost. Contact local schools of design to see if they have intern programs for their students. You may be able to get free assistance, perhaps even students working under the direction of their teacher. If the school does not have a formal internship program, ask the dean or a professor to recommend a very talented student. Your costs will probably be minimal.

You might also find a full-time window trimmer who works for a large department store and is looking to moonlight, or a talented interior designer or decorator who has a flair for doing store windows.

Many retailers and their employees have become skilled window decorators. While it takes time from their regular duties, it does save the store money. If you will be doing your windows in-house, contact your suppliers to see if there is any assistance they may offer. It might include handbooks or videotapes on decorating techniques. A supplier might have a consultant, who could visit your store to run an informal seminar and offer other assistance; or they may even have window designs you can follow.

Making the Windows Work for You

With major decisions made on the look your windows will take and who will decorate them, it is time to put those windows to work for you. They have to help you sell your products, motivate window-shoppers to come into the store, and leave an impression of the store on the minds of passersby.

Here are some tips on how to accomplish this:

- Use your windows to tell what's going on inside the store. Always feature your sales, special events, and thematic promotions in them. For example, if you are running a "Back to School" promotion, decorate the window with school logos, books, blackboards, and school desks as well as your featured products. Also use banners to reinforce the message.

- Be ingenious on how you display your products. Sometimes use props instead of mannequins and fixtures. Display waterproof boots by having them stand in a large pot of water. Try a child's jacket draped around the back of a kitchen chair, just like the child would do at home. How about a woman's hat on top of a lamp shade? There is no limit to what you can do.

- Change your windows frequently. People will stop looking at the same old window if it is there too long.

- Develop a daily feature so that passersby will be enticed to look at them each day. A product of the day, joke of the day, trivia question of the day, or special password of the day good for a surprise gift or discount. A fun feature guaranteed to attract people on a regular basis is to hide a mascot (a Teddy bear or some other stuffed animal) in a different place in the window each day. People will talk about the window, and it should get good media coverage. A local disc jockey may pick up on it and make it his or her pet.

- Keep your windows clean. Dirty, unwashed windows are a turnoff and bad for your image.

Other ideas for window displays to support promotions, sales, and special events will be found throughout the book.

If You Do Your Own Window Displays

If you are dressing your own windows, as many retailers do, you should develop a relationship with a local distributor, designer, or producer of window display materials. Get on the mailing lists of some of the national companies in the field. You will be able to get just about anything you need to decorate a window including mannequins, mannequin parts, banners, turntables, oversized formed plastic products, seasonal displays, lights, classic columns, pedestals and platforms, and animated characters.

But don't confine yourself to the traditional window-dressing materials. You can use just about anything in a window. Sometimes by simply repainting, you can use a prop again and again.

Antique dealers, art galleries, and furniture stores are ideal places to borrow materials for your window displays. You can usually get them to lend you what you need so long as you give them credit in the window.

You can make your mannequins more attractive by adding jewelry and other accessories. Borrow what you need from other merchants, giving them a credit in the window.

If you are running a sports promotion, try borrowing equipment from local sports teams (see chapter 13). You can probably get old newspaper headlines from your local daily.

Your historical society and local library are good sources for display material. So are the veterans' organizations, boy and girl scouts, and garden clubs. Make contact with local hobbyists and collectors who will probably be very happy to lend material for your windows. Finally, don't overlook local junk yards or the garbage dump. You will be amazed what you can sometimes find at these locations. All you will need is a little paint and you have a first-class window prop.

ENTER THE FRONT DOOR

The first impression campaign should continue with your front door. It is only a small piece of the picture, but an important one, which is all too often ignored.

How many retailers have a sign on the door that says, WELCOME, PLEASE COME IN AND BROWSE, or THROUGH THESE DOORS WALK THE NICEST PEOPLE IN THE WORLD? Probably very few, yet such signs are inexpensive to have made and would probably bring in additional traffic.

Use the front door as a continuation of your window. If the windows are promoting a sale or special event, have a sign on, or over, the door relating to the event: WELCOME TO OUR SPRING CLEARANCE SALE, or MEET JAMBO THE MAGICIAN, etc. Sometimes a sign isn't necessary to serve as a bridge. If for example, you are promoting St. Patrick's Day in the window, all you would need on the door are shamrocks.

Not only should you have a welcome sign of some type on the outside of the door but you should also have a THANK YOU sign on the inside that the customer sees on the way out. It might read, THANK YOU FOR SHOPPING WITH US, THANKS FOR YOUR SUPPORT, HAVE A SAFE TRIP HOME, or WE APPRECIATE THE TIME YOU SPEND WITH US.

Other than the single sign, your front door should be clean and provide a clear view into the store. You want the passerby who is turned on by the window to have a good view of the interior of the store when he or she approaches the door.

INSIDE . . . A CUSTOMER FRIENDLY STORE

Designing the interior of the store requires special talents and is a job that should be done by a professional. Even if you do not have plans, or the money to renovate your store, it still might be a good idea to consult a store designer for suggestions on how you might improve the selling floor. A retailer should always be looking for ways to improve the interior of the store to make it easier for customers to shop and find the merchandise they came to buy. A designer can assist you in that area.

Even without a designer there are many steps you can take to make shopping an easier and happier experience.

■ Your merchandise should be organized in such a way that customers will quickly find what they want. One technique is to have the various sections of the store numbered, and directories up front, in the middle, and in the rear of the store identifying in which section specific products can be found. Another technique is grouping merchandise. In men's clothing stores, you might do it by size with regular, short, and long each having its own section. In a food store you might have all your low-calorie and sugar-free products in a special section. If you have a recipe program, indicate next to each ingredient the section letter or number in which it can be found.

■ It is important that your products be displayed so that you can maximize their appeal within the store. Identify those with very strong eye appeal and use them as a major focal point. Always have an interesting product or display featured up front and visible from the outside of the store. It should be aimed at attracting the attention of passersby, and at grabbing the interest of customers walking through the front door. Try color-coordinating displays and merchandise.

■ Whenever you have a limited sale, or if you have a regular sale table, it should always be in the rear of the store so that customers will have to pass all of your other product displays to get to the bargains. You'll never know how much additional business you will pick up this way.

- Cleanliness and neatness throughout the store should be a must. Your sales help should be trained to tidy up and replace product automatically when it is out of place. Customers react positively to a clean, neat environment, and negatively to a messy and dirty one.

- The aisles should be wide enough for customers to walk through without bumping into displays and counters, as well as for disabled people to maneuver in them easily.

- Movement control within a store should be an important goal for all retailers. While it is not always easy to achieve, you want to develop a pattern of movement for your customers so that they will be exposed to key product areas as they move from Point A to Point B. You should study their movement habits before you develop your plan. Indeed, in developing your plan you may discover that it is easier to move your key product areas within customers' existing shopping patterns than it is to change their habits.

- Avoid placing product higher than a five-foot-tall person can comfortably reach (unless your clientele is primarily male; in that case add an extra seven to eight inches). Also many people cannot or do not like to bend. Try not to place product lower than one foot off the floor.

- Lighting is important, especially when fashions, home furnishings, and other color-oriented products are sold.

- Some retailers believe that adding pleasant scents to a store will improve customer moods, but that can backfire if customers have allergies to the scents.

- All store personnel should wear name tags, and the tags of salespeople should identify their areas of specialization when appropriate. This would be particularly important when selling consumer electronics products, major appliances, etc.

- If you have cashiers, cash registers are usually placed at the front right-hand side of the store near the exit. If you attract large numbers of shoppers during certain periods, you might mount one or more cash registers on wheeled carts and place them at strategic areas around the store in order to ease the traffic flow. If your salespeople handle the actual transactions, you might have the registers scattered around the store so that your people do not lose time being away from their sections.

- If your budget permits, you might consider having a host at the front door to greet customers as they enter the store and thank them on the way out. The greeter can also be your security person.

- Some of the manufacturers of products you sell may provide displays for use with their merchandise. These may be permanent displays, or for short-term promotional use. They may be given to you free, at cost, or as part of a package if you purchase a certain amount of merchandise. If you are thinking of using any of these displays you must decide how and if they fit into the decorative environment of the store. If they overwhelm your other displays, you may opt not to accept them.

IN-STORE SIGNS THAT SELL MERCHANDISE

Your interior signage should not only contribute to the ambiance and image of the store but also to the sale of the merchandise. Signs that don't help sell are really not doing their job.

There are many things that your signs can do:

- They provide pricing information.
- They provide product information.
- They direct or lure customers to particular products, specials, or sections of the store.
- They promote coming events.
- They complete the story you started to tell in the window.

Your signs can take on several forms.

- They may be neon and used on the walls to identify the various departments or sections of the store.
- They may be in the form of moving message boards and provide information on specials and sale items as well as coming events. The signs can range in size from a single-line crawling message to a wall-mounted, five-lines-at-a-time display.
- They can be banners appropriate for the season of the year, or heralding a specific sale, a special event, or a holiday.
- They can be distinctive price/size tags on the product with the store logo or name.
- They can be price, sale price, or percentage-off signs for your counters, display tables, or racks.
- They can be counter, display table, or rack signs with a series of one-line descriptions of the features of a specific product.

- They can be self-standing with an easel backing so that they can be placed on counters.
- They can be "as seen" signs. Manufacturers will often supply point-of-purchase material of print ads, along with the tag line, AS ADVERTISED IN TIME MAGAZINE, etc. They may also offer p-o-p of the product with the line, AS SEEN ON SUCH-AND-SUCH SHOW ON NBC. These p-o-p materials are usually provided in easel format and are aimed at creating additional customer excitement and credibility for the product.
- They can be signs of all types, shapes, and forms provided by your manufacturers and distributors. They all want to help you sell through to the customer and will provide all types of point-of-purchase aids and signs.
- They can be odd-shaped signs like arrows, circles, stars, or puffs. The odd shapes, along with color, are aimed at grabbing the attention of customers.

The type of point-of-purchase signs that you have made for your store should reflect a "look" that is present in all your signage. If you have a featured color scheme (the windows, walls, display cases, etc.) you should use those colors on your p-o-p materials, too.

Printed signs or those professionally handmade are always preferable to the handwritten ones so often used. There are several ways to approach your signage needs:

- You can have the signs designed and printed locally.
- You can purchase colorful stock signs and have the pricing information and messages printed locally.
- You can use your computer or purchase a special sign making system and make your own.
- You can use local art students to create some of your special signs and/or hand letter the stock signs you purchase.

There are various types of talking signs available including push-button activated displays that feature audio or video point-of-purchase messages. Speak to your manufacturers or distributors to see if they have any available.

OTHER PARTS OF THE BIG PICTURE

There are other steps you might take to help enhance your in-store image among customers:

- Use only recyclable packaging materials. Most of your customers will have a favorable impression of the store if you do.
- Place a suggestion box in a prominent place within the store. Acknowledge every suggestion and give gifts to those people whose suggestions you implement.
- If you have celebrities—local or national—who are customers, ask them for an autographed picture and permission to display it in the store. Many customers are impressed when they learn that they shop at the same store as celebrities do. Also, if any customers send you letters complimenting you on your products, service, or individual employees, post them in a heavily traveled section of the store.
- If you have the space, you might have a small lounge/sitting area in the store for customers to take a brief break. You can serve coffee. This will work in certain types of stores, usually upscale ones. The downside of a lounge/sitting area is that it may become a hangout, attracting the same people all of the time. So if you set one up, let everyone know that you are doing it on an experimental basis. This will give you an out in case you have to close it down.
- If you supply merchandise to prominent groups in the area (the ballet, theater company, orchestra, athletic team, school, etc.) try to get permission from them to let you call yourself the group's "Official Supplier." Then promote it in-store and externally. You could have signs throughout the store proclaiming, OFFICIAL SHOE SUPPLIER TO OURTOWN BALLET, OFFICIAL POSTGAME CATERERS TO THE OURTOWN TIGERS, OFFICIAL STATIONERS TO OURTOWN COLLEGE, etc.
- If you, or the store, receive awards from the community, religious, business, government, educational, or professional organizations, display them in a prominent place in the store.
- Consider placing a literature rack somewhere in the store. The rack might contain consumer material as well as specific use and care information on products you sell. For example, if you sell clothing, you might have material to take home on how to remove stains, if you sell electrical products, you might have literature on safety and how to avoid overloading circuits. You could also have material on local health screenings

and various booklets on subjects of interest that are available from the federal government.

LOOK TO YOUR SUPPLIERS AS YOUR PARTNERS

Throughout this chapter retailers have been encouraged to seek out the manufacturers of the products they sell, or their distributors. Many will offer a variety of assistance packages to store owners in a broad range of categories including store design, marketing and merchandising, promotions, signage, special events, advertising, public relations, and training.

Let your suppliers know that you are very interested in promoting their products and would appreciate any help they can give you. Ask what support programs they can offer.

You might also encourage your suppliers to use your store to test promotions, which they might want to try before rolling them out regionally or nationally.

8

—■ ■ ■—

Making the Big Decision:
Which Programs to Conduct

WHILE THERE MAY be more than a thousand promotional ideas within the pages of this book, by no means is each one of them suitable for every retail establishment. Rather, they comprise a universe of ideas from which retailers can select those appropriate for their stores. Entire categories may be eliminated by some retailers as not appropriate for the store, its product lines, or its customers. Or they might be just too expensive for the store's budget. On the other hand some retailers may find workable suggestions in all categories.

Only you are in the position to decide which promotions to try at your store. And you should make these selections only after a careful analysis of customer attitudes and your costs.

MATCHING THE PROMOTION TO THE CUSTOMERS

Before you even begin work on the financial feasibility of a promotion, you must be convinced that it will be attractive to your customers and to your potential customers as well. This is where your role as matchmaker comes in.

Chapter 4 discussed the data readily available in your community as well as other information that can be developed locally. This information will help you profile your actual and potential customers. Once you have profiled them, you will have a better idea of the promotions to which they will react positively.

In addition, while a promotional idea is still in its embryonic stage, your sales staff should test customer reaction to it. You should also poll your customers by telephone as well as some of your targeted potential customers.

Information to Get from Regular Customers

- Try to determine if regular customers will visit the store during the promotion solely because of it.
- Will regular customers postpone a visit to the store until a promotion starts? Or, will they avoid the store during promotions?
- Will added crowds at the store during the promotion upset the regular customers?
- What promotions do your regular customers prefer? Special events, seasonal themes, sales, contests?
- Try to determine, by themes, which promotions your regular customers prefer (sports, exhibits, entertainers, psychics, etc.)?
- Would regular customers prefer lower everyday prices to promotions?
- Do promotions have any effect on how regular customers feel about the store?
- What do regular customers think of proposed promotions outlined to them? Would they look forward to them?

Information to Get from Potential Customers

- What do they think of promotions?
- Will they visit a store for the first time because of a promotion?
- Will they visit it even though they may not be looking to purchase a product?
- What promotions would attract them to a store? Special events, seasonal themes, sales, contests?
- What themes would attract them? Sports, nostalgia, psychics, exhibits, holidays, entertainment?
- If they visit a store because of a specific promotion, would they visit it a second time after the promotion is over?

- Would they prefer to patronize a store that offers everyday low pricing rather than periodic promotions?
- What do they think of the proposed promotion outlined to them? Would they look forward to attending?

ANSWERING THE FIVE BIG QUESTIONS

1. Will this promotion attract new and/or repeat customers and/or incremental business?
The obvious answer must be yes. A promotion should only be conducted if it will attract customers and business. The type of promotion you select, your pricing during the promotion, and those to whom you market each promotion will determine your success in attracting new customers and building incremental sales. It must be a promotion that appeals to your target audience.

2. Will the new customers it attracts be the customers you want to attract— people who will come back to the store after the promotion is over?
This is where you have to be careful in selecting a promotion. A good rule of thumb is not to hold events that will draw large crowds unless you feature products in the popular price range. Even if you meet that criteria, you have to be careful that your promotion draws people who are going to come back. There must be a relationship between the promotion and the type of customers attracted to your store.

An upscale men's clothing store with a sports memorabilia display will probably attract many sports fans, but very few will ever come back. However, if the store runs a promotion featuring just golf memorabilia, it will probably attract the people who fit its customer profile and generate repeat business. Thus promotions upscale retailers run will undoubtedly appeal to a narrower audience with all of the promotional efforts aimed directly at that group. Its goal would be to draw a smaller number of quality prospects to whom the sales force can give more personal attention, and work toward converting into regular customers.

3. Will the promotion enhance the overall image of the store, or will it possibly detract from it?
This is the easiest question to answer since you have total control over it. You know what image your store has, or at least what you want it to

have. Measure the proposed promotion against it and see if it will detract from your image. If you are known as a conservative store, do not conduct an "off-the-wall" promotion with psychedelic lighting that will draw a teenage crowd. By the same token, if you draw a young upbeat clientele, don't schedule a promotion to attract a middle-age audience. Your customers undoubtedly like the image of your store because that's why they shop there. So by tailoring promotions for them, based on their likes, you will be enhancing the overall image of the store.

4. Will it hurt existing business by attracting so many new customers that your sales force will have a hard time properly tending to the needs of your regular customers?
This is a possibility if your store becomes so packed with people that shopping becomes difficult and your regular customers will not get their usual good service. You must try to select promotions that can fit comfortably into the store, and will not draw masses of people who cannot be properly served.

Another way to approach the problem is that when you schedule promotions that you expect will draw large crowds, hold a preview day or night for your regular customers. This way, they will feel important, have first crack at all the merchandise, and get the VIP treatment. It will also enable your sales force to spend more time during the promotion cultivating new customers.

5. What is the bottom line? Will it be cost efficient? And how cost effective will it be when compared to other promotions you could run?
You will need to develop quite a bit of data to answer this important fifth question. If you have been compiling sales statistics over the years, you may already have this information. If you have not, you should be collecting sales data on a regular basis since it is so important to your promotional planning process.

The data you should develop include:

Cost of Promotion/Percent of Annual Budget

One of the first things you have to do is price out very carefully the exact cost of the promotion. You must factor in all of the basic costs from planning to execution. This includes:

- Entertainers/personalities (magician, clown, etc.)
- Platform rental, if needed
- Public address system
- Decorations, costumes, props, etc.
- Advertising and promotion (only factor in the costs of advertising and promotional materials purchased exclusively for this promotion)
- Prizes, if it is a contest
- Extra security
- Additional staff salaries (temps, or overtime)
- Refreshments, gifts for customers (both optional)
- Contingency allowance
- Contribution to a charity (if a tie-in with a nonprofit organization)

Once you have added up all these expenses, figure out what percentage of your annual promotion budget will be used for this event. Also figure out your estimated profitability, using the profitability figures from past promotions.

Store's Sales History During Promotions

If you have been keeping good records of your sales by week or month, you will be able to get an idea of what your average sales figures have been over the past few years during the specific period(s) you are planning one or more promotions. Note whether you were conducting a promotion during this period in past years. You should also determine the percentage of your annual sales that usually occur during this month.

Square Footage Needed Versus Available Space

You must carefully calculate the amount of square footage needed for this event, including space for customer-spectators. Then calculate the amount of nondisplay space available. You will then be able to determine how much additional space may be needed.

At this point, you must decide whether it will be worth committing the additional space to the promotion. What is the potential income lost by eliminating the display space during the promotion period? If you do not already have this information, start tracking sales from the display area involved over a period of days similar to those during which the promotion will run. Will the additional business generated by the promotion more than make up for the loss? Would any loss be minimized by shifting the products from the eliminated display area to another area in the store? Could you have them temporarily replace less profitable products on display?

Experience Factor

What has been your experience regarding similar promotions or any promotions held during this period of time? Approximately how many additional customers were attracted to the store, and how many of them became regular customers?

Staffing Requirements

You must factor in the staffing requirements for the promotion or event. This includes both planning time and the event itself. If additional people are needed, or staff members are paid overtime, costs must be calculated and added onto your budget.

Targeted Goals for the Promotion

You should set some practical profit and customer goals for your promotion.

- Is your main objective to use the promotion to introduce new customers to the store?
- Is it to increase gross sales, or net profits? If so, by how much? And are these reasonable figures?
- Is the objective just to focus attention on the store, or to enhance its image without caring about sales figures and income?

You must put some dollars-and-cents estimates against these questions. For example, you must place a monetary value on a new customer. Based on experience, how much additional revenue will a new customer generate in a year? You must also estimate how much additional revenue will be generated by the promotion. You should be able to use figures from past promotions to get these numbers.

Additional Income

Will any of your suppliers contribute promotional dollars for the event? If so, now much? Will an increased buy-in of products entitle you to better pricing?

Other Items

There are additional factors to consider before making your final decision:

- Make certain that the promotion dates do not coincide with any religious holidays celebrated by a large number of your customers.
- Avoid scheduling a promotion if people are expected to be on vacation. If there are large industrial plants in your area, check to see when they shut down for vacation.
- Be flexible and factor in snow days in case your area is hit with a storm.
- Don't schedule an event for a day when there's a big local high school or college football game scheduled in the city, especially if the whole town turns out for games.

MAKING THE FINAL DECISION

It is now up to you to make that final decision.

- You should be totally convinced that the promotion you select will appeal to your audience.
- You should be convinced that it will accomplish its goals: to attract new customers, create excitement, increase sales, and enhance the image of the store.
- You should also be convinced that there will not be any financial surprises, that you will be able to come in on budget, and that income from the promotion will be within the parameters of your estimate.

9

■ ■ ■

Creating Exciting Holiday and Seasonal Promotions

"WHAT AN EXCITING STORE!"

"The place comes alive!"

"It's theater!"

You don't have to be a retail giant to generate these enthusiastic customer reviews.

No matter what your size or product line may be, you can—and should—make your store an exciting place in which to shop, a place where customers will want to hurry back and visit more frequently, buying more products and spending more money.

You can accomplish this through a combination of excitement-generating vehicles: lively in-store promotions and entertainment, eye-catching displays, theme-related sales and special events, and a warm, friendly atmosphere. Do it and you will win over the loyalty of customers who will appreciate the pleasant change of pace they experience at your store compared to the usual routine they encounter elsewhere.

The various holidays of the year, the four seasons, and other significant periods are ideal vehicles to develop these exciting week-long—or even longer—storewide promotional events.

GETTING MAXIMUM EXPOSURE
AND OPTIMUM RESULTS

In order to gain maximum exposure as well as optimum results for your in-store promotions, you should be thorough in carrying out your themes so that they are evident throughout the store, in your advertising, on your Web site, and in your publicity.

Store windows should reflect the holiday or seasonal theme the customers will find once inside the store. The theme decor should be included on the front door, too. This might include, for example, shamrocks on St. Patrick's Day, red hearts on Valentine's Day, pumpkins on Halloween, Santa around Christmas, American flags on Independence Day

In-store decorations should include the colors (if there are any) usually associated with the theme or holiday. Posters and other decorative materials should clearly tell the customer what the theme is all about.

But decorations should not be the only way to carry out the theme. Depending upon the type of store, your sales staff might wear appropriate dress and/or accessories, or buttons relating to the theme promotion (KISS ME I'M IRISH, etc.).

Drawings for prizes related to the theme can be held daily or weekly. Your suppliers should be asked to donate product for prizes. If you advertise a promotion and promise to include the donor's prize in the ads, as well as in the windows and in the store, chances are that you may be able to get attractive prizes donated locally from noncompetitive sources (a travel agency, restaurants, area resorts, major appliance dealer, etc.). Budget and space permitting, light refreshments could also be served. If you can fit it into your budget, you might also want to give away small favors related to the theme. Most important, and only if appropriate, hold a sale keyed to the theme of the promotion. Some of the theme promotions occur during traditional sale periods.

In developing your promotional plans, it would be advantageous to do so by quarter. List all of the possibilities over each three-month period; and select the ones that you feel, based on your planning criteria, meet your needs as well as those of the customers. Perhaps plan to have one theme promotion a month, complementing it with other types of promotions (special events, sales, contests, etc.)

THE FIRST QUARTER OF THE YEAR

If you had to give the first quarter of the year a name, it would be The Sale Quarter. It starts off with the ending of the post-Christmas sales period, and the beginning of the traditional white sales, then slides into the Presidents' Day sales, and in recent years the sales have continued through March, when it got warmer and the Easter-buying season began.

While there are some great promotional theme possibilities for this period, some retailers might want to take a conservative approach and not put as much money into promotions this quarter as they would during the second quarter with its heavy gift-giving holidays.

Here are some of the first quarter promotion opportunities:

Happy New Year!

An ideal theme to run from the day after Christmas through the first week of the New Year. It is a fun promotion that will appeal to people of all age groups and enable you to turn the normally hectic post Christmas clear-the-shelves sale period into a launch of the New Year with fully stocked shelves of new products as well as your clearance items.

Built around a New Year's Eve party theme, the decor in the windows and throughout the store might include streamers, confetti, balloons, Happy New Year signs, pictures of the New Year baby, noisemakers, hats and taped music. (If taped music is played, you are required to pay an annual licensing fee.) Also such signage as OUR NEW YEAR RESOLUTION: TO KEEP A HAPPY CUSTOMER, or MAKE A RESOLUTION TO SHOP AND SAVE AT (STORE NAME).

You might also consider "fun" newspaper headlines "forecasting" events for the year ahead: "Local High School Star Signs $100-Million Dollar NBA Contract," "Washington Finishes with Trillion-Dollar Surplus," "$10,000 Dividend Checks Sent to All Taxpayers," "Martian Space Ship to Land at (local park) Sunday," "Tom Cruise Buys House on (local street)."

Dress the sales help in either formal or party wear and have them wear typical New Year's Eve hats. Serve light refreshments and beverages.

As far as merchandise goes, in addition to your Christmas sale items, feature products related to New Year's Eve, the New Year, and the winter season. If you feel it is necessary to run a sale during the promotion, themes to consider include: "Start the New Year Off with a Bargain," "First Sale of the Year," "Ring in the New Year Sale," "Our 2004 Sale—$20.04 Specials."

This event would be the ideal time to give away calendars or diaries imprinted with the store's name. If you have firmed up your promotion schedule for the year, it should be included in the diary or on the calendar. Prizes for drawings could include champagne, baskets of fruit and/or cheese, or some of the store's products.

As an added dimension to the promotion, each evening during the last hour of business (or some other appropriate time of the day), consider staging an actual "New Year's Eve" celebration. Hold a countdown to "midnight," toss confetti and streamers, pass out noisemakers and hats to your customers, serve champagne and other snacks, and just have a good time. You might make all or some of these parties exclusive for frequent buyers as a way of thanking them for shopping your store. Daily newspapers, television channels, and radio stations should be invited to cover your mock New Year's Eve party. Try to get them to cover it as early in the week as possible since it would help attract more customers to the store while the promotion is still on.

Elvis Presley's Birthday

Bring Elvis into the house on his birthday, January 8. Put posters of the King all over the store and windows for this one-day promotion and encourage everyone to shop in their best fifties or sixties outfit. Perhaps have an Elvis look-alike on hand to entertain, or an Elvis look-alike contest. You might even be able to cosponsor an Elvis sound-alike contest with a local radio station. Encourage residents to loan Elvis memorabilia for a window display. See if you can tie in with local record stores, getting them to provide Elvis recordings.

While this is only a one-day promotion, you can probably get a tremendous amount of advance publicity, draw a big crowd to the store, and get follow-up publicity as well as new customers. You can build your customer base by giving everyone who makes a purchase at the store that day "Elvis Bucks," good for a discount on their next purchase at the store. The coupons should expire in thirty days.

Martin Luther King, Jr., Day

This would be a time to pay your respects to Dr. King. Photographs of Dr. King, quotes from his speeches, perhaps newspaper headlines and front pages covering his marches, and quotes from other Americans about Dr. King should be displayed in the store as well as in the windows. There should be no commercialism attached to this display, and you might even give a percentage of the sales that day to a civil rights organization in Dr. King's name.

The Super Bowl

The most publicized sports event in the United States gives you an opportunity for a final farewell to the football season. You have to be careful on the use of the name since it is licensed by the NFL. Check and see if any of your suppliers have a license to use the Super Bowl name and logo and if they do, ask for any p-o-p materials they may have. In recent years advertisers have gotten around the NFL policy by calling it "The Big Game." All you really need is a generic football motif: helmets, blown-up action photos, footballs, jerseys, and banners. Your customers will get the idea. You might order some Super Bowl programs and offer them as door prizes. The purpose of the promotion is to create additional excitement in the store.

Chinese New Year

In cities with large Chinese populations, the Lunar New Year is a colorful event with dragon dancing, fireworks, and a lantern festival. Giving the store an oriental look, featuring any made-in-China products you carry, passing out fortune cookies to customers, or giving dinners at local Chinese restaurants as door prizes can all be part of your salute to the Lunar New Year. Even if you do not have a large base of Chinese-American customers, the popularity of Chinese food is so widespread that everyone will enjoy the fun. As an added feature you might have a Chinese tea-leaf reader at the store. You might even be able to find dragon dancers in town who would make an appearance.

National African American History Month

Proclaimed by the president, February is National African American History month and like Dr. Martin Luther King, Jr., Day, it would call for a noncommercial tribute or display in your window and/or in-store. If you advertise, you might have some copy about the month. If you do plan to have some type of display or exhibit, it would be a good idea to put it together with the assistance of local African American leaders or educators.

Valentine's Day

According to Hallmark Cards, next to Christmas, Valentine's Day is the second busiest holiday period for greeting cards in the United States. It is also an important gift-giving day.

Gift purchases usually fall within a rather limited number of categories: sweets, flowers, jewelry, men's furnishings, lingerie, and other intimate products. However, this does not mean that a retailer carrying other products cannot capitalize on this gift-giving day through clever promotions.

A Valentine promotion should run for a week to ten days, ending February 14. The in-store and window decor should be hearts, cupids, and the color red. Also consider getting blowups of short love poems, Valentine's card verses, and/or graffiti-like statements on love (combinations of words and symbols that you might get local graffiti artists to prepare). Photographs and posters of lovers holding hands, embracing, or walking down the beach together would also add to the decor. Sales help should wear as much red as possible, and have Valentine pins on their clothing. Female sales help who own necklaces or earrings with hearts on them should be encouraged to wear them. Sweets served from heart-shaped boxes or heart-shaped cookies would make ideal refreshments. Background music? Love songs, of course.

If your store does not sell the traditional products people usually buy as Valentine gifts, try some unique approaches: hold a "Red Sale," offering special prices on all red products in the store; offer gift certificates packaged with a small box of chocolate candy; take pictures of customers against a red, heart-shaped background and insert them into special Valentine cards to accompany a gift or gift certificate.

In-store drawings might be for boxes of candy, bottles of wine, flowers, dinners for two at local restaurants. (Try to get dinners donated in turn for in-store promotional exposure.) As favors, give heart-shaped key rings inscribed with the store's name, small packets of candy hearts, and other heart-shaped novelties.

Contests you might consider can include "An Ode to My Valentine" poetry contest, "Miss Valentine 200X." Set a "rule" that only people wearing something red will be admitted to the store on Valentine's Day. Without red, there will be a $2.00 fine payable to the American Heart Association. Notify media about this a week before February 14.

Presidents' Day

Celebrated the third Monday in February, it is traditionally a very big sales period. You can celebrate it as a one-day event, a three-day weekend event, or run it from February 12 to 22, covering the birthdays of both Abraham Lincoln and George Washington. If you are running a Valentine promotion, you can always start your Presidents' Day event February 15.

Traditional decor would include pictures of, and memorabilia associated with, Lincoln and Washington: posters and jumbo pictures of the Washington Monument, Lincoln Memorial, Mount Vernon, and the White House; American flags, stovepipe and tricornered hats; powdered wigs and colonial costumes on mannequins. If there is a Lincoln and/or Washington High School in the area, try to borrow banners and any display materials the schools have.

While the focus on Presidents' Day is traditionally on Washington and Lincoln, there is no reason why you cannot use it as a tribute to all former Presidents of the United States.

Salespeople can join in the spirit of the promotion by dressing in the outfits worn by Washington and Lincoln. You might also have employees or actors dressed as Lincoln and Washington greeting customers and posing for pictures with them.

Cherry pie has been associated with George Washington, and you might serve it along with coffee. Try to get a local bakery to contribute the pies, or at least provide them at a good discount. Patriotic songs will make excellent background music.

Since Presidents' Day sales usually offer tremendous savings, this is a good time to put on sale closeouts and other products that you can afford to offer at a significant markdown. Talk to your suppliers about any specials they may be able to provide. In holding such a sale, be certain it does not degrade the image of the store.

Sales themes you might use: "Your George Washington Dollar Buys More," "Stretch Your Dollar Sale," "We're Chopping Our Prices," "Presidents' Day Values," "A Lincoln Penny Goes a Long Way," "One-Cent Sale," "We're Cleaning Out the House." You might give each customer a new Lincoln penny glued to a small card, announcing it as a "good luck coin," from your friends at (store name).

If you hold drawings for prizes, they might be cherry pies. You might also try to get an airline, hotel chain, or travel agent to donate a weekend trip to Washington as a grand prize. Your chances for getting such a trip donated increase if you are going to advertise the promotion in local media.

Special events, which might attract media coverage, would include the presence of Washington and/or Lincoln look-alikes, the presence of the Lincoln and/or Washington High School bands, cheerleaders, or drill teams. If you expect very large crowds on Presidents' Day, or they develop before you open your doors, alert local newspapers, radio, and television. They may want to cover the crowd pouring into the store when it opens.

Mardi Gras

Give the store a New Orleans look and feel as you celebrate this pre-Lent festival. It provides a chance to have a costume party in the store (let your staff get into the spirit) and maybe a costume contest among your customers. Perhaps have the party for your frequent customers after the store closes. See if you can get a small New Orleans jazz band to play in the store during the promotion, serve pralines, and try to get a local travel agent to provide a trip to New Orleans for the door prize. Try to get New Orleans posters from the city's Convention and Visitors Bureau, or perhaps the travel agency can help you.

St. Patrick's Day

This is an important event if you have a very large Irish population in the city, in the neighborhood in which you are located, or among your customers. An ideal period is from the weekend prior to March 17 through the day itself since, like most holiday-oriented promotions, it should not run beyond the day of the holiday. While the promotion will be most attractive to people of Irish ancestry, in many cities everyone becomes Irish on March 17.

The window and in-store decor is green, green, and more green. And don't forget the shamrocks, leprechauns, maps of Ireland, posters of Irish tourist attractions, posters announcing the local St. Patrick's Day parade, shillelagh, and other memorabilia.

Salespeople should be wearing the green and should top it off with green St. Patrick's Day hats, shamrocks, and St. Patrick's Day pins. You might also want to have an employee dressed in a leprechaun outfit to greet customers and pose for pictures with them. This could attract media interest as a pre-St. Patrick's Day photo opportunity. Try to get the media to cover a "dress rehearsal."

Any Irish-made merchandise should be featured as well as green products. It is not necessary to hold a St. Patrick's Day sale, but if you do, names to consider might be "Bargains from the Old Sod," "A Green Sale" featuring green products, or "Celebrate St. Patrick's Day Sale."

Irish coffee is an ideal refreshment to serve but also offer non-alcoholic beverages. Many people of Irish ancestry are very sensitive about the image of Irish people linked to heavy drinking, so be careful not to promote alcoholic beverages during this event. If you have the budget, consider giving customers shamrocks (live or fake), St. Patrick's Day buttons, or green St. Patrick's Day hats as favors. There are great tapes of Irish music available to get into the swing of the promotion. You may also want to get a bagpiper to play at the store during the promotion. It should be a good drawing card and could attract local television coverage.

If there are active groups in the community, you should consider setting up a special evening at the store for the local Hibernians, Irish Historical Society, etc. It could be a special sale or just a social event with Irish entertainment, prominent Irish community leaders, and local government officials in a preview salute to St. Patrick's Day.

If you decide to hold a drawing for prizes, offer products imported from Ireland. And, while it might be difficult to arrange, you might try to get an airline, hotel chain, or travel agent to provide a trip to Ireland as a grand prize.

If you will be featuring many products made in Ireland, you should try to get a feature story in a local newspaper's lifestyle page. Also contact local magazines, weekly newspapers, mass-circulated Irish newspapers, radio, and television. If you can get the media to run the story prior to St. Patrick's Day, it will bring people to the store.

Winter Festival

This is a theme to use anytime during January, February, and March, even if you do not sell winter related products. It is a way to create excitement during the cold weather days. As with most promotional themes, it should not run more than ten days to two weeks.

The decor throughout the store and in the windows can include anything that depicts winter: ski posters, ski equipment, ice skates, snow boards, hockey sticks, sleds, cold weather clothing on mannequins, snow shovels, pot belly stoves, artificial snow, blowups of pictures or posters of igloos and Eskimos, thermometers showing below zero readings, a fireplace, etc.

The sales staff should be wearing ski sweaters, and any refreshments served should be hot: coffee, tea, toddies, warm wine.

Feature any winter and cold weather products you have in your most prominent displays. If you have the appropriate product mix and clientele, set off a corner of the store and call it "Warm Weather Bound," featuring products customers would normally take on a vacation in the sun belt.

If you have suitable outside space, have an ice carver on hand, and sponsor a snowman-building contest. It could be among youngsters, or mothers/daughters, or fathers/sons; perhaps a different combination each day. Have them dress the snowmen and award a prize for best-dressed snowman. It is the type of photo op that will appeal to the media.

If you plan a sale around your Winter Festival, consider themes like "We've Thawed Our Prices," "Hot Bargains on a Cold Day," "It's Snowing Savings," "Winter Wonderland of Savings," "Meltdown to Spring Sale," "The Thermometer and Our Prices Are Dropping." You might also institute "Snowy Days" sales, offering special discounts to all shoppers when it is snowing during the sale.

Try to tie in your Winter Festival with a ski area or local ice skating rink and ask them to give discount tickets to your customers. Other giveaways might include car window ice scrapers with the store's name on it, inexpensive room thermometers, plastic paperweights with snow scenes in them. Prize drawings might be for cold weather products (ear muffs, thermal gloves, and socks, etc.), ski equipment, and a weekend at a nearby ski resort if you can get it donated.

A way to attract attention to your winter promotion is to have a person dressed in a snowman's outfit handing out circulars outside the store or in the general area. Before doing this, however, make certain that it fits in with the image of the store, and does not violate any local ordinances. It would be a good photo op for media. Another good photo op to set up during the promotion would be to have one or two models in bathing suits in the window on a snowy or very cold day.

THE SECOND QUARTER OF THE YEAR

Three major gift-giving periods occur during the second quarter: Mother's Day, Father's Day, and graduation. In addition, April showers may bring May flowers, but April also brings out the customers who have been hibernating all winter and were "too cold" to get in the mood for spring shopping.

Easter/Spring

An Easter display and/or promotion is almost a "must" for most retailers since it represents an important holiday and a change in season. It appeals to almost all people and all age groups, and is often the first real shopping done by many people since the Christmas season. Easter displays work well for the ten- to fourteen-day period leading up to Easter Sunday. Then, the theme can be converted into a spring promotion by taking out the symbols associated only with Easter like bunnies, eggs, and jelly beans.

Decor is spring and Easter: pastel colors, parasols, Easter eggs, tulips and other spring flowers, Easter bunnies (chocolate and stuffed), bonnets. The smell of spring in the air. Easter and spring songs make good background music, and jelly beans are good refreshments.

Easter and spring-oriented products should be featured, as well as those associated with the outdoors, such as rainwear. If you do choose to run a sale, themes might include "Easter Savings," "Spring Savings," "Winter Closeouts," "Easter-Egg Hunt Sale," "Savings from the Easter Rabbit," "Spring Ahead to Bigger and Better Bargains." Also consider a "Rainy/Snowy Day Sale," which kicks in on rainy days. (See chapter 11.)

Gifts to give customers would include: chocolate Easter eggs, dyed eggs, spring bulbs ready for planting, flowers, small plants. If you have a drawing for customer prizes, consider Easter dinner (arranged through a local restaurant), large solid chocolate bunnies, stuffed bunnies, umbrellas, tickets to baseball games (see chapter 13 for sports promotion information). Sales help should wear the light colors of spring. Saleswomen could wear bonnets, and salesmen boaters. Have an employee in a rabbit's costume greet and pose for pictures with customers, as well as hand out jelly beans, to add in-store excitement. The costumed rabbit standing outside the store and touring the neighborhood will attract people to the store. It might also draw media attention. So might an Easter egg roll or an egg hunt for youngsters or an "unusual" Easter bonnet competition among customers. Another opportunity for publicity is to set up a photo opportunity at the local airport, railroad station, or bus depot a week before the event as the costumed rabbit arrives in town. It would be a natural for television and the daily newspaper.

Live chicks and bunnies should be on display only if they have been borrowed from a farm or educational organization, will be well cared for at the store, and will be returned to the farm or organization at the end of the promotion. Touch base with the local humane organization to make certain that such a display is not against the law. In most areas it is against the law to give away or sell chicks or bunnies; even if it is not illegal, such a practice might promote boycotts or demonstrations against your store by animal rights groups.

Cinco de Mayo

May fifth is a Mexican national holiday recognizing the anniversary of the Battle of Puebla in 1862, when greatly outnumbered Mexican troops defeated the invading French forces of Napoleon III. With a large number of people of Mexican heritage living in the United States, it might be appropriate to celebrate the day. Naturally, it is a big day for Mexican restaurants in this country. Your promotion might include Mexican music, the colorful clothing and costumes of Mexico, travel posters, Mexican drinks and dancing. A retailer might be able to co-op a promotion with a Mexican restaurant by offering discount coupons to customers to the restaurant, and in turn the restaurant could provide food for the store's promotion, and perhaps even arrange for a band to drop by the store.

Mother's Day/Father's Day

Both are important shopping periods for retailers who carry products that are appropriate gifts for mothers and/or fathers. Ideally, promotions for both days should run for about ten days so that two Saturdays are included.

Appropriate Mother's and/or Father's Day signage should be displayed. Some should be saluting parents, others should have some "sell" in them: DON'T FORGET MOTHER ON MOTHER'S DAY, HAPPY FATHER'S DAY, WE SALUTE (CITY)'S MOTHERS, THANKS FOR EVERYTHING, DAD, EVERY DAY SHOULD BE MOTHER'S DAY. A window or in-store display might feature a mannequin in a relaxed position and a sign reading THANKS, MOM, FOR EVERYTHING YOU HAVE DONE FOR US. You should also set a display of photographs of area mothers and fathers during the appropriate promotions. Take their pictures when they shop the store. It is an effective way to pay tribute to your customers.

Consider taking pictures of sons and daughters who purchase gifts for their mothers and/or fathers against an appropriate backdrop (HAPPY MOTHER'S DAY, etc.). The picture can then be enclosed with the gift. For those wanting to send gift certificates, develop a special gift wrapping (with a small box of sweets or a rose). With each gift purchased, enclose an invitation for the recipient to come by the store the following week or so to have their picture taken so they can send it to the purchaser of the gift with a thank-you note. It is not only a nice gesture but can also result in an additional sale to the parent. Also have each gift-giver enter his or her parent in a drawing for prizes, and also invite all parents shopping at the store to enter. The ideal prize would be a weekend at a nearby resort (again, try to get the resort to donate the prize) or dinners at local restaurants. You might also want to sponsor a local Mother- and Father-of-the-Year contest, award, or awards luncheon. You will get good media coverage through this type of sponsorship.

One weekend day for each promotion should be aimed at encouraging parents to bring any younger children in the family so that they can do their Mother's Day and Father's Day shopping. On the set-aside day, fathers could bring in their children to do their Mother's Day shopping; and the following month it would be set aside for mothers to shop with their children for dad. Make it a fun experience for the children.

Armed Forces Day

With the nation more dependent upon its citizen-soldier reserve forces, and patriotism at a new high, a salute to the Armed Forces could be a very appropriate promotion, especially if there are reserve units or military bases in your area. A good time for the promotion would be the period around the third Saturday in May when Armed Forces Day is celebrated.

Honor those on active duty, in the reserve and National Guard, ROTC and retirees. The decor should be patriotic and military with American flags, recruiting posters, historic pictures and art, mannequins in uniform, displays of medals and insignia, and even equipment. If you have a parking area, you might be able to get a unit to display a vehicle in it. You may also want to build an exhibit around a local war hero, Medal-of-Honor winner, etc. Local veterans' organizations may have historic equipment they will let you exhibit. Play the music of military bands and Sousa's marches (he led the Marine Corps band).

Your objective for this promotion is to get those either connected to the military or who support the military to visit and shop at the store. Prominent signs should herald the event as a SALUTE TO OUR ARMED FORCES. As a giveaway, consider American flag pins.

You may want to use the occasion to promote U.S.-made products. Offer a discount to all members of the Armed Forces, Reserves, National Guard, ROTC, retired military, and members of local veterans' organizations. Promote the event through flyers and other announcements sent to the specific organizations, asking them to post the flyers on their bulletin boards.

You should also consider holding a reception at the store on the eve of the opening for the key personnel of the military and veterans' organizations.

You might want to consider donating a percentage of gross sales to an organization like the USO, or toward the restoration of a local war memorial.

Graduation

June is graduation month for virtually every type of school from graduate school to prekindergarten and is, therefore, a significant gift-giving period. While adults are the givers, the products are for the students. If you carry products for any of the graduating age groups, you should consider a graduation gift promotion. Check and see when the schools in your area are holding their graduations and run your promotion around those dates. A graduation promotion should run about two weeks.

Decor should be caps and gowns, diplomas, photographs of local schools, yearbooks, school logos, pennants, and other items associated with the schools. In your windows, you might also feature class pictures, pictures of class leaders, pictures of the salutatorians and valedictorians. Banners and/or signs might read, WE SALUTE OUR GRADUATES, BEST OF LUCK JUNE GRADUATES, HERE'S TO BIGGER AND BETTER THINGS, GRADUATES.

Merchandise to promote should include all products that will appeal to graduates. Since the bulk of the graduates will be from grade school through college, that means products that will appeal to ages fourteen to twenty-two. You may want to invite customers purchasing gifts to enter the graduate's name in a drawing for prizes, which could include savings bonds, athletic equipment, or tickets to local entertainment events.

You might also want to sponsor an award for a graduate at one or more of the local schools. Another element of your promotion might be to donate a portion of each sale to area schools, letting each customer select the school to which the contribution on his sale should be made. This will create a lot of good will for your store, and enable it to get good publicity in local media.

THE THIRD QUARTER OF THE YEAR

Summer vacations and backyard pools and barbecues preoccupy consumers until around mid-August when they begin the back-to-school shopping season. To pull people into the stores in July and early August, reach into the bag of special events, innovative sales, contests, and other promotions outlined in other chapters.

Independence Day/Summer

Kick off your Independence Day/Summer display late in June. Once July 4 has passed, drop the Independence Day–related materials, and you can have a good summer promotion for another couple of weeks.

For Independence Day bring the patriotic look to your windows and throughout the store: red, white, and blue; American flags; posters and pictures of the Liberty Bell and the Statue of Liberty. Add other looks of summer: picnic basket, a grill, pails, shovels, sand and beach umbrellas; banners from local day camps and beach clubs; a baseball bat, ball, and glove.

An employee dressed as Uncle Sam can greet customers at the door and pose for pictures with them. Salespeople should dress in patriotic colors till July 4 and then switch over to a casual summer or even beach look if it doesn't compromise the image of your store.

If the promotion will include a sale you have a lot of options: "Firecracker of a Sale," "Fourth of July Sparklers," "Beach Bargains," "Star-Spangled Sales," "Sun and Fun Sale." If you want giveaways, consider small American flags, flag pins, flag key rings; or red, white, and blue sun visors. Patriotic marching band music till July 4th, then switch to summer songs. If you have a drawing for prizes, give away tickets for summer activities (outdoor concert, boat ride, amusement park, baseball game); or red, white, and blue beach blankets or coolers.

After the July 4th weekend, encourage customers to display their beach and vacation pictures on one of your walls; consider running a "Best Tan in Town Contest" for customers. It is the type of event that will probably get you media coverage. Sometime during the summer months, set aside an area and call it "Letters from Camp." Encourage customers to post humorous letters they have received from their children who are away at camp. The letters can draw media coverage.

If you carry summer fashions, you should consider staging fashion shows at local beach and swim clubs. It is a good way to extend your reach into the community and draw people to the store.

Christmas in August (CIA) Sale

The Christmas shopping season begins earlier and earlier each year. Many stores hold Christmas-in-July sales. We prefer Christmas in August since a CIA sale offers greater mystique. The initials CIA are catchy and are going to grab a lot more people's attention, including media, than a plain old Christmas-in-July sale.

Those dog days of August are a wonderful time to bring out your Christmas decorations, Santa, and even some ice carvings and artificial snow. The only difference between December and August is that you should feature your current product line and not your Christmas line, with a few exceptions.

Arrange media coverage for Santa's arrival at the store (on horseback, perhaps), the lighting of the tree by your mayor or some other official, photo opportunities between Santa and children, and local choral groups singing carols.

You should structure your CIA event so that customers who purchase a product receive an incentive to return during the Christmas shopping season. Perhaps if they purchase a sale item, they receive a coupon good for a 10 percent discount, and if it is a nonsale item, a coupon good for a 15 percent discount.

If you have high-end products in your usual Christmas line, perhaps you can make a deal by giving a discount during the CIA sale to anyone who leaves a nonrefundable 25 percent deposit toward the gift, which will include free gift-wrapping.

Labor Day/End of Summer/Back to School

The period between the last fifteen days of August and the second or third week of September presents an opportunity for several promotional themes. The back-to-school period begins rolling out in mid-August while Labor Day weekend usually signals the end of the summer beach season. And, while summer is not officially over until late September, most people think of it as ending on Labor Day weekend.

Your decor can take on several forms: a last-fling-of-summer look with snapshots from local beaches, including one without a soul on it; signs saying FAREWELL SUMMER OF 200X and WELCOME BACK FROM THE BEACH. The back-to-school look can include text books, school yearbooks, banners and pennants, varsity sweaters, jackets, blackboards, and enlarged photographs of local schools. Seeing the local school material and colors in your window will be an instant attention-getter from alumni. To make an even greater impression on customers, have your sales staff wear school jerseys or baseball caps. Get tapes of the school songs and play them as background music.

Themes to consider: "End of Summer Specials," "September Savings," "Fall Preview," "Back from the Beach Bargains," "Back-to-School Savings," "Blackboard Specials," "Student Sales Corner," "Classroom Classics," "3Rs Sale."

Customer gifts might be sand dollar key rings, local team football schedules, book covers with the store logo, rulers, or ballpoint pens. You might have special gifts for students who received all A's on their June report cards. And have a drawing for tickets to local high school and/or college football games.

Among ways to attract media coverage would be to donate a percentage of profits during the promotion to one or more schools in the area, holding a party for students who finished the June term with all A's and awarding gift certificates to the "Teacher of the Year" at each school.

National Hispanic Heritage Month

By Presidential proclamation, Hispanic Heritage Month runs from September 15 to October 15 and is the time to honor the very large Hispanic population in the United States. This should not be a sales event but rather a tribute to the contributions Hispanics have made to this country. The best way to plan this in-store tribute and window would be to seek out Hispanic leaders in the community and put together a committee to help develop the display and tribute. You should hold a reception for the Hispanic leaders at the store before the exhibit opens. Consider taking advertising in any local Spanish newspapers as a salute to Hispanics in the community. If there isn't any Spanish language newspaper in the area, advertise in the daily.

THE FOURTH QUARTER OF THE YEAR

This is the quarter of all quarters, when you pull out all the stops for what should be your biggest selling season of the year. Not only do you have the massive opportunities for Christmas but Halloween is also becoming a very important selling season with estimates of sales of $5 billion to $6 billion with adults getting into the act, too.

Fall/Columbus Day

Fall begins in late September, and Columbus Day is celebrated the second Monday in October. The latter is a traditional sales day (weekend, or even week). You might start off with a fall promotion in late September and lead into the Columbus Day event the Thursday prior to the holiday.

Decor includes the colors of fall, fall foliage, leaves, football (team uniforms, pennants, helmets, "game" balls—all loaned from local schools), pictures and posters featuring Columbus and his ships, and scale models of the ships. If baseball is popular in your area and there is interest in the play-offs, you might include some baseball memorabilia as part of your window and in-store displays.

Salespeople should wear fall clothing or local football jerseys. And, for Columbus Day weekend, have them wear Columbus Day buttons.

There is a variety of merchandise to promote during this period, and it all depends upon your customers, the merchandise you carry, and your approach to the traditional Columbus Day sales period. Fall products, of course, are a natural at this time. Some retailers promote their winter products in October, some even start their Christmas promotions that month, and others use the Columbus Day sales to unload summer products. In addition, products made in Spain and Italy can have special appeal. Possible themes: "1492 Sale" with a special selection of product on sale for $14.92 or $14.92 off on each product, "Fabulous Fall Buys," "Discover Columbus Day Values," "Discover a New World of Values," "October Extravaganza." Since it is also the heart of the football season, songs from the top colleges, as well as local high schools, would make good background music.

If you plan to hold a prize drawing, offer dinners at local Italian restaurants.

An event that will attract media attention is one with ridiculous prices on a limited number of products (five television sets at five cents each). People will line up all night and make a mad rush to the items when the doors open (a made-for-television news event). However, be certain that such an event does not compromise the image you are trying to develop for the store. Another media possibility would be an announcement that a percentage of Columbus Day profits will go toward cleaning or rehabilitating a local statue of Columbus or for a scholarship in his name at a local high school. Both the announcement and the presentation of the check can make the news. You may also be able to locate a descendant of Columbus or a crew member and have the person "cut the ribbon" to open the store on Columbus Day. Another possibility would be to hold a reception at the store for the local Columbus Day parade committee, inviting city officials and the media.

Halloween

Your Fall Festival can take on a new and even more colorful look for Halloween, which is fast becoming one of the most important shopping periods next to Christmas. Start about two weeks before trick-or-treat night.

The traditional orange and black colors should reign, along with pumpkins, witches, brooms, costumes, and face masks of all shapes, sizes, and colors. TRICK OR TREAT signs and other Halloween greetings should be scattered around the store and its windows. Serve punch but call it Witches Brew. You might want to serve cookies resembling a pumpkin face, and even pumpkin pie (especially if you can get a local bakery to provide them).

Fall products are usually featured, as well as anything that will appeal to children. It is also a good time to start your fall sales. Possible themes: "Trick or Treat Sale," "Broomstick Bargains," "Orange and Black Sales" featuring products containing those colors, "Falling Prices," "Fall Closeouts, and Winter Previews." Products you might want to feature at regular pricing could be grouped under the heading "Halloween Headliners."

Give out small "trick-or-treat" bags of candies, or large empty "trick-or-treat" bags for children to take on their rounds. The store's name should be prominently displayed on the bag. If you are going to have a drawing, pumpkin pies are the ideal prizes.

All types of special events can be held in connection with Halloween: a "Witches Brew" recipe contest, a pumpkin-decorating event, a costume contest, art contest, storytelling contest. Have the contests broken into different age categories, even an adult category.

You might also try to get the largest pumpkin in town for your store window, or a very large one, which is uniquely decorated. Sponsor a pumpkin-pie baking contest, and invite local media personalities to judge it. By having a witch or warlock make in-store appearances, you will create a lot of excitement and get media attention.

Veterans Day

Celebrated November 11, it honors the veterans of all wars and is a traditional sale day. It offers retailers several possibilities: a traditional sale, or a promotion with emphasis on honoring and attracting veterans, as well as active military and reservists. It can be similar to the Armed Forces Day promotion suggested for May. Call the promotion "Salute to Veterans of All Wars," and the sale "Veterans Day Specials."

Decor should include banners borrowed from the local veterans' organizations, uniforms of all the services, and perhaps historic U.S. uniforms worn through the ages. The local veterans' groups might be able to help you find them. The patriotic posters of past wars, pictures and newspaper front pages and headlines would attract attention both in the windows and inside the store.

As part of the promotion, you might bus over veterans from a local veterans' hospital, giving them money for a sales spree. It will get you favorable exposure in media.

Work with the local veterans' organization, asking them to notify their members of the event. Also consider holding special sale preview nights for the various groups, donating a percentage of the evening's take to them.

Media will be interested if you have an interesting collection of military memorabilia on display and/or if you are going to donate a percentage of profits to repair or clean a local veteran's statue or memorial. Even more media interest might be generated if the store's staff goes to the statue or memorial prior to Veterans Day and cleans it, or the surrounding area. Media will be interested if you invite the oldest living veteran in the area, or a veteran from each of the wars since World War II to participate in some type of ceremony at the store.

Thanksgiving

With the Christmas selling season starting earlier each year, Thanksgiving promotions and events have become less popular among some retailers since their Christmas decorations have been up for several weeks by the time "turkey day" arrives.

If you choose to run a Thanksgiving promotion, it might focus on getting more customers to do their Christmas shopping earlier than usual. Run it for about ten days prior to Thanksgiving and offer some specials for the early buyers. Reduction on gift-wrapping, pre-Christmas discounts on certain products, turkeys as door prizes, possible discount on December purchases based on dollars spent during Thanksgiving promotion, etc. You can also use the promotion to clear off your shelves of any fall products you still have on hand.

There are plenty of decorative materials available to give the store a Thanksgiving motif. Most can be purchased at local party stores. If you are portraying Indians, be certain to do so with accuracy and without exaggerating their physical appearance or dress. If you serve refreshments, try cranberry juice or cranberry juice cocktail. And, you might want to have someone dressed in a turkey costume at the door, or just outside the door, greeting customers.

Be sure to have some "tease" signs around the store announcing some of the upcoming Christmas events.

Christmas Season

It is called the Christmas season, but it encompasses three different holidays: Christmas on December 25; the eight-day observance of Chanukah, whose exact starting date varies from year to year; and Kwanzaa, the seven-day, African American festival, which begins on December 26. A Chanukah tradition is to give children a gift on each of the eight days.

This is the season to pull out all stops. In more recent years, some retailers have started the Christmas season as early as late October. Pricing strategy might be to start off with a pre-Christmas sale for a week or ten days, then go for full pricing and if product doesn't move, cut prices a week or two prior to December 25.

In addition to Christmas decorations, it is important to include decor from both Chanukah and Kwanzaa. How much you devote to each holiday would depend upon your customer base.

If your store is large enough, or if you have a sizable outdoor area, you might have a different church choir or school choral group singing carols each day. If you have a large Jewish customer base, you might set up an oversized menorah and have a different customer's child light a candle each evening at sundown.

A live Santa can be used as a profit center: charge for photographs with him, also for special gifts he gives to children who visit with him. Or, if you prefer, you might want to use your live Santa as a goodwill ambassador to greet customers and pose, free of charge, for pictures with customers and their children. You might also loan the Santa out for personal appearances in the community at events where you will get good exposure, and have him visit local television shows with gifts for the hosts.

If your store has unique Christmas decorations or gifts, if your Santa is an unusual person, or if you plan a special philanthropic event

(Christmas gifts or shopping sprees for the less fortunate), you may be able to get local media coverage. An excellent media-oriented idea for a store that sells toys is to set up a panel of a half dozen young children sometime in October and have them test the new toys and games and select what they consider the "top ten" of the season. You could hold a press conference at the store to let them make the announcement or arrange special newspaper interviews and television appearances.

BE SENSITIVE TO RELIGIOUS AND ETHNIC HOLIDAYS

When considering holiday and ethnic promotions, it is important to be sensitive to the traditions connected to them. For example, it would be inappropriate to run a sale in connection with Martin Luther King's birthday, the Muslim observance of Ramadan, or the Jewish High Holy days of Rosh Hashanah and Yom Kippur.

You should become familiar with the many religious, ethnic, and foreign country holidays of your customers. Seek the advice of local religious and ethnic leaders, as well as foreign consulates (or prominent representatives of foreign-born groups in the community), regarding what would be appropriate to do on such holidays. You may find that holidays of foreign countries, which are celebrated by large segments of your community, can be developed into interesting promotions. This could include Chinese New Year, St. Patrick's Day, Fasching (Germany and Austria), Carnival (Brazil), Cinco de Mayo (Mexico).

10

---■■■---

In-Store Special Events
That Draw Customers

PEOPLE LIKE ENTERTAINMENT whether they are sitting at home watching television, out of town, or even shopping. Holiday and seasonal promotions, already discussed, provide a happy ambiance. But they represent only two of the promotional steps you can take to attract new customers and keep old ones coming back.

In-store special events will also create that additional excitement so appealing to customers.

There is a whole range of special events you can conduct. They include an annual anniversary celebration, personal appearances by celebrities, entertainment, exhibits and displays, psychic readings, and international product promotions.

Before settling on a special event, there are several things you must consider:

■ Will it appeal to your customers and potential customers? If they are serious shoppers with little time to spare, they probably could care less about special events at the store. They just want to get in, shop, and get out.

■ Will the event overshadow its purpose: to attract people to your store to make a purchase? If the event will require so much floor space that customers do not have full access to the merchandise, don't hold it.

- Will the event create too much noise or other distractions that will disturb shoppers?
- Will the event bring in enough additional revenue to cover its costs?

A special event should only be scheduled after you are convinced that it meets your criteria and objectives.

AN ANNUAL EVENT: YOUR ANNIVERSARY

Whether you have been in business one year, eleven years, or more than one hundred years, pull out all stops to celebrate your anniversary each year. It offers you unlimited marketing opportunities, as well as a chance to create excitement and gain additional visibility for your store in the community.

Even though a one- or three-year anniversary may not appear to be impressive, it is in retail when you consider the turnover rate. *By focusing attention on your anniversary, you are demonstrating to your customers and the community that you have a stable, successful operation.*

While milestone anniversaries—your twenty-fifth or fiftieth, for example—might last an entire year, your annual celebration can run anywhere from a weekend to a month. It all depends on how long you want to celebrate and maintain the momentum.

The key theme of your anniversary celebration should be to thank your customers for making your store a success. Here are some ways to celebrate your anniversary with your customers.

An Anniversary Sale

The easiest and most logical way to celebrate your anniversary each year is to hold a special "Anniversary Sale." It focuses on your success, and offers your customers the opportunity to share it with you since they made it possible. Use this "Thank You" theme in your advertising, in your windows, and in your store. Make your customers feel they are part of the family.

In planning the anniversary sale, contact your suppliers and see what support they might provide. It might be in pricing, special products, or some other area of marketing. You might start a tradition of rolling prices back to your founding year. If the business is more than twenty-five years old, the rollback concept might be too costly to do across the board. Instead, you might have just a select number of products at their original pricing, with smaller discounts on the rest of the products on sale. If you expect to have an anniversary sale every year, you might have an artist design a special anniversary logo, which can be updated each year by just adding the new anniversary number.

Re-creating Your Founding Year

If appropriate, you should re-create the atmosphere of your founding year. Have the store employees dressed in the styles worn during the founding year and decorate the store and its windows with memorabilia from the founding year. This could include newspaper front pages, political campaign buttons from that year's election, pictures of what the store looked like when it opened, etc. This will work best if it is a twenty-fifth or older anniversary. Contact your local historical society and newspapers for help in locating appropriate items.

A Special Collector's Item

You might want to develop a special collector's item as a giveaway for each anniversary. While it should be inexpensive, it should be something your customers will save. It could be a small commemorative pin with the store name, the anniversary number, and year. In addition to changing the number and year each year, you might also change the color. Once you reach a milestone year, you might want to change the design for the next decade. Alternatives to the pin might include a commemorative drinking glass or mug, or drink coasters.

Special Anniversary Events

You should pay tribute to your customers and employees during your anniversary month. Invite your customers to nominate candidates for "Employee of the Year," and then select the winner from among the finalists. Hold a special reception at the store to honor the winner, inviting all the employees and their families. Also present employees awards for length of service.

You should hold one or more similar receptions for your best customers, serving birthday cake and champagne, and holding a drawing for door prizes.

It is not necessary to get into an expensive customer event unless you are celebrating a milestone like your twenty-fifth or fiftieth anniversary. For a twenty-fifth or fiftieth anniversary, you may want to buy out a performance of a local theater company and invite your best customers to attend, or reserve a section of seats at a sporting event or concert.

Launch a Significant New Program

An anniversary period is always a good time for a retailer to make a significant announcement regarding the business. It could be a new merchandising policy, an expansion program, or even the addition of one or more product lines. You could also use the anniversary to introduce your own credit card, a new credit policy, new hours, a new manager, a frequent buyers program, a home delivery service, or even a product-of-the-month club.

Give Something Back to the Community

Your anniversary is always a good time to announce you are giving something back to the community for making your success possible. It could be a contribution to a charity or nonprofit organization, the launching of a community involvement program, or the sponsorship of an award. Chapter 16 offers many ideas on how to get involved in your community by giving something back.

Get Official Government Recognition

For a milestone anniversary, obtain public recognition. Ask the mayor and/or local city government legislature to issue a proclamation or legislative resolution honoring the store. Try to arrange for the presentation at the store and invite media coverage. Also ask state legislators who represent your district to arrange state recognition. If it is a twenty-fifth or fiftieth anniversary, they might be able to get the governor to issue a proclamation and arrange a presentation ceremony. Also ask your congressman's office to insert a statement honoring your store in the Congressional Record.

Anniversary Publicity

If you are celebrating a milestone anniversary, you can probably arrange good media coverage: a newspaper feature story and/or business page story, and perhaps a segment on local television news. The thrust of the publicity would be the growth of the store and how business today differs from what it was like when it first opened.

LIVE ENTERTAINMENT

Special events featuring live entertainment are usually weekend promotions, though some may be single day events held during the week and aimed primarily at housewives. Some of the special events can be part of an ongoing series.

Costumed Characters

Costumed characters have already been suggested for some of the holiday and seasonal promotions in chapter 9. They can also be used anytime during the year to generate in-store excitement.

There are several approaches to take:

■ Rent a generic character costume from a local theatrical costume house. Most offer a variety of costumes, ranging from animals and clowns to knights in armor and astronauts. Use one of your employees, or hire a local performer or member of a college theater group to wear the outfit during the event. Needless to say, the person should relate well to people and exhibit a "little ham" in his or her performance.

■ It is also possible to rent costumes depicting various comic book characters. Since this type of costume will have instant recognition, it will be very effective in attracting traffic.

■ Arrange to have one of the costumed mascots from a local sports team appear. You might be able to get him at no cost if you develop a joint promotion with the team. It might involve distributing ticket information in store, a mailing to customers, or an agreement to advertise the appearance.

■ Check your suppliers to see if they have any licensing agreements to use cartoon characters. If they do, they may be able to arrange an appearance.

Get maximum use of these costumed characters:

■ Have them right near the front door (or just outside the entrance) so that they can greet customers and attract the attention of passersby.

■ If city ordinances permit, you might have the costumed character walking through the neighborhood streets, leading passersby back to the store in Pied Piper fashion.

■ If you use a team mascot or well known character, consider taking pictures of them with customers who make a purchase. Also encourage the mascot or character to sign autographs.

■ One function the costumed character can perform is to keep children entertained while their parents are shopping.

■ If your budget will permit, hold a drawing among all who visit the store during the costumed character's appearance. The prize: a free appearance at any event the winner selects. It could be a child's birthday party, or even an adult's surprise party.

■ You might have an auction among your customers for an appearance by the character. The proceeds would go to a local charity or to assist a very sick child.

■ If you have an unusual costumed character, inform newspapers and television. They may want to cover. Any costumed character provides a good photo opportunity, especially when he has a very young child looking up at him.

Live Music

Depending on your available space and customer base, you might want to feature live music in the store. But you should be convinced it will enhance business, and not divert attention from the selling floor. It could be on a regular schedule (Tuesday nights, Saturday afternoons, etc.) or just on special occasions. An advantage for having it on a regular schedule is that you may be able to develop a loyal group of "Music Night" customers. You could have a pianist, cellist, accordionist, or even a small combo if you have the space. While most retailers will probably want soft background music, those who cater to young audiences may want to feature louder music. By billing "Music Night" as a showcase, you might be able to get a local music school to provide student talent. While you will be getting amateur talent, the school will recognize this as an opportunity to enhance its image and will undoubtedly provide its best talent at no cost to you. Let local disc jockeys know about your live music plans. If you try the music night approach, see if you can get local music critics to drop by and review the talent. Only invite them when you know you will be having above-average talent.

Magicians

Magicians fascinate people and can be used not only to draw people to a store but also to specific products.

The performance should be carefully choreographed so that customers are "forced" to move around the store and given time to shop. Otherwise they will stick with the magician, and you will end up losing sales. One effective scenario is for a brief performance in the window, with an announcement that it will continue inside in five to ten minutes. Inside, the magician should again perform and announce that the show will continue in a different section of the store in another ten minutes. The magician should be instructed to include plugs for various products and specials in his act. He should also use some of your products, if possible, as props during the performance.

Try to develop a unique news angle for the magician's appearance to get media coverage. For example, perhaps the magician will "saw his or her one thousandth person in half" at your store, or will be retiring the rabbit that has been with him for ten years.

Before hiring a magician, watch a live performance to make certain he or she is the right person for your store.

A Caricaturist

An artist drawing caricatures of customers is always a popular attraction. People enjoy being the subject of such drawings and will display the finished product at home or at work. You might want to have a caricaturist on hand on a regular basis, during special promotions, or just once in a while. If you offer caricatures on a regular basis, pick a slow day or time period, using the caricaturist as a traffic builder. Offer a caricature only when a purchase is made. Somewhere on the caricature, the artist should work in the store's name. This will give you exposure if the subject keeps it on display. Work out the possible price with the artist. Estimate the number of caricatures to be drawn, then determine whether you should hire him by the day, hour, or caricature.

To add fun to the event, ask customers for permission to display the caricatures in the store or window that week. Display them under a banner reading, SALUTING OUR CUSTOMERS. THANKS FOR YOUR SUPPORT. Promote the appearance of the caricaturist with a sign in the window and a caricature of a famous person.

Free Psychic Readings

A favorite attraction for stores with a large female customer base would be free psychic readings. You could have a special one-day event, a monthly event, or even more frequently if it draws customers. You might schedule it for a slow afternoon each week, having a different psychic each week. A tarot card reader, handwriting analyst, palm reader, tea-leaf reader, etc. If it will be a one-time event, or two or three times a year, you might have all of them at the same time. Readings should be offered only when a purchase is made. You might make an exception for your best customers, sending them an invitation to drop in for a reading at a specific time. If they drop in for the reading, they may end up making a purchase. Determine how many readings a psychic can do in an hour. That will give you a better idea whether you should negotiate a full-day or a per-customer rate.

Promote appearances with in-store and window signage. You may be able to get some media coverage on these appearances if you position them properly. Try to arrange to have the psychic make his predictions for the year, forecast results of a sporting event, the economy, academy-award winners, etc. An advance release to media promising these forecasts might bring out camera crews and reporters.

Balloon Sculptor, Origami Artist, Juggler, and Others

There are a variety of other entertainers who can create an exciting atmosphere at your store. The list of potential performers is limited only by your ability to find them in your city.

- Balloon sculptors are a big favorite among children. They provide fun and entertainment wherever they perform, and people get to take home the balloons they sculpt into hats, toys, and animals.
- Origami artists let customers take home the novelty items they make

from paper. Hire one who will not only demonstrate this Japanese art but also conduct a workshop and show your customers how to do it.

- Jugglers, if you have the space, will grab your customers' attention. Not only have the juggler perform, but have him teach your customers some of the basics of juggling.

- Mimes fascinate. They have been successfully used in store windows as live mannequins, as well as inside to demonstrate fashions and products. They hold people spellbound as they go through their routines.

- A puppeteer can be used in your window and then lure people into the store to see the rest of the show, and shop. The technique is similar to that suggested for magicians.

- Clowns appeal to people of all ages. An ideal clown for in-store promotion would be one who is a combination magician, mime, and comedian who can keep everyone happy and laughing.

One way to find these performers is to check out who is entertaining at local children's parties, women's clubs, and other organizations. You can also check the Yellow Pages.

There may be some interest from television channels to cover some of these appearances, especially if it is a slow day for news. They might like the concept of customers learning juggling or the art of origami, a unique juggling act, the puppeteer whose real profession is medicine, science, or politics, etc.

Pets Are a Customer's Best Friend

Even if they do not have one at home, most people are attracted to pets. A smart retailer will consider in-store promotions to help build traffic. If you have the space, and it will not inconvenience your customers, occasionally let the local humane society or one of the pet rescue groups bring in kittens and puppies available for adoption. Advanced publicity by the group(s), as well as window and in-store signage, will help build a crowd.

Once or twice a year you may want to stage a dog and/or cat show, inviting customers to bring in their pets. Hold it in the store or your parking area, if you have one. Award ribbons or prizes to the winners who do the best tricks. Set up some fun categories: "Biggest Smiler," "Least Obedient Dog," "Worst Dining Habits," "Loudest Meower," "Slowest Eater," etc. Local media enjoy covering pet stories.

You might also hold a pet photography show, letting your customers display pictures of their pets in store. You can award prizes in such categories as "Most Unusual Pose," "Nicest Costume on a Pet," "Cat with the Widest Eyes," "Most Unusual Pet," etc.

CELEBRITY PERSONAL APPEARANCES

Personal appearances by celebrities will always create excitement and attract traffic. However, before you book a celebrity, you should evaluate the expected results and weigh them against the cost of the promotion.

Will the appearance sell products, gain new customers, and build incremental sales? Will it gain important positive exposure for your store in the community?

Tips for Getting Celebrities

Celebrity appearances usually involve a fee. However, there are times when you may be able to arrange a celebrity appearance gratis, or at a greatly reduced fee. Check your suppliers to see if they have any celebrities under contract for personal appearances. If they do, they may arrange an in-store appearance at no cost, providing you place a large order; or they may offer to split the cost with you.

Also contact local entertainment promoters to see if they have any celebrities coming to the city to perform. They may be able to arrange a free appearance if it will help promote the celebrity's performance, or if the celebrity is promoting a book or product you carry. You might also purchase tickets to his or her performance and give them away at a drawing at the store, with the celebrity picking the winning numbers.

If your product line appeals to the celebrity, you may be able to pay him with product in lieu of cash. This will save you money since the product value would be calculated on the basis of the retail price.

You should contact local charitable organizations that may have a working relationship with celebrities. Offer a percentage of the sales that take place while the celebrity is in the store to any organization that arranges a free appearance.

Local celebrities, including television news anchors, weathermen, and sports reporters; newspaper cartoonists and sportswriters; authors; local chefs; retired athletes; college coaches; disc jockeys and other radio personalities, may be willing to make appearances for smaller fees than national celebrities and probably more willing to take product in lieu of fee. If you advertise on television, in the daily newspaper, or on the radio, you might be able to get the media celebrities from those outlets free of charge. The chefs will not charge a fee since they will be promoting their restaurants.

Using the Celebrity

Celebrities can be used in a variety of situations:

- Signing autographs
- Doing sales pitches or demonstrations of products they endorse, recipes, etc.
- Holding question and answer periods with customers
- Modeling clothing
- Conducting a drawing for door prizes
- Having their pictures taken with customers

Autographs or pictures should necessitate a purchase, or even the purchase of a specific product especially if the celebrity is associated with one.

Read chapter 13 for information concerning the use of sports personalities. Some of the ideas in that chapter can apply to nonsports personalities, too.

Publicizing a Celebrity's Appearance

Whenever you will have an in-store appearance by a celebrity, send out an advance press release as well as a media advisory inviting coverage. If it is a show business personality, send the material to the entertainment page editors and columnists, the entertainment reporters on radio and television, and disc jockeys. Try to get a disc jockey to do a live interview with the celebrity at your store.

DESIGNERS' OR SUPPLIER PRESIDENTS' APPEARANCES

Depending on your product lines, you may be able to develop exciting special events featuring designers and the presidents of your supplier companies.

Designers

Customers like to meet and talk with the designers of dresses, jewelry, scarves, furniture, suits, and even the appliances they purchase. Some of the designers, of course, are well known celebrities and will attract large crowds. However, even unknown designers will draw people to your store. A designer's appearance should be in connection with a promotion for his or her product and should be arranged through the manufacturer or distributor. The appearance may require an advertising commitment on your part, a significant product order, and/or the designer's transportation expenses. Local media will probably be interested in covering the event, especially if it is an appearance by a fashion designer. Contact the lifestyle and/or fashion editors at newspapers and producers or hosts of local women's programs on radio and television. Send advance information as well as invitations to cover the event.

Company Presidents

Some stores run "Presidents' Day" promotions that have no relationship to the February holiday. These promotions feature the chief executives of the companies who manufacture the products the store sells. They appear at the store to greet customers and/or demonstrate their products. Of course, the greater volume you do with a company; the better the chance you have of getting its president.

You might want to hold a single "Presidents' Day" for all your suppliers. This probably has the most promotional impact. Or you may want to invite each one on an individual basis, setting aside one afternoon or evening a month for an individual president's appearance. Logistically, the latter will be easier to handle and better suited for smaller-sized stores.

When a president will appear, his or her company may spend some money in local media to promote the appearance. Chances are, however, they will probably try to get you to pay some of the costs. You should agree to arrange publicity interviews for the chief executive with local media while he or she is in your city. Business page editors should be contacted, as well as radio and television news desks. If there are any local business programs or business reporters at local stations or channels, contact them. If you hold a single "Presidents' Day" promotion, you will have to plan it well in advance to assure everybody's availability.

During the promotion, each president should be stationed at a booth, table, or section where his company's products are displayed. A sign should identify the company, and its president should wear a name tag. Space permitting, you may want to have a central assembly point for formal presentations by each president. This is not necessary, however, if there is enough space at each company table.

EVENTS THAT EMPHASIZE PRODUCT SALES

It is vital to your business to hold special events that specifically target the sale of your merchandise.

Private Shopping Night

Set aside special nights for groups you are trying to cultivate as customers, as well as for regular customers during various holiday seasons. Serve champagne and other refreshments, have door prizes, and perhaps distribute with the invitations one or more coupons for single item discounts. Have your sales help primed to offer special attention to the customers.

Hold special nights for singles, husbands (before Valentine's Day and Christmas), wives (also before Valentine's Day and Christmas), senior citizens, government employees, local Rotary Club, schoolteachers, etc. You can set aside such nights of personal shopping for just about any group you think has customer potential.

These nights also have potential for media coverage. "How men meet women at singles night shopping event," "How women interact with each other as they shop for Valentine's Day gifts for their husbands," "Seniors still shopping with passion for Valentine's Day gifts after forty years of marriage," etc. Television might cover some of the special nights.

Welcome Back Party

Once a year, consider holding a "Welcome Back" event for former customers. Select from your mailing list the names of the customers who have not been to the store for more than six months and invite them back for an evening of refreshments, champagne, and special discounts.

Promoting Products from Around the World

Special events developed around products made in a specific foreign country, or a particular state or region of the United States, offer unlimited promotional opportunities.

If, for example, you carry many French-made products, consider holding a "French Week" or "French Month" promotion. The entire store should take on a French theme. Display travel posters and other scenic pictures as well as video tapes. Contact the French Consulate or trade commissioner (if one is located in your city), or the French Embassy in Washington, D.C. Outline your plans and ask for their assistance. They may be able to arrange for a French trade association to supply wines and cheeses or even a trip to France as a door prize. Also ask the firms supplying you with French products to provide money for the promotion as well as other support. They may be able to arrange for some French entertainers to appear at the store.

To launch the promotion, arrange a special reception with the French Consulate or Embassy, whose ranking officials might co-host the function. Invite city officials, leaders of any local French societies, French professors from local colleges, key customers, and representatives from supplier companies.

The French promotion is just an example of a foreign-country promotion you might conduct. Develop such promotions on countries from which you carry a substantial number of products and who have a good image in the world marketplace.

Similar promotions might focus in on states or regions of the United States from which you carry significant product. You should discuss arranging these domestic promotions with the manufacturers as well as the various state trade and industrial promotion divisions.

Publicity opportunities for this type of promotion are numerous. If food, fashion, or wine are involved, the lifestyle sections of newspapers will probably be interested in covering your event. Send to the lifestyle editors an outline of what will be featured and the times of any special events. Try to get an on-air radio personality to do a show live from your store. Television news programs might also be interested in covering, especially if they can do an interview with an authority on the subject (French wine expert, French government trade official, etc.). You might also put together a small basket of samples of some of the products on display to send to on-air radio personalities, disc jockeys, and hosts of local daytime television programs.

Fashion Shows

If you sell men's or women's clothing, jewelry, hats, bathing suits, or shoes, you might consider holding fashion shows during the year. The ideal time is at the start of the selling season for the fashions you plan to feature. Jewelry can be shown just about anytime during the year.

There are several ways to schedule a fashion show. Ideally, it should be held in the store. However, if you do not have the space, you might rent a hotel ballroom, an auditorium, or some other hall. It should be located near the store, and customers should be encouraged to visit the store right after the show for refreshments and to purchase product. Try to get the manufacturers to underwrite the show, or pick up some of the expenses.

It is always best to use professional models. However, sometimes it is very effective to use the sales staff or even customers. Those in attendance might relate better to "plain people" than they would to professional models. Moreover, customers will be flattered to be asked to model.

The best time to have the show is in the early evening. Another possibility is to have mini-fashion shows on relatively busy days, Each show would last ten to fifteen minutes. They would be informal, with the models walking through the aisles and showing the fashion when they came upon customers.

Invite the local fashion writers at newspapers and magazines to cover your shows as well as local television news and hosts of women's radio programs.

Product Reviews

Similar to fashion shows, these can be held whenever a new product line or significant products are introduced. Some examples might be the new

Christmas toys just as the Christmas selling season is about to begin; new consumer electronics products when they come to market after the Consumer Electronics Show; new appliances; and new furniture.

These product previews should consist of demonstrations by representatives of the manufacturer, or your sales staff. Customers can inspect the products, try them, and ask questions. These product previews can be held over a weekend with demonstrations on an ongoing basis, or every hour on the hour.

Inform media about these previews, especially if any products are unique and haven't been available in the city till now.

OTHER CROWD-PLEASING EVENTS

A Tethered-Balloon Ride

If you have outdoor space, one weekend you might offer tethered-balloon rides to customers who spend a minimum of $100. Few people have probably ever taken a balloon ride, and the adventure associated with ballooning should make the ride a big attraction.

The balloon is tied down and only rises a short distance into the air. However, this short trip becomes something special to someone who has never experienced it, particularly if you also take a picture of the customer in the balloon gondola.

It is a tradition to drink champagne after a balloon ride. So if your budget can afford it, you might give each customer a split of domestic champagne. Or perhaps you can get a local liquor store to participate in the promotion and provide the champagne.

Media will love this promotion, especially if you let them take a ride and even broadcast from the gondola. Invite columnists, on-air radio personalities, and local television hosts as well as the news sides of radio and television, and the daily newspapers.

Children's Story Hour

This could be a weekly, or even a daily event—especially if you have many customers who shop with young children. Have a storyteller keep the children occupied while the parents shop. Arrange this special feature for a two-hour period daily, or for a full day on Saturday. During the week, schedule it for late afternoon after school lets out since many of the children will probably be in the lower grades of school. By promoting this convenience, you may find that many more mothers with children will become new customers. Try to hire a schoolteacher or college student to be the storyteller.

Petting Zoo and Pony Rides

If you have outside space, set up an annual petting zoo and pony ride day one Saturday. It is a great promotion to attract young families to the store. You might take pictures of children on the pony and either give them to the parents, or sell them at cost.

Memorabilia of All Kinds

This might include movie posters and pictures of old-time stars; old dolls and doll houses; toys from the twenties, thirties, and forties; old newspaper front pages or headlines; historical pictures and materials about your city; old advertisements; World's Fair items; old opera costumes; and theatrical and other entertainment posters. This material can probably be borrowed from local collectors, the historical society and museums, the local newspaper(s), advertising agencies, the opera company, and theater company. You could have one memorabilia exhibit, covering an era (the twenties, thirties, etc.), or individual exhibits in each category.

One method of collecting the material would be to ask local media to help you find collectors who will loan display items to you. They might run a small story about what you are seeking and even agree to become the cosponsor of the exhibit. You might ask local disc jockeys to request help from their listeners; it could result in good publicity months before the exhibit.

Art and Handicrafts

These exhibits could include artwork and handicrafts by local professional artists, members of the Art Student's League, schoolchildren, scouts, the handicapped, and senior citizens. They could range from watercolors and oil paintings to wood carvings, sculptures, and even photography. Shows could be organized with just one group or open to everyone. You might get more media attention if each show featured the works of a different category: local high school students, senior citizens, professionals, works of local artists, members of the Art Student's League, etc. If you plan to give awards, have the art critic from the newspaper(s), as well as museum curators do the judging.

Other Old Collectibles

You will be amazed what people collect, and what people are interested in seeing on display. Consider exhibiting some of these products, especially if you sell their modern day counterparts: household products including old irons and other small appliances; stoves; washing machines, washtubs; personal products including old razors, women's hair curling and straightening devices, shaving mugs, beer steins, and even barbed wire. The latter is very popular out west.

Because of the individuality of these collectibles, the local media will probably give good coverage to such exhibits. Just let them know in advance of the event that you have something that warrants coverage. Also send stories about the event ten to fourteen days before it will start and ask that information be included in events listings and announcements.

Joint Exhibits

Some local libraries and museums may cooperate by loaning exhibit materials for display at your store. Sometimes they may loan you several pieces that relate to a current exhibition at the museum as a means of drawing attention to that exhibit. This will not only help promote the museum but will also draw people to your store to see part of the exhibit.

Always have an opening ceremony and invite the curator of the museum or chief librarian to "cut the ribbon." Invite the media, including art critics to review the "mini-show." Also try to get the exhibit listed in the events columns of newspapers and local magazines, as well as on radio and television.

If you display art borrowed from museums, you will have to provide security so that the material is not stolen. You should also have insurance to cover any loss or damages to borrowed property.

The purpose of any special exhibit or display is to get people into the store. So, while you should promote the exhibit in the store windows, only show a few examples of what can be seen inside the store. Use the windows to tease people into entering the store.

HEALTH SCREENINGS

Health screenings are an effective way to draw people to your store. It is usually relatively easy to tie in with a hospital or medical group since they can get good exposure and public relations out of the project. What type of screenings you do, when you do them, and how you do them will depend upon your customers and the amount of space you have in your store.

Here are some ideas:

■ Once or twice a year, hold a health fair offering screenings and providing health information on various diseases and illnesses. This will only work if you have the space to set up tables for the various tests, as well as for representatives of the various groups, who would distribute literature and answer questions.

■ February is heart month and an ideal time to sponsor cholesterol and blood pressure screenings, as well as distribute nutritional information. This would require less space than the health fair. Some organizations zero in on Valentine's Day for their heart month promotion. This would be an ideal event for a health food restaurant, or one that specializes in low-cholesterol meals.

■ Some retailers make their stores available for flu shots and other inoculations, with customers paying a minimal fee. Seniors are usually covered by Medicare. There are medical services that conduct such inoculations. Basically all the retailer has to do is provide the space and promotion.

PROMOTING YOUR SPECIAL EVENTS

The success of your special events program will depend upon how well it is promoted. If it is an ongoing program with at least one different event scheduled weekly, chances are the knowledge of it will spread by word of mouth.

But that might not be enough to assure its success. You should strongly promote events through your store windows, through flyers, bill stuffers, advertising, your Web site, and a quarterly newsletter listing all special events, promotions, and sales during that period.

And don't forget publicity!

Many of your events will be newsworthy, and local media may run advance information about them if you ask. See chapters 21 and 22.

You should also reach out to groups in the community that may have a special interest in a specific event. These groups may range from hobbyists, pet owners, and artists to senior citizens, expectant mothers, and businessmen or -women.

11

—■·■—

The Right Sale for the Right Place

"H O L D A S A L E and they will come."

In normal periods, sale days rank among the top traffic-builders in virtually every segment of retail. They bring in customers and move merchandise, though not necessarily at the profit margins most retailers would hope to achieve. Once the sale is over, regular prices and regular profits prevail. And, hopefully, new customers will be a result of the sale.

In recent years, however, the picture has drastically changed. Sales now play an even more significant everyday role in retail marketing strategy, and there is no indication when and if this trend will reverse itself. Giant discount stores keep the pressure on everyone else in retail to cut prices in order to compete. The depressed economy has also made a greater number of consumers more price conscious and sale oriented, forcing a much broader base of retailers to take a more aggressive sale strategy, something they really cannot afford to do.

Unfortunately, the small retailer can become a big loser when an aggressive sale program is adopted. It is why the smaller retailer must carefully develop a sale strategy that does not cut too far into profit margins, nor cut into the long-term image he or she should be developing for the store among its customers.

No matter how creative a sale is, no matter the number of customers it attracts, it should not be considered successful by a retailer unless the merchandise moves at a fair price. And merchandise will not necessarily move at a fair price during a sale unless the customers *perceive* they are receiving a good buy. They need a base from which they can compare pricing, and they will not get that measuring stick at a store where everything is on sale virtually every week. Thus, if you believe in weekly sales on everything in the store, you are probably going to have to offer pricing at such a low level that you will not be able to make a decent profit.

Thus a good businessperson will avoid weekly across-the-board sales. Knowing everyone likes a bargain, the savvy retailer will continue to run sales from time to time throughout the year. But, they will be carefully structured.

By featuring only a limited number of different products at a sale and getting full price for everything else in the store, the retailer is providing his customers with that measuring stick that enables them to perceive that they are getting a good deal from a merchant who carries quality products, and who will be around a long time. Those are the people you want to attract to your sale and convert into regular customers.

How you promote the sale will depend upon what your goal is. Is it just to create a little excitement among your present customer base? Is it to attract new customers? Or is it to close out seasonal products?

Sales aimed at your present customers or specific target audiences should be promoted through in-store signage, mailings, and personal calls by salespeople.

Sales aimed at the general public, which should have a special customer-only preview the eve of the sale, should be promoted through advertising, handbills and flyers, bulletin board posters at nearby offices and industrial plants.

There are two important consumerism rules to follow when holding a sale: If specific products are on sale, be certain to have plenty in stock. And offer rain checks to customers if you run short so that customers can still get the product at the sale price.

Chapter 9 has information on how to create exciting in-store promotions around holidays, seasons of the year, and other annual events. Included are ideas for conducting sales in connection with those promotions.

THE EASIEST SALE TO STRUCTURE

The easiest sale to structure is one that requires you to just look at everything in your store. Look at every color. Look at every size. Look at every shape. Look at every type of product. Then act.

We're talking about a series of one-day sales, each featuring a particular category of products. These one-day sales can be held one day a week, one day a month, on consecutive days, or even every single day during an entire month.

One day put everything that is red on sale, on a second day everything blue, the next day, green. Then when you get tired of colors, put everything that is round on sale one day, everything that is square another, everything rectangular the third day. Everything with flowers in its design another day, glass items still another day, and wall plaques the day after that. It offers you endless opportunity to shine the spotlight on each of the different categories of products you sell. Naturally, you will zero in on the slower-moving products in each category, holding back the products for which you can get top price.

A New York City gift shop, Flights of Fancy, has really perfected this type of sale. It conducts it each September as its only sale of the year, its "Confusion Sale." Every day another category of product is on sale at 20 percent off. It might be stationery one day, wine-related products another day, puppets and stuffed animals the third day. (See promotional flyer on page 134.) On the last day of September everything previously on sale and not sold is offered at 35 percent off. To make this month-long event even more appealing, anyone making a purchase during the sale receives a coupon good for a 10 percent discount in December.

THIRTY SALES THAT WILL BUILD TRAFFIC

Happy Hour

Happy Hours have been a mainstay for building business at bars so why shouldn't retailers try it, too? Every store experiences slow periods of the day or week when customers just don't seem to be around. It could be the first two hours each morning, sometime in midafternoon, or perhaps every Thursday morning. One way to counteract slow periods is to run specials, or sales, during those hours. As a start, limit them to two-hour

Sunday	Monday	Tuesday	Wednesday	Thursday	Friday	Saturday
	A Rebate For Savings! Mon.–Fri. 11 to 7 PM, (open till 8 PM on Wed.) Sat. 10 AM to 7 PM, Sun. 12 to 6 PM Absolutely No Day Switching... and no gift wrap on Sidewalk Sale Items (Please note: This Sale in no way reflects the political views of Flights of Fancy)					**1** Harry Potter's Train to Hogwarts @ Platform #9 1/2 Anything Magical **20% OFF**
2 Be Kind to Writers Day All Cards, Stationary & Paper Stuff **20% OFF**	**3** Labor Day **Closed**	**4** Where have All The Flowers Gone Day All Potpourri & Incense **20% OFF**	**5** Be Late For Something Day Clocks & Watches **20% OFF**	**6** Here Is My Handle, Here Is My Spout Day All Teapots & Pitchers **20% OFF**	**7** National Ex-Lover Day (Things your "ex" never bought you) All Jewelry **20% OFF**	**8** Singer, Patsy Cline's Birthday Sing a line from one of her songs and get **20% OFF**
9 Grandparents Day All Glass or Crystal or Silver **20% OFF**	**10** Let There Be Light Day All Lamps & Nite Lights **20% OFF**	**11** Bald Is Beautiful Day Anything Smooth or Shiny **20% OFF**	**12** Olympic Hero, Jesse Owen's Birthday All Sports-Related Items **20% OFF**	**13** Come On Baby Light My Fire Day All Candles **20% OFF**	**14** Good Neighbor Day Any Gift For A Friend **20% OFF**	**15** Sidewalk Sale! Anything Outside **50% OFF**
16 National Fish Day Everything Listed **20% OFF** Just for the Halibut!	**17** Bacchus' Birthday All Wine-Related Items **20% OFF**	**18** Rosh Hashana All Judaica **20% OFF**	**19** National Narcissist Day All Picture Frames & Mirrors **20% OFF**	**20** What Accent? Day All Pens and Pins **20% OFF**	**21** Last Day of Summer All Windchimes & Picnic Bskets **20% OFF**	**22** Sidewalk Sale! Anything Outside **50% OFF**
23 National Dog Week Gifts for your Pet-20% Off **30*** Last Day Of Sale **35% Off**	**24** Jim Henson's Birthday All Puppets & Stuffed Animals **20% OFF**	**25** Only 91 Days 'till Xmas All Xmas Items **20% OFF**	**26** Johnny Appleseed's Birthday All NY Items & Anything with Apples **20% OFF**	**27** Make A Wish Day All Fountains **20% OFF**	**28** Confucius' Birthday Anything Asian **20% OFF**	**29** Broadway's Mama Mia previews in one week **(Congrats Brent!)** Any Gift for your Mama (or Mia) **20% OFF**

periods maybe twice a week. The sale can be on specific products, or a straight percentage discount on anything in the store. Promote your "Happy Hour" via window and in-store placards, mailings to senior citizen organizations, PTAs, and other groups whose members may have the time to do off-hour shopping. While you may be cutting down on profits during the two-hour "Happy Hours," it is better than having to pay salespeople when no one is in the store.

The Rainy/Snowy Day Sale

Since business is usually slow during inclement weather, you might institute a policy that when it is raining or snowing outside, prices automatically come down inside. Establish a firm rainy/snowy day discount and promote it throughout the year. It might kick in after one inch of snow falls, or after it has been raining for one hour.

Use window and in-store signage, direct mail to customers and groups, and perhaps some advertising. An ideal way to promote the sale is through the sponsorship of one or more local radio weather reports. You may be able to arrange, in advance, to purchase time on these weather reports whenever it is raining or snowing. Or you might be able to arrange a buy time on one of the radio talk shows. You should also have an announcement on your Web site and a recorded telephone announcement so that customers can check and see if the promotion is on that day. Like "Happy Hour," the purpose of this sale is to get people into the store during a dead period.

Temperature-of-the-Day Sale

Another sale aimed at bringing people into the store during less favorable weather periods would be one that kicks in when the temperature dips below, say twenty degrees, in the winter or rises above ninety-two degrees in the summer. The exact temperatures will depend upon your climate and your objectives.

Heavily promote this temperature concept just before and during the winter and summer seasons. Use in-store and window placards, bulletin board mailers to nearby businesses, flyers at the cash register, mailings to customers, and in all regular advertising.

On days the sale kicks in, have an announcement on your Web site, and on a recorded telephone message. You should also have a big banner or sign in your window. Good themes for this sale include "Our Prices Drop with the Temperature," "Cool Prices on a Hot Day," "Come In and Watch Our Prices Melt" "Warm Up to Our Cold Day Specials." Use the same media approach as recommended for the Rainy Day/Snowy Day Sales.

Your Birthday Sale

Make your customers' birthdays special occasions by inviting them in during their birthday week for a special "Happy Birthday Discount." It might be good for one product, or for the first $100 of purchases. If you have a program that enables you to track customer sales, you might tailor the discount so that better customers get a bigger discount. You might also give a small gift to your better customers.

Frequent buyers club members as well as VIP membership card holders should be automatically enrolled to receive the birthday invitation. In addition, you might have applications for the "Birthday Club" at the cash registers.

Invitations to use their "Happy Birthday Discount" should be sent to customers about one week before their birthday week.

Customers Pick the Sale Products

Once a year, let your customers structure a "Customer Appreciation Sale." Give them a ballot listing products you are willing to place on sale and let them vote for the three products they would like to see on sale. Tally up all the votes and then place the top five or top ten (you decide the exact number) on sale during "Customer Appreciation Week." In your promotion materials for the sale start right off by saying, "We asked you what you would like to see on sale and after counting the votes, here's what you asked for."

Surprise Special of the Week

For a three-day period each week feature a different product at a special discounted price. Do not advertise the product or the price but promote the concept, letting it be known that there is a "Surprise Special of the Week" every Tuesday through Thursday (or whatever days you select).

The objective is to get customers to visit the store weekly to see what the special will be. Have a placard in the window announcing "Sales Special of the Week Available Today."

Weekly Senior Citizen Day

Many retailers offer special discounts to senior citizens, often setting aside a slow period (one morning each week) for them. Since seniors are usually flexible with their time, it enables retailers to build traffic during a period when they can use more business. Seniors are reachable through senior clubs, senior citizen centers and housing, newsletters, and other publications. Contact your local government senior citizens office and see if it can provide you with the addresses of local senior citizen organizations.

Late Night Sales

From time to time you might want to hold a "Late Night Sale," to accommodate night owls and men and women who get off from work at midnight. This could be an effective way to introduce your store to a whole new segment of customers. Promote the event as a "happening" and perhaps even have live music. Have flyers at police stations and firehouses, hospitals, restaurants, and plants that have late shifts. Also promote through the media, especially disc jockeys and radio talk show hosts, predicting a large turnout of singles. If budget permits, you may want to do some advertising on late night radio.

Full Moon/Half Moon/New Moon Sales

The positions of the moon provide you with good themes to run sales. You might run one or several different "Moon" theme sales each year. The featured phase should be displayed in the window and throughout the store, down to full-, half-, and new-moon-shaped price tags. Themes might be "Take a Full Moon (10 percent) discount," or "Half Moon Sale . . . Buy One and Take Half off the Second."

The horoscopes page in newspapers is a good place to advertise this type of sale.

Your Lottery Sale

With interest in state lotteries high, you can create your own "lottery," in which everyone is a winner. After a purchase, the customer receives a scratch-off ticket that determines how much he or she gets off on the purchase. While everyone gets something off, some get a bigger discount than others. To make this sale even more interesting, you might have several 100-percent-off tickets.

Blood Donor Discount

In conjunction with the local blood bank, offer a special discount to anyone who donates blood during a specified period of time. Plan this drive with the blood bank's marketing and public relations staff since they probably have good contacts with the media. They may be able to get free public service time on radio and television to promote the drive.

They may be able to get the mayor, a popular disc jockey, or a local television news anchor to launch the drive by donating a pint of blood. The ideal time for the promotion would be during a slow donor period or when there is a shortage of blood in the area.

Private Sales for Private Groups

An effective way to attract special groups of new customers is to hold a private sale strictly for them. Keep the store open after hours exclusively for the specific group and offer an across-the-board discount or special sale prices.

Such private sales could be for people who live or work in the store's building or complex; for employees of a firm that recently relocated to your city; for the members of local business clubs, medical and dental societies, local chapters of professional societies, and teachers, etc. Select groups from which you will reach people who fit into your target customer audience.

Arrange these events with companies' human resources departments or the program chair at business clubs and organizations. Prepare invitations for the group to include in its next mailing, or see if you can get the group's list so that you can send invitations personally.

You should serve light refreshments for the special sale and have a drawing for door prizes.

Tax-Time Savings Sale

This is a good sale to run around the April 15 tax deadline. "Tax-Time Savings Sale" reaches consumers at a time when they may be short on cash and looking for ways to ease their expenses, or just looking for a bargain to reverse the usual April 15 doldrums. A subtheme might be "Relieve Tax-Time Blues."

Your in-store and window displays might include blowups of Internal Revenue forms with the sale announcement superimposed. You may also try to cross promote by asking local tax preparers to permit you to leave sale flyers at their locations. You may even hire someone to distribute flyers outside the local Internal Revenue Service offices. Media usually do all types of tax-savings stories around this time of the year. You might try to get your sale included as an anecdote. As with most sales, it is important to only offer some of your merchandise at sale prices.

Welcome to Our Town Sale

Each quarter, hold a special evening "by invitation only" sale and reception for new residents of the community. You may be able to obtain names and addresses of new residents through your county clerk's office or other government offices, which handle real estate transfers and voter registration, as well as real estate firms, welcome wagon, or a local mailing-list firm.

This get-acquainted sale should feature a percent-off coupon good toward the purchase of one item. Invitees should be signed up for your frequent buyer's club or VIP membership card. It is a chance to establish a rapport with new members of the community.

The Diet Sale

This is a two-part promotion. The first part is "Sign Up for Our Diet Sale—the More You Lose, the More You Save." During the one-week period, customers weigh in and sign up for the sale, which will actually be one month later. The enrolled customers weigh in again during the sale week and get a percentage off a single product, based on the number of pounds lost. (Eight pounds lost mean an 8 percent savings, etc.) Cap the discount at 10 percent to 15 percent. However, anyone who loses more than the maximum ten to fifteen pounds should be entered in a drawing for prizes. In addition, the person who loses the most weight should get a grand prize, perhaps a discount, which is double the percent of pounds lost, or a gift of some value.

This type of sale is a natural for media coverage—both the sign-in as well as the final weigh-in. Try to interest a local television news channel to interview a few customers during the initial weigh-in. They can talk about how they plan to lose their weight, what product they have their eyes on, and how much they hope to lose. Have the media back to cover the second part when they can follow up with the same people.

You can have all kinds of fun with this. You might run a parallel contest among local disc jockeys, with one dollar donated to a charity for every pound lost. Another contest might be for customers to guess the cumulative total pounds lost during the promotion. This, too, will attract media interest.

You might be able to interest the American Heart Association, a local hospital, or some other health group to cosponsor the promotion. It would give it a lot of credibility and a lot more exposure.

Reduce the Deficit Sale

With municipal budgets out of whack because of the economy, a "Reduce the Deficit Sale" is bound to get good coverage in local media. This is a promotion aimed at demonstrating both good citizenship and good pricing for your customers. You could offer a 5 percent off sale to your customers, donating an additional 5 percent to the city treasury. Have a City Hall press conference to announce the promotion, and a City Hall ceremony when you present the check to the mayor.

February 29th Sale

Leap year comes every four years but that doesn't mean you cannot celebrate it every year. What about all the people who were born on February 29. Is it fair to them to have a birthday only every four years? So, celebrate February 29 during the last four hours you are open on February 28. Invite everyone born on February 29 to attend a birthday party at the store, and let them participate in a special sale open only to February 29ers.

Promote your search for people born February 29 in your window, in-store, in small space advertising on the horoscope pages of newspapers, through disc jockeys, and other media. And do not forget to invite media to cover the event.

When February 29 appears on the calendar, have a real Leap Year sale, inviting all your customers to participate.

Roll Back the Prices Sale

Rolling back the prices on some of your products to your founding year was covered in chapter 10. You can also conduct a "Rollback" sale for any year you want. If might be for a historic year (the end of World War II), one tied to a show business personality (the year of Elvis's first hit record), or even the birth year of one of your customers. Invite customers to enter their birth year in a drawing, with the winner receiving a prize. In rolling back prices, do it for only a few products and see if you can get a special buy-in price or promotional allowance from the manufacturer.

The "Good Old Days" Sale

Like the "Rollback Sale," "The Good Old Days Sale" is aimed at bringing back the memories and pricing of past years. Examples of "Good Old Days Sales" might be a "Gay Nineties Sale," a "Fifties Sale," or a "Roaring Twenties Sale." Decorate the store to re-create the image of the era with salespeople wearing the clothing of the period. Drop some prices to what they may have been in those good old days. Your windows should also reflect the period you are featuring. In planning the promotion, you might contact the local historical society or a local museum for assistance. They may be able to loan to you costumes or other material to exhibit in-store or in the windows. This type of sale is aimed at creating excitement and attracting new customers to the store Your special pricing should only be available on, at most, one-third of your products.

Special Student Sales

The young people of today are the customers of tomorrow, so do all you can to cultivate them at an early age. There are a variety of sales you can conduct for students at the local schools. They include a "Graduating Seniors Sale," an "All A's Sale" for students with perfect report cards," an "Always There Sale" for students with perfect attendance records.

Reach the students through advertisements in the school newspapers. You may even sponsor a competition among area schools, offering special prizes for the school with the most all-A students and the one with the greatest number of perfect attendance students. The prizes might include donations to the respective schools' scholarship or recreation funds.

Cheaper by the Dozen (More or Less) Sale

Quantity is the name of the game here. This is an ideal sale for lower and medium-priced products. The more you buy of an item, or series of items, the less you pay. You might set the break point at six. For every additional six units purchased, the prices are further reduced.

Carload/Truckload Sale

Park a large truck in your lot. Around it, have cartons of product stacked on pallets. Have demonstration models in the store. When a customer purchases a product, he or she has to go to the truck area to pick it up. A huge sign could keep a running tally of the number of sales that day; or in countdown mode, the number left of each product. The public perception will be that the store probably got a good price because it bought a truckload, and is passing the savings on to the customer.

The Daily Knockdown Sale

This is not a sale for every store, especially not one with an upscale customer base. It is aimed at closeouts, irregulars, and damaged goods. The store has an announced policy that each day, or every third day, you reduce the prices on the items displayed in a special area. Each time you knock them down another 10 percent to 20 percent. If you cannot sell a product at the end of the set period, hold a drawing among customers, and give it away.

Two for the Price of One Sale

Restaurants do it, some entertainment venues do it, too. So it is no wonder that some retailers occasionally run "Two for the Price of One" sales. Purchase one product and the second one is free. The free product is the least expensive of the two. A variation is the "One-Cent Sale," which is popular at stores selling low-ticket items. The customer pays full price for the first unit, and only one cent for the second one. Again the one-cent product is the least expensive of the two. In planning such sales you have to be careful that you only include products that would enable you to still make a profit on each purchase.

Buy One, Pay Half Price for the Second Sale

A similar sale has the customer paying full price for one product (the most expensive) and half price for the second. This can be a popular sale among an upscale audience and should enable the retailer to make a fairly nice profit as well as give the consumer the satisfaction of finding a bargain.

Grandparents Day/Mother-in-Law Day Sale

Grandparents Day (the first Sunday in September after Labor Day) and Mother-in-Law Day (the fourth Sunday in October) are not as commonly celebrated as Mother's or Father's Day but provide a good promotional opportunity for a retailer. Have special gift certificates printed up for both occasions, encouraging customers to purchase one for each grandparent and another for each mother-in-law. Each certificate would entitle the receiver to a 10 percent discount when he or she uses it.

Father-in-Law Day Sale

No one has created a Father-in-Law Day yet so maybe you should. You can be the first one in your area to run a special "Father-in-Law Day" sale (pick any day you want), and offer the same gift certificate deal as suggested for Grandparents and Mother-in-Law Days.

Bonus Buys More Sale

If local companies award midyear or year-end bonuses to employees, run a "Bonus Buys More" sale. Since people have a tendency to spend bonus money on items they normally could not afford, feature upscale products in your sale. Make the offer full price for the more expensive product and half price for the other one.

The "Next Season" Sale

When a customer purchases a product one season at a full price, give him or her a discount coupon good toward a purchase during the next season. Run such a sale at least once a season. While you should make your customers aware of this promotion in advance of its dates, you should surprise your nonregular customers by just giving them the coupon after they pay for their purchase.

Name a Sale After a Person

Retailers have named sales after their sales's manager (Jimmy Smith's Sale), after their salesman of the year, even after a retiring employee. How about naming one after a customer? Run a contest inviting any customer who wants to have a sale named after himself or herself to enter his or her name. Hold a drawing to come up with the winner. Then promote the story through local media. The customer should receive a nice wad of shopping money and be invited to select three or four items he or she feels the store should put on sale. It probably will get good play in newspapers, television, and radio.

PROMOTING THE VALUE OF YOUR SALES PROGRAM

If you have an aggressive year-round sales program with significant savings for your customers, you may want to heavily promote this fact in the community. On the other hand, if you have an upscale customer base, this is not something to publicize.

For those who do want to promote the value their customers received, here are some of the ways to do it:

■ Compute the amount of money customers collectively saved as a result of your sales the past year. Then get the amount of money in $10 bills, or in gold, and display it for a day in your window. Have armed guards all over the place. Contact media, especially television, to cover the event. This will be a very effective way to position your store as a place where customers can realize huge savings through its sales.

■ Display a huge bankbook listing each of the year's sales, and next to each sale list the amount of money collectively saved. On the bottom line, run the total. The bankbook too can be displayed in the window or in the store. As a matter of fact, this can become a permanent fixture on a year-round basis. As each sale ends, enter the cumulative customer savings. Keep updating the chart after each sale.

■ Business page editors might be interested in a year-end story on the total customer savings, and even periodic updates. This might also be a good subject for talk show appearances.

CUSTOMER PROMOTION CALENDAR

If you can plan your promotions well in advance, it would be advantageous to provide your customers with some type of calendar. It could be a full twelve-month calendar, with sale days imprinted on the appropriate dates. Or, if you do not plan that far in advance, you might issue a quarterly calendar.

Another way would be to provide customers each quarter with a sheet of self-sticking circles, each imprinted with another event. They can then place them on their own calendars.

12

■■■

Everyone Loves a Contest

EVERYONE LOVES A contest. They enjoy participating and, of course, the anticipation of winning.

Carefully structured contests, offering meaningful prizes, will not only create excitement among existing customers but will also build additional store traffic. Even people who do not ordinarily enter contests will participate if the prizes are perceived to be valuable, or something they want.

Before conducting a contest, be certain to consult with your attorney since there are various rules and regulations governing contests.

There are basically three different types of contests retailers might consider:

- A sweepstakes. No skills are required. A person just enters his or her name and a drawing is held to pick the winner(s).
- Games of chance. Again, no skills are required. A person spins a wheel, scratches off a game card, or picks a capsule from a drum.
- A skills contest. The customer does something to win. It may require guessing something or a special talent.

EVERYTHING YOU NEED TO KNOW ABOUT
RUNNING A SWEEPSTAKES

Sweepstakes contests may be held in connection with promotions, sales, other special events, or by themselves. The more expensive the top prizes are, the more interest there will be in the sweepstakes.

To keep costs down, try to get suppliers, other merchants, and companies to provide the prizes, or at least give you a good price on them. In turn you will have to offer good window and in-store promotional support. You will find that the more you agree to spend to advertise and promote a sweepstakes, the easier it will be to obtain prizes.

Let your imagination take over when naming the sweepstakes.

It may carry the same name as a promotion or sale, or it could be named after the grand prize, "Holiday in France," "A Night Out on the Town," "Shopping Spree Madness," etc. Or, it can be named after anything else. "Lucky Days," "Dreams Come True," "Reach for the Sky," "The Big Win," or "A Needle in the Haystack."

Your sweepstakes can take on several formats: Customers can enter by writing their name, address, and telephone number on an entry form or a slip of paper. They can enter by submitting their business cards. Use this format if business people and firms make up your customer base. If you have the mechanism, customers can be entered automatically each time they make a purchase. However, remember that a purchase cannot be a condition for entering a sweepstakes.

A modified form of sweepstakes is the daily drawing for prizes you might hold during holiday and seasonal promotions and special events. The daily drawings would be from among customers who had registered that day at the store. You might then save each day's registration slips for a grand drawing at the end of the promotion.

If any of your suppliers is running a national sweepstakes, you might run a local version. Right next to the national contest information and entry forms, promote your own contest. Have a special form, which customers can use to enter. Posters promoting your version might read, "Enter XYZ Company's Automobile Sweepstakes . . . and Our Local Drawing for Six Months of Free Gasoline." While your prizes may be more modest than the national sweepstakes prizes, they should relate to them. If the national contest is for a trip, you might offer a set of luggage. If the national grand prize is a house, you might offer maid service for a year. Be sure to touch base with the supplier holding the national sweepstakes before announcing your local tie-in.

For all sweepstakes, require that entries be dropped off at your store. The names and addresses from the entries should be used to develop a mailing list and/or to track where your customers live. This latter information will help you develop your marketing plans.

Some suggested sweepstakes:

- Offer as a prize the winner's weight in a product. It might be chocolate, soap, shoes, bubble bath, ice cream, apples, etc. Ideally, it should be a product you sell, but if you do not have an appropriate one, find a "fun" one. The weigh-in should be at the store, where first the person is weighed and then the product. Made for television and newspapers!
- Try to purchase programs from major events (Academy Awards, Super Bowl, Grammy Awards, World Series, etc.) and offer them in individual sweepstakes. Let people enter the sweepstakes for a two-week period prior to the event. Have the drawing on the day of the event. It will probably take a couple of weeks before the programs are delivered to you. You may want to have several winners for each event.
- Shopping sprees are good sweepstakes prizes. Are people staying home because of the cold weather? Get them out by conducting one-week sweepstakes offering a shopping spree as first prize. A shopping spree can also be given away as a prize in a skills contest as described later in this chapter.

MAKE YOUR GAMES OF CHANCE PAY OFF WITH INCREASED SALES

Games of chance can work effectively with special sales. They can be used to determine how much discount a customer gets on a purchase. They can work well on customer appreciation days, and with other giveaway promotions, which determine which prizes an individual gets.

There are several ways to run games of chance:

- Rent a carnival or roulette wheel, or a one-armed bandit (providing this is legal in your area), and invite customers to try their luck. What number or combination comes up determines the percent discount. Make the highest odds numbers or combinations, the highest discount figure (50 percent or 75 percent) in order to enhance interest in the promotion.

- Use lottery type scratch-off tickets to determine discounts or prizes. They can be printed to meet your specifications, or you may be able to buy stock cards.

- You might also encourage customers to bring in their losing state lottery tickets for a "second chance" door prize. Develop a discount structure based on the lottery serial number printed on each ticket. Perhaps the third digit from the right determines the discount. If you plan to run a "Second Chance" contest, be certain you check to see if it must be cleared with your state's Lottery Commission. If you run such a contest and it has the approval of the Lottery Commission, contact area shops that sell lottery tickets and offer to provide a sign: YOUR LOSING TICKETS MAY WIN YOU A PRIZE AT (NAME AND ADDRESS OF YOUR STORE).

- You can also have capsules with numbers in them, or numbered tickets, and let customers pick one from a large container. This is the easiest and least expensive way for a game of chance drawing. It also gives you greater control over the amount of the discounts to be offered since you place the numbers in the container.

- You might consider using a "Treasure Chest." A customer is given a key and if it opens the chest, he or she is the winner. The customer then selects one of the envelopes in the Treasure Chest to determine which prize he or she has won. Another way, if the key opens the Treasure Chest, the person becomes a finalist for a big grand prize. Then have all of the finalists come back to get another key with only one key that will fit the lock. The person getting the lucky key is the big prize winner. If the prize is a very big one, local television might cover the finals to capture the reactions of the winner.

- Several one-, five- and ten-dollar bills could be circulated around the city as "Special Prize Money." Post the winning numbers inside the store so that people have to come in to see if they have a winner. Each winning bill should have a value that can be applied toward the purchase of products in the store.

- For Chinese New Year, serve tea and fortune cookies to your customers. While most of the cookies will have the customary fortune, some should contain the good news that the customer has won a prize. Among the prizes can be merchandise from your store, dinners for two at local Chinese restaurants, and various inexpensive Chinese-made products (fans, chopsticks holders, decorative soup spoons, etc.). Contact some of the Chinese restaurants in the area to see if they will provide the dinner prizes free of charge in return for promotional signage at the store. See Chinese New Year in chapter 9.

USING SKILLS CONTESTS TO DRAW CUSTOMERS

These contests generate a lot of fun and interest because they require a customer to use their skills or their talent. They range from guessing and costume contests, to poetry writing and photography competitions.

Guess the Number of . . .

Guessing the number of items in a bowl or cylinder has challenged Americans of all ages and has been a popular retail contest that is easy to conduct. The winner is the person who comes the closest to guessing the exact number of items in the bowl.

You can run such a contest from time to time or on a regular monthly basis.

If you run it monthly, consider awarding a grand prize for the year in addition to the prize for each contest. It would go to the customer who comes up with the closest correct guess for the cumulative number of items displayed over the year. Run this cumulative contest during the last quarter of the year. Let everyone know the correct numbers for the first nine months so all they have to do is add their guess for the last three months. Set mid-December as the closing date for the cumulative contest.

Different items you might consider for your monthly guessing contests include:

- January: Ping-Pong balls
- February: chocolate kisses
- March: M&M's
- April: jelly beans
- May: golf balls
- June: pennies
- July: peanuts (in their shells)
- August: dimes

- September: quarters
- October: Halloween candies
- November: bubble gum
- December: candy canes

Initially, you might have the container in your window, inviting passersby into the store to enter the contest. Then, if the space permits, move it inside the store, keeping the sign in the window. If you run this contest throughout the year, you may be able to get a newspaper or television channel to run a picture of the cylinder each month. It is the type of a light sign-off item a news show might do. The newspaper might look at it as, "It's that time of the month again."

There are all types of items that can be included in "Guess the Number" contests, and some retailers might want to feature products more closely associated with the store. For example, a sporting goods store, which sells a lot of fishing equipment, might have customers guessing the number of worms in a pail; a men's store might have a cylinder of cuff links; a jewelry store a cylinder of rings, etc.

Costumes and Fashions

During the year, run a "Costume Day" or "Costume Night" contest and party, inviting customers to shop in costume and compete for prizes in such categories as "Best," "Most Original," "Funniest," etc. Other fashion-oriented contests might be an "Easter Hat Preview," "Trick or Treat Chaperon Wear," "Sloppy Wear," etc. Visible contests like these are designed to draw media coverage.

Poetry Contests

These can be fun and attract good media coverage. Invite your customers to write an ode to your store, their favorite salesperson, or a particular product ("An Ode to My Jeans," etc.). You can establish a theme for the contest so that all poems will be on the same subject, or let people write whatever they want so long as it is under a set number of lines.

To judge the poetry, arrange for a panel to include an English professor or high school English teacher, a disc jockey, a newspaper columnist, a local television personality, and a librarian. Have a read-off of the best poems at the store. It should get local television coverage. In addition, you might arrange to have some of the contestants read their poems live on local talk or disc jockey shows.

Groundhog Day Shadow Game

Will he or won't he? That is the question of the day. For a week prior to Groundhog Day (February 2), invite customers to guess whether or not the local groundhog will see its shadow. On a tote board in your window, provide a running total of the vote. After the groundhog has made his appearance, conduct a drawing among those who came up with the right answer. If you do not have a local groundhog, use the "Punxsutawney Phil" sighting to determine your contest. His shadow-search results are always well publicized on network television news programs and in daily newspapers.

Furnish media, especially disc jockeys and talk show hosts, with daily updates of the voting at your store. Try to get a newspaper to run a daily tally box near its weather forecast. Also try to get a television weatherman to give daily updates.

Look-alike Contests

"Look-alike" contests are a good way to create in-store excitement, and they can be very appealing to television news programs, which means good publicity for your store. There are two types of contests: one open to all look-alikes of famous people, the other for just a look-alike of a specific person (Elvis, Jackie Gleason, Lucille Ball, etc.). If you open it up for all famous people, you might have specific categories for judging (television, motion pictures, sports, politics, etc.).

Try to get a local television personality, a disc jockey, a newspaper columnist, and an elected official to serve as judges. Have the event at your store.

To attract candidates, contact local modeling schools, send flyers to companies to post on their bulletin boards, and send material to radio, television, and newspapers. Try to get local radio and television media to encourage people who look like any of their personalities to enter. They could have a lot of fun doing this.

Halloween Art Contest

When Halloween rolls around, invite your customers' children to participate in an art contest. Have them submit their work and display it in the store, as well as in the windows. Set up a prize structure based on age brackets (Under six, six to eight, nine to eleven, etc.).

Pumpkin Decorating Contest

The Halloween season also lends itself to a pumpkin-decorating contest. Invite everyone, young and old, to participate. Display the pumpkins at the store and give prizes to the winners. Have three categories of judging: subteens, teens, and twenty-plus.

Recipe Ingredient Contest

This is an ideal contest for a restaurant to conduct. Take one of its popular dishes and run a contest among diners letting them guess the ingredients in the dish. The contest could be run on a regular basis, with the winner of each contest getting a free dinners for two (or four).

Cherry Pie Contest

Since cherry pies are so often connected with George Washington, sponsor a cherry pie baking contest around Presidents' Day. After you have picked the winners, serve the pies to your customers.

Decorate a Doghouse Contest

This is an ideal contest for a pet store to conduct. Sponsor a contest to find the best-looking doghouse in town. Have people decorate the outsides of their doghouses and submit a photograph of the finished product. Hold the finals, with the actual doghouses on hand, at the store on a Saturday afternoon. You will probably get good media coverage.

Calendar Contest

If you have the budget to produce an annual customer calendar, consider illustrating it with art by area youngsters. Sponsor a contest inviting them to submit art on either a specific subject or a variety of possible subjects (their pet, the street they live on, their school, their teacher, their room, the city, the playground, etc.). Select the twelve best and use each to illustrate a specific month. A savings bond should be given to each winner.

Use press releases to announce the competition and encourage entries. Send copies of the release to school principals and ask that they forward it to art teachers.

When the twelve winners are selected, have a press conference at the store to unveil the pictures.

Do-It-Yourself Greeting Card Contest

This contest is designed to bring out the talent in your customers. Invite them to design a greeting card for one or more upcoming holidays. It might be Valentine's Day, Halloween, St. Patrick's Day, Thanksgiving, or Christmas—you pick the holiday. Have two divisions: computer generated cards, and hand-designed cards. Display as many as possible in the store, and award prizes to the best ones. You might even let customers be the judges, having them vote for their three favorites.

Vacation Picture Contest

It is a great "End of the Summer" event. Invite customers to display their favorite vacation photographs. Establish several judging categories: scenery, on the water, at the beach, the city, etc. Award prizes in each category and set up a special display area for the winners. Try to get the local daily newspaper photo editor, a local professional photographer, and a photography instructor to judge the contest.

You might also repeat it in the wintertime with three categories: "Christmas Time," "Fun in the Sun," and "Snow Scenes."

Shopping Spree Contest

Shopping sprees are always fun, and usually are covered by media. The most popular version, usually conducted by supermarkets and department stores, gives the winner a fixed amount of time (anywhere from five to ten minutes) to shop. He or she can keep everything they have brought to the cash register during that period. This version will work if you have smaller ticket items. If you have higher priced items, you might cut the time down to two to three minutes, or set parameters: only one of each item can be taken.

Another version allocates a budget for the spree. If the winner goes over the amount, he has to give double the overage back (i.e., if $500 over a $2000 budget, a $1000 return in merchandise). If the winner is under the budget, the under amount is donated to the person's favorite charity. To enter the contest, people have to write in twenty-five words or less "Why I Like to Shop at (name of store)" or just have them answer a question in one word: "The first thing I will take during my shopping spree will be————."

This promotion is a natural for television coverage because it is so visual.

Super Savings Guessing Contest

From time to time when you hold a sale, you might want to reinforce the value of that sale through a unique contest. Let each consumer estimate the total savings by customers during the sale. The person who comes the closest to the correct amount is the winner of a gift certificate.

"Best Tan in Town" Contest

As the name implies, customers compete for the "Best Tan in Town" title, a good contest to hold in late July or August. While any store can sponsor such a contest, this is an ideal one if you sell bathing suits, sportswear, health foods, or cosmetics.

Sand Castle Building Contest

Bring piles of sand to your parking lot and invite customers to compete. The concept is that since you couldn't get to the beach today, we brought it to you. A great July event but you might also try it sometime during the winter. The winter version will create a lot of excitement and media interest.

Home Video Contest

Invite customers to enter a home video contest. Let them submit three-to five-minute tapes on a specific subject: the children, Thanksgiving dinner, a day at the beach, etc. Invite a local television producer to select ten finalists. Then, hold a special weekend "(Name of city) Home Video Festival" at the store and let the customers vote to pick the three winners. You should also approach local television to see if they would be interested in running the winning entries on one of their news programs.

13

■ ■ ■

Sports as a Promotional Vehicle

THERE IS PROBABLY no more exciting or glamorous vehicle to use in marketing your business than sports. What makes sports so appealing is both great public interest and the variety of sports and promotions available. There are professional, semiprofessional, and amateur; college, high-school down to Little League. Team sports include baseball, football, basketball, hockey, soccer, volleyball, lacrosse, and softball. Some popular individual sports are boxing, horse racing, tennis, golf, swimming, hunting, fishing, bowling, Ping-Pong, ice skating, and gymnastics. And very important, both sexes enjoy sports as both spectators and participants.

However, because of the glamour and personal emotions connected with sports, you *must* be certain that a sports promotion is appropriate for your store and your audience, and will be the *most cost-effective way* to reach that audience. Also there could be a danger in overdoing it. Do not run sports promotion after sports promotion unless you have a customer base of sports fanatics. It is time to evaluate and ask "The Five Promotional Criteria Questions," found in chapter 8.

Furthermore, you *must* take into consideration the sports atmosphere in your community. What are the favorite sports and teams of your customers and potential customers? Who are their favorite athletes? In some areas, a semiprofessional or amateur team may have a very strong following. Or a coach or retired athlete may be the most respected sports figure in the area.

You must also recognize the growing popularity and importance of women's participation in sports both on the team level and through individual performances.

Most important, make your decisions on what is going to help business, and not on what you personally like!

Here are some of the ways you can use sports to promote traffic, sales, and recognition for your store.

SPORTS PERSONALITIES' IN-STORE APPEARANCES

Personal appearances by athletes and those associated with sports can be good traffic builders.

However, such personal appearances should be carefully scheduled and programmed to achieve your objectives. You want to avoid a mass invasion of people who want to meet the personality, or get an autograph, without any thought of making a purchase. In addition, you do not want the personal appearance to interfere with customers who come to shop who are not interested in the celebrity.

Thus personal appearances by athletes should be connected with the sale of a specific product, or minimum dollar amount. Only those who make the required purchase should get the chance to meet the athlete and get an autograph.

If you have a small store, or you feel an in-store appearance would be too distracting to business, you can schedule the appearance away from the store, at a local auditorium or hall. However, to gain admission, the customer must have made the required purchase at the store that week, in order to receive a ticket.

Whom to Schedule for a Personal Appearance

That is a decision you have to make yourself. You must determine which person will attract the greatest number of potential customers and meet the marketing goals of your store. If you want to attract an older audience, you might opt for a retired athlete; if you sell athletic equipment, it might be a team trainer, who could conduct a question-and-answer period on conditioning; around Super Bowl time, it might be a local college football coach discussing the upcoming game.

Here is a list of possibilities:

- Professional athletes from teams in your area, from visiting teams in town for a game, or those who live in the area during the off season, or who are retired.
- Team managers and coaches, both professional and college.
- Individual performance athletes: boxers, jockeys, golfers, tennis players, auto-racing drivers, ice skaters, gymnasts.
- Trainers from both professional and college teams are ideal for certain types of retailers, including shoe and athletic-shoe stores, sporting goods stores, drug and medical supply stores, and stores catering to senior citizens.
- Team broadcasters and local sportswriters.
- Former college greats.
- Team executives if they have a very high profile in the area.

When a Fee May Not Be Necessary

You will probably have to pay an appearance fee to get most sports personalities. In some cases, when you have the right product mix, you might be able to pay in merchandise instead of money. But there are exceptions to fee arrangements:

- When the appearance is in connection with a book he or she has written.
- When the appearance is in connection with a product he or she endorses. It is important for every retailer to determine what personalities its suppliers have under contract for in-store appearances and how they can arrange such an appearance.
- If there is a connection with an upcoming sports event. The promoters of individual performance events often bring athletes connected with the event into a city on an advance promotion trip. Try to strike a deal by offering promotional windows, in-store promotions, or other activities calling attention to the event in exchange for providing the athletes at no cost. The appearance could be during the advance trip, or even during the event itself. These events might include tennis matches,

golf tournaments, rodeos, auto races, ice shows, gymnastics competitions, etc.

- If they feel it will help ticket sales, some professional teams might arrange appearances by their players or coaching staff. They may also cooperate if you purchase a large block of tickets for a game, or a significant number of season tickets.
- By tying in with charitable organizations. Many charities have access to professional athletes who will make special appearances on their behalf, providing funds are raised. You may be able to arrange such an appearance by agreeing to give a percentage of sales that day to the charitable organization.

Using the Athlete at Personal Appearances

Some of the activities to consider during an appearance include:

- Signing autographs. You might set this up so that a customer who makes a minimum purchase receives an autograph on a card. A larger purchase might bring an autographed photo. A still larger purchase might earn the customer an autographed baseball, basketball, football, or hockey puck, depending on the athlete's sport. Sometimes the athlete might autograph the product with which he is connected.
- A photograph with the athlete. This should require a substantial purchase.
- Conducting the drawing for prizes. If you sponsored a sweepstakes, have the athlete pick the winning tickets.
- Holding a question-and-answer period, letting the athlete answer customer questions.
- Using the appearance as a fund-raiser. Charge a nominal fee for all autographs, and donate all the money to a local charity.
- Conducting a clinic in your store, if you have the space. If not, consider scheduling the clinic away from the store but require a ticket for admission, which the customers can get by making a purchase at the store.
- Using the athlete to model clothing or fashion accessories if those products are sold at the store.
- Inviting certain athletes to skills competitions. For example, set up a basketball net outside your store and have a basketball player shoot ten

free throws. Then invite customers to try to top his record. If any do, give them a certificate that reads, "I out-shot (name of player)." The athlete does not have to be present after he takes his shots.

■ Prior to major sporting events, arranging for a local sportswriter or sportscaster to conduct a forum at the store, discussing the participants, predicting the outcome, and conducting a question-and-answer session with customers. If you advertise in newspapers, radio, or television, try to get the advertising departments to arrange the sportswriter and sportscaster appearances as part of your promotional allowance.

TICKET GIVEAWAYS

Ticket giveaways and drawings for tickets to sporting events always create excitement. To enter a drawing, a person has to visit the store and register (Note: The law usually requires that a purchase is not necessary to enter a contest). It may be a one-time drawing for a specific game, or it might be a series of drawings held on a weekly basis for different games. You should automatically enter all members of your frequent buyer's club in each drawing. You might want to purchase one or more season tickets and hold a drawing for each game.

A giveaway can be tied to a purchase. A free ticket is given to each customer who purchases a high-priced item, or buys more than a specified dollar amount of merchandise during a month. You can usually purchase blocks of tickets at discount so the perceived value of the gift is more than your costs. You may also be able to make a deal with the team by trading off space in your ads or your windows for free tickets or for a deep discount.

A third possibility is a sweepstakes to an out-of-town sporting event. While the major events (the Super Bowl, Kentucky Derby, Indy 500, Masters) could be very expensive to sponsor, there are other possibilities to get local cosponsors. A minor league baseball team in your city might sponsor a trip to see its big league affiliate play. A professional team might sponsor a trip to one of its away games. You should also approach airlines, hotel chains, and local travel agents to see if they will cosponsor the prize. They may agree if you will heavily advertise and promote the sweepstakes and their participation in your ads, flyers, store windows, and mailings to your frequent customers.

EXHIBITS AT THE STORE

Interesting sports exhibits attract traffic, as well as media coverage. For example, prior to a local auto race, try to arrange to have one or more of the race cars on display in front of your store. Inside, you might have drivers' helmets and racing outfits. Part of the deal would be to sell some of the licensed products of the racing team. Perhaps you can even have the driver appear for a few hours. Invite your best customers to have their pictures taken with the driver as well as people who make a significant or specific purchase(s) that day. A thoroughbred or trotter, along with the jockey, driver, or trainer might make an outside-the-store appearance. Contact a local track to arrange such a promotion.

Inside-the-store exhibits and displays to consider include:

- Sports memorabilia. Make it an "insider" display, inviting customers to display memorabilia they may have. If that's not possible, find a single collector in the area who might be willing to show his or her collection.
- Sports art. Offer local artists the chance to display their works. Invite the local art schools, galleries, and local museums to participate. This type of exhibit could cover all sports, or you could schedule a series of art exhibits around major sporting events, limiting the art to the specific sports. Baseball at World Series time, Super Bowl in January, horse racing to coincide with a big national or regional race, etc.
- Local teams. Local professional and college teams might loan you uniforms, trophies, equipment, memorabilia, and other material. It could coincide with the start of a specific sports season. You might be able to get a coach or players to appear at the opening of the exhibit. In turn, they might ask that you make their schedules and ticket information available to your customers. You may also want to consider displays from local high schools, semiprofessional, and amateur teams if they have strong local support or are heading to state tournaments. The same with Little League teams, especially around tournament time. These local team exhibits will probably generate the greatest interest at the start of the season and during play-offs and tournaments.
- Single athlete display. Build an exhibit around a current athlete or a retired athlete, who lives in the area. He or she might loan you trophies, newspaper headlines and clippings, personal uniforms or equipment, and other memorabilia. Hold a preview reception for your best customers, and have the athlete on hand. You might also want to have the

athlete appear on a shopping day at the store to sign autographs and pose for pictures.

■ Newspaper headlines. In conjunction with your daily newspaper, arrange a display of headlines of famous sporting events of the past. Include international and national events as well as major events in which local teams participated.

With the increased popularity of women's sports, you might include an exhibit on the achievements of local women athletes and teams.

When you hold a display, always send material in advance to local media so that they can run the information in their Events columns and broadcasts. Media should also be invited to a preview the night before the opening if you have athletes on hand. Also invite your best customers. (See chapter 21 for more information on how to get publicity.)

MAJOR SPORTING EVENT ATMOSPHERE

If you have a very sports-oriented customer base, go all out to re-create in store the atmosphere of the major sporting events while they are taking place: the World Series, Super Bowl, Final Four, Indy 500, a college bowl game, Kentucky Derby, etc.

For legal reasons, you might not be able to use the exact name of the event unless you pay a licensing fee. If your suppliers have a licensing arrangement, they will be able to get you point-of-sale material with the event logo and name. However, if they do not, it is possible to get around it by providing the hoopla without the name. Your customers will easily catch on when they see the football decor and references to "The Big Game," or the horse-racing decor and "The Big Race," and the World Series scenario referred to as "The Best of Seven."

Use banners and blowup action photos, newspaper headlines of past years' results, equipment associated with the sport, team pennants, jockey silks, uniforms, and memorabilia. You might have your salespeople wearing team caps, jersey tops, or some other piece of clothing associated with the sport.

To add excitement, you might run an in-store "Guess the Final Score" contest. Or, you could run an advance drawing to select twenty-five to fifty customers to watch the event on television at a private party hosted by a local sportswriter or sportscaster.

AT THE ARENA OR STADIUM

There are a multitude of ways a retailer can get involved in promotions at sporting events. While most usually involve professional sports, colleges and amateur leagues are becoming more aggressive in attracting sponsorships. Most will involve a sponsorship fee or a commitment to purchase tickets. Arrangements can be made with team marketing departments.

- Sponsor a race at a local horse or trotting track. The track will name the race after your store. Let your customers know when it will take place. Try to arrange special discount tickets for your customers as well as special seating. Perhaps hold a drawing to select a number of winners to be your personal guests at the track. You might consider distributing discount coupons to your store at the track that day or night. Or, perhaps the track will let you hold a drawing for merchandise among those present at the track.
- Sponsor a skills competition for fans at the event. Some basketball teams invite one or more fans to take a halftime, half-court shot. If the ball goes through the hoop, the person wins a car, a big cash prize, or other merchandise. If you sponsor such a competition, you should purchase an insurance policy to cover the cost of the big prize. Another basketball competition allows a fan to attempt sinking ten consecutive free throws. A season-long, dribbling relay competition can be very entertaining and can include a wide cross section of people. At each game teams representing different groups—firemen, police, teachers, lawyers, doctors, dentists, stockbrokers, housewives, carpenters, families, etc.—compete, each team member dribbling the length of the court before handing off to the next member. The team that finishes first goes on to the next round. The tournament concludes with the finals on the evening of the last home game of the season.
- Minor league baseball teams are among the most receptive of all sports teams to sponsors of in-stadium events. Minor league baseball is very family oriented and encourages fun-type events that can involve children as young as three and four or senior citizens. They have races around the bases for children, throw the ball into a peach basket contests, adult distance throws, team relay races. Football opportunities include throwing the ball into a target, kicking a field goal (the greater the distance the bigger the prize), and punting. The marketing departments

of the teams will usually solicit local firms to underwrite these types of competition, as well as other sponsorship packages. The teams are also open to sponsors' suggested events. There are several ways in which the participating fans are selected. Sometimes lucky seat numbers are drawn, often a lucky number printed in the game program is used. And sometimes fans have to register at a locale away from the arena or stadium in advance of the game. If you underwrite any competition, get the team to agree that all sign-ups must take place at your store. It is a good way to build in-store traffic and gain exposure.

Other opportunities for arena and stadium promotions include:

- Giveaways. Budget permitting, you might consider sponsoring a giveaway day or night for one or more teams. The giveaways—all imprinted with your store's name—can range from T-shirts, hats or bats, regular size or miniature balls to travel bags, umbrellas, or sunglasses. Since they also carry the team logo, most giveaways are kept and used, giving your store's name good exposure on a long-term basis.
- Lucky number prizes. In addition to using program lucky numbers to pick fans to compete in skills contests, the numbers are also used for drawings during the game for cash prizes and merchandise. If you sell women's products, then you might want to concentrate on the programs of women's sports teams.
- The team mascot. Some teams seek sponsorship for team mascots. This, too, might be something to look into, especially if you can use the mascot for in-store events and book it into other promotional events that you are promoting away from the store.

A POTPOURRI OF OTHER OPPORTUNITIES

An In-Store Sports Trivia Contest

Use photographs and other nostalgia items for visual identification for an in-store trivia contest. Shoppers who want to participate receive an entry form on which to write the answers to the questions posted at each item. Since the items and questions are scattered around the store, participants will be exposed to your entire product line. Give merchandise prizes to the winners. Invite local radio and television sportscasters and sportswriters to compete in a special category and act as judges. If there is a local all-sports station in the area, see if you can get it to be a cosponsor.

Player Awards

It may be possible for your store to sponsor one or more of the various awards given to local team members. It might be "Player of the Week or Month," "Rookie of the Year," "Most Valuable Player," "Most Improved Player," etc. These awards can be structured for professional teams as well as for college, high school, and amateur teams. At the school level, be sure to have separate awards for male and female teams. You may also want to sponsor the awards for an entire league (amateur, Little League, etc.).

If you do sponsor such awards, be certain to include your store's name in the title. Plaques and trophies are the appropriate awards for nonprofessional teams and players. Such awards can be presented at games, or at an annual awards banquet. Store merchandise or gift certificates, along with plaques or trophies, might be given to professionals and presented at games so that your store will receive good exposure before the fans, and on television coverage. Or you might make a donation to the winning athlete's favorite charity.

You might also sponsor a "Most Popular Player" contest with fans casting their ballots at your store. The contest might be among players of a professional team, or on a college or high school team. It depends on which team is the "big team" in town. Or, you might let the fans pick the "Most Popular Player" from among all the athletes in town, whether they be professional or amateur, male or female.

Teams and Leagues

In almost every city there are opportunities to sponsor amateur teams and get your store's name on their uniforms. Those teams include softball, bowling, baseball, basketball, football, and soccer as well as Little League. Sponsorship costs may vary from city to city and sport to sport. It might require paying for uniforms, equipment, field or arena rental, and officiating fees. It might also include travel expenses to tournaments and other incidentals. If you become a sponsor, make certain that you promote the team in-store. Try to get your customers to think of it as their team; get them to go to the games and become involved. There may also be opportunities to sponsor an entire league.

If local media covers Little League and other amateur sports leagues, you probably will get sports page exposure. And if your team goes all the way to the state tournament, interest will mount along with your exposure. Most of all, your customer-fans will feel even closer to the store.

A Bicycle, Walking, or Foot Race

Individual recreational competition has become more popular throughout the nation among people of all ages. Most of these events are either sponsored by nonprofit organizations as fund-raisers, or by individual companies. Sponsorships, whole or part, offer retailers a chance for good community exposure. The events are already organized and sponsors are asked to donate money, prizes, and free giveaways for competitors (T-shirts, sun visors, hats, etc.). Giveaways have the event and sponsor's name; and since they are used after the event, sponsors get good long-term exposure. Some of the events to consider sponsoring are bicycle races and bikeathons, walking races and walkathons, road races (from short ones to marathons), triathlons, and three-on-three basketball team competition.

If you do agree to be a sponsor, insist that competitors pick up or drop off their entry forms at your store. And if you are the sole sponsor, or the sponsor putting up most of the money, insist that your store name be the only one in the event title.

Player Achievement Awards

Sponsor season-long, player achievement contests among the major amateur teams in your city. For example, in baseball give awards for the longest home run hit and the longest hitting streak by a home-team player during the season; for the most strikeouts in a season by a pitcher, or for consecutive strikeouts in a game. In basketball, it could be for the most points scored in a game, the most blocked shots in a game, the most assists in a game, or the most minutes played in a season by a home-team player. The football competition could be based on the longest punt, pass, and most yardage gained in a game.

Try to get local media to keep a running scoreboard on these achievements. Also keep a scoreboard in your store or in its window. At the end of the year, present the winners with appropriate prizes.

Weekly "Pick the Winners" Contest

If it is fan participation and enthusiasm you want, a weekly "Pick the Winners" contest will do the trick. Require that entry forms be picked up at the store or on your Web site and/or dropped off at the store. If the form is on the Web site, place it so that it is not linked to the home page but rather to the second or third page of the site so that the person has to scan the site till they come to the entry form. For baseball, contestants might have to pick the local team's cumulative runs and/or hits for the week. For football, contestants would pick the scores of ten to fifteen games each week. For basketball, contestants would guess the cumulative points scored for the week by an area team, or for several teams. For hockey, contestants would pick the high scorer of the week and the number of goals scored by that player. Offer store merchandise or gift certificates as prizes.

An alternative to being the sole sponsor would be to cosponsor the contest with a local newspaper or radio station. If a newspaper is the cosponsor, negotiate with the newspaper to print the entry coupon in the paper each week but the coupon has to be dropped off at the store unless you are located in a large city.

Ticket Stub Promotion

A good ongoing promotion involves special discounts to fans who present ticket stubs at your store or restaurant twenty-four to forty-eight hours following a game. There are several offers you can make: the same discount no matter who wins, or the score; a discount if the home team wins; a discount based on the point spread; or a discount if the home team scores over a certain number of points or runs.

Your discounts can be across the board on all products, or on a special selection of products. It is an ideal fast food promotion: two hot dogs for the price of one; a free soda when you buy a hamburger; if the team scores over a certain amount of points, a free slice of pizza; if it doesn't, then a free soda if you buy the pizza, etc.

If you run a ticket stub promotion, you will probably have to run an ad in the team program. Also try to get the team to give you space on the back of the ticket stub and in public address announcements.

Nights at the Game

Most baseball and basketball teams promote special "nights" for which a company can purchase a large block of tickets at discount. Consider sponsoring such a night, perhaps in tandem with one of your suppliers. Either distribute the tickets to your most frequent customers, hold a drawing among entries received at the store, tie a free ticket to the sale of a product, or offer tickets at discount to customers. "(Name of store) Night" can be a fun customer evening. Most teams will acknowledge groups on their scoreboard and in public address announcements, and sometimes on their radio and television game coverage. Some teams have special dining or picnic areas for groups that purchase a certain number of tickets.

The night will have some perceived value to your customers since you can pass along the discounted ticket price. If you purchase enough tickets, you may be able to negotiate a free souvenir or game program for your customers. You may be able to develop this night into an annual event that customers will look forward to attending each year.

A Players' Wives Fashion Show

If you sell fashions or accessories, you might want to hold an annual fashion show using professional athletes' wives as models. To get the most out of the event, tie in with a local charity, and run the show as a fund-raiser. Charge admission and give all proceeds to a local charity. Invite the media to cover the event. It should get good newspaper and television pickup.

Programs from National Sporting Events

It is usually possible to purchase programs in bulk for major sporting events such as the Super Bowl, World Series, All-Star Game, Bowl Games, etc. Since they are collector's items, you might want to obtain some and offer them as premiums to customers who make certain purchases.

USE YOUR SUPPLIERS' CONNECTIONS

Check with the manufacturers who supply your merchandise to determine if they are tied in with athletes, teams, or sports promotions. If they are, examine how your store can become involved. Your suppliers may also have professional athletes working for them, and you may be able to arrange to have them appear at your store.

If you have ideas for sports promotions or tie-ins that you would like to conduct, invite your suppliers to participate. Perhaps an idea you present might be adopted by a supplier as part of its marketing support program. If so, your store may be the place selected to try it out since it was your suggestion.

14

■■■

Building Repeat Business and Incremental Sales

TWO INGREDIENTS OF the formula for success of any retail establishment are to get its present customers to keep coming back to purchase more goods and products and to increase the amount of each sales transaction in the store. This is true whether you run a department store, a women's clothing store, boutique, supermarket, sporting goods store, stationery store, or even a bakery.

It is true that a combination of factors will normally be responsible for attracting the repeat customers: satisfaction with purchases, quality of merchandise, pricing, treatment by sales help, store ambiance, location, and store hours, etc. But specific programs can also be developed in order to both generate and accelerate this repeat business and incremental sales.

REWARDING YOUR CUSTOMERS

The most effective technique for encouraging both repeat business and incremental sales is through the establishment of customer reward programs. Not only do they reward the customer but the retailer comes out a winner, too. The amount of data gathered on each customer through each recorded transaction enables the retailer to carefully tailor programs aimed specifically at individual shoppers.

There are three programs that enable retailers to reward customers:

- A reward or savings card program
- A frequent buyer's program
- Bonus bucks

The latter program, bonus bucks, is the simplest way of rewarding customers but does not provide you with any data on the customer. It is based on giving customers certificates worth a dollar toward a future purchase at the store for every "X" dollar amount spent by the customer. You decide the amount required. It is a quick way to reward a customer and get them to come back to buy something else. To expedite a return visit, you might place a six-month expiration date on certificates.

REWARDS/SAVINGS CARD PROGRAM

Some call it a savings card, others a bonus card or a rewards card, still others a courtesy card. No matter what it is called, its purpose is to reward customers and to learn as much as you can about them. All customers are encouraged to sign up for this free-of-charge card. How the stores use the card varies.

- Practically all stores require that a customer present the card to get the discounts on the products on sale.
- Others use it as a rewards program card. Not only does the customer need it for the product discounts but rewards are given when they reach a certain sales plateau. A food store, for example, might give a free pound of shrimp after the customer accumulated $300 in purchases. Thus, the customer is encouraged to use the card every time he or she shops. Naturally, under this type of program, the store receives a thorough picture of the customer's purchasing pattern.
- Some stores use the shopping information they receive to reward consumers with coupons good specifically for products they are interested in or related to the type of products they are purchasing.

Thus, the bonus/savings card is a very effective marketing tool, maybe even more effective than the conventional frequent buyer's program if you carry a multitude of products, since it is capable of providing customers right at the checkout point with coupons for products in which he or she has shown an interest, and which can be used during his or her next visit. It helps you get that customer to come back to the store to purchase something he can use.

FREQUENT BUYER'S PROGRAM

There are a variety of ways to conduct a frequent buyer's program. Only you know your profitability structure and how much you can invest in such a program. To make this determination factor in all of the costs, including administrative, promotional, and awards. Your goal should be initially to realize a profit as good, or nearly as good, as your current profit. Once the program gets off the ground, and you have covered your start-up expenses, your profits should increase as your volume increases. A well-promoted frequent buyer's program will not only attract repeat business from present customers but also attract new customers to the store.

However, you should monitor your program very closely to make certain that it is meeting its objectives and not becoming a drain on your profits. In order to protect yourself in case the program is not financially viable for you, have your attorney include a disclaimer in the rules given to all participating customers. It should state that the program can be canceled at any time, without prior notice, by the store. Your rules should also contain an end date for the promotion. You can always extend that end date once you decide the promotion is working to your satisfaction.

STRUCTURING YOUR FREQUENT BUYER'S PROGRAM

There are several different ways to organize a frequent buyer's program:

Formally Structured

It can be formally structured with a membership card scanned at your register; monthly e-mail statements; printed rules and redemption information; and/or a catalog. Numbered membership cards should be given to all customers who register for the program. The application should be signed by the customer and include a release statement drafted by your attorney.

Stores that carry higher priced items will probably find it advantageous to run such a formally structured program. Because it is computerized, the formal program will give a retailer all types of information about each customer's buying patterns and enable its sales staff to be of greater assistance.

Informally Structured

Logistically, an informal program can be a nightmare. Customers are required to save their cash register receipts for redemption purposes. And unless you use an outside fulfillment firm, someone is going to have to add up all the receipts when the customer brings them in.

Since computers are not used to track purchases and no monthly statements are issued to customers, it is a very low-budget program and ideal for a smaller store with a limited customer base or a store that sells small ticket items.

Ideally, have customers redeem their receipts when they reach certain specific increments ($10, $25, etc.). Redeem the receipts by giving them a rebate of perhaps 5 percent or 10 percent of the value turned in. Rules for this program should be posted in the store near the checkout desk.

Specific Product Program

A third type of program is aimed at promoting repeat business by targeting the sale of one or more specific products: If you purchase a half dozen pairs of shoes over a set period of time, you get the seventh pair free; if you buy eleven quarts of milk in one month, get the twelfth quart free; after purchasing ten shirts, get the eleventh shirt free.

Each customer is given a special card when making his or her first purchase of an item. The rules for the program should be printed on the back of the cards. Subsequent purchases are recorded on the card and when the required number has been made, the customer turns it in for his or her free product. Or, you can offer a significant discount toward the purchase of a different product. It is one way to get the customer to purchase something he or she might ordinarily not buy at your store.

This specific product program is ideal for shoe stores, dry cleaners, shoe repair shops, haberdashers, nail salons, hair stylists, coffee shops, pet stores, video rental stores, and other retailers who want to increase unit sales of products or services. It requires little administration on the retailer's part, but it does not give the retailer any insight into the customer's buying habits.

GUIDELINES FOR SETTING UP THE PROGRAM

Never lose sight of the objectives of your frequent buyer's program: to develop both repeat business and incremental sales. You want customers to come into the store more frequently than they have in the past, and you want each cash register transaction to be higher than before the program started. In order to accomplish these objectives and gain immediate impact, you may want to consider including several conditions in the rules.

- A specific number of points must be earned, or purchases made, each quarter in order for the membership to remain active.
- All of a customer's points must be redeemed within a certain time frame. In the formal program, it might be within twelve months of being awarded. In the register receipt program, it might be every quarter. In the special product program, it might be every six to nine months. The purpose of this rule is to motivate your customers to increase the number of purchases they make during a period of time so that they can step up to a higher prize plateau, or not lose points.

Awarding Points

Programs are usually set up to award one point for every dollar spent. When the card is swiped at the register, the points are automatically entered into the computer. In addition to all the customer information you will obtain by computerizing the system, you will also have better budget control since you will be able to determine, on an ongoing basis, the number of customers who are active in the program, as well as the number of outstanding redeemable points. You will also be able to identify customers who have not visited the store recently. In such cases, you might drop them a note letting them know how many additional points they need in order to reach the next plateau. It also gives you the opportunity to send a monthly points statement to customers along with information about special sales and promotions, news about the store, and how they can win bonus points.

Bonus Points

In order to motivate customers to make additional store visits and purchases, consider offering bonus points for specific products purchased. Points should be awarded to encourage customers to purchase certain slow-moving products, during certain special promotions, or when introducing a new product line. Contact suppliers and ask them to absorb the cost of setting up these special promotions for your frequent buyer's program members.

Bonus points can also be awarded immediately to a "sponsoring" member, who brings in a new member, or after the new member reaches a certain plateau. Or a combination of both: Award some points to the "sponsor" at the time of the first purchase and additional points after the new member reaches a certain plateau.

During very slow periods (when people are away on vacation, during a very cold winter, or during heavy snow storms), bonus points can be used to provide a need incentive.

In your cash register receipt program, program your cash register so that every fiftieth or sixtieth tape has a "lucky star" printed on it, entitling the holder to a set number of bonus points. Since every point you award costs you money when it is redeemed, be certain that the additional business generated will more than make up the costs. It is not necessary to offer double or triple bonus points unless you have a supplier picking up the costs. Instead, offer 25 percent or 50 percent bonus points.

The Awards

The award structure should be based on your profit margins, promotional budget and the other factors discussed earlier in this chapter. There can be a great deal of flexibility on what you offer as awards, and how you handle the redemption of the points for prizes.

- Store discounts. After a customer reaches a certain point level (for example, a thousand points), he or she receives a percentage discount on all purchases during the next six months or year. At the next plateau (perhaps fifteen hundred points), the percentage discount or even the time frame increases. The only award(s) in this type of program is discounts on all future purchases. The redemption procedure is simple to handle.

- Store products. In this case you place point values on some or all of your merchandise, and customers select their award(s). This can be very cost efficient since you compute the redemption value on the retail price of a product for which you paid wholesale. A possible negative side is that you may be taking a sale away from the store since the customer might have purchased the product anyway. This point value procedure is also simple to handle.

- Fulfillment house. Let the frequent buyer select an award from a fulfillment house catalog. Your store would issue certificates to customers confirming the number of points when they want to redeem them. Customers would send the certificates, along with their orders, directly to the fulfillment house, which would then bill the store.

- Travel awards. Contact resort hotels within a two hundred-mile radius of your city that attract guests from the same economic bracket as your customers. They may be willing to offer you heavily discounted rooms, or even free rooms, for your program, especially if you are promoting the program through media advertising and direct mail and agree to promote the hotels in that advertising. You could then position your frequent buyers program as a "vacation program," offering hotel stays each time a member reaches a certain plateau. By signing up a number of resorts in the area, you will make your program even more appealing to your customers. Redemption would have to be done at the store, with a certificate given to the frequent buyer, who would have to make his or her own arrangements with the resort. In setting up such a program, be certain to have your attorney draw up a formal agreement with the resort(s), spelling out exactly what each member will get free of charge, and make sure that each member understands what the stay includes.

- Tickets to special events. The circus, ice shows, rodeo, theatrical productions, as well as sports teams usually offer discount tickets to groups. Often, the more you buy the greater the discount. Tickets to these events can also serve as awards. You could purchase them at the special group rate and redeem them for earned points based on the box office price. Discuss this program with box office managers in order to persuade them to give you the flexibility of returning any tickets that are not claimed by any of your customers.

■ Savings bonds can also be effective frequent buyer awards since their value is usually perceived to be the redemption price, which is more than the actual cost to the store.

■ Gift certificates. You may let your frequent buyers redeem their points for store gift certificates, or for certificates to be used at local restaurants. You should negotiate a good discount with the restaurants for their certificates (at least half price) in return for the promotional exposure, as well as the new customers, who may be introduced to the restaurant through the program.

Promoting Your Frequent Buyer's Program

For a frequent buyer's program to be successful, it must be publicized among your current customers as well as your potential customers. You should promote enrollment and the program's value to customers, as well as the incentives offered to collect more points.

There are many ways to accomplish this:

■ Media advertising. Themes might include: "Customers Save Money and Earn Merchandise Through (store name) Frequent Buyer's Program," "Frequent Buyers Earn Merchandise and Gifts at (store name)."

■ Direct mail and/or e-mail to customers, as well as on your Web site.

■ In-store and window signage.

■ Tie-in with charitable/nonprofit organizations. Set up a program to encourage members and supporters to donate their earned points to the charity so that the points can be redeemed for products needed to support the charity's activities. Each cooperating group will undoubtedly promote the program among its members and supporters, which will result in additional business for your store. To make it an even more attractive promotion for charitable and nonprofit organizations, use a special fulfillment catalog that offers business-oriented products (office supplies, equipment, etc.). Or convert the points into cash contributions to the charity. Media should be notified if you are permitting your customers to donate their points to charitable groups. Arrange for a photo op with a prominent community citizen, who is involved in one of the cooperating charities, and the director of the organization when he or she obtains a frequent buyer's card and pledges x-number of points. There is another media opportunity when the organization redeems its points for products.

■ Promotional incentive program among members: Award a special prize (merchandise or bonus points) to the member who records the most points each month, also a prize for the most points recorded in a year. If you can afford it, or arrange to have it donated, offer the high-point leader a trip to a popular resort area. Another special prize might be awarded to the first customer who reaches a certain plateau (perhaps one thousand points). It should be an amount within reach of a considerable number of customers and used to jump start the program. You want those customers to be motivated by the promotion and to expedite their purchases or go on a shopping spree. Once the first plateau is reached, rerun the promotion at a second plateau (perhaps two thousand points). Promote these incentive programs through your monthly e-mail point statement, through circulars distributed in-store, through in-store signage, and on your Web site.

KEEPING THE FREQUENT BUYER HAPPY

There are many other techniques that can be used to develop repeat business and incremental sales. All of the items listed in this section can be employed either as part of the store's frequent buyer's program or for its total communications program.

Customer Communications

It is important to maintain good communications with all your customers but especially with your more frequent buyers. They have shown their loyalty to you, and showing your appreciation to them could result in an even closer business relationship.

■ Send birthday and/or anniversary cards. Obtain these dates when the customer enrolls in your formal program, signs up for your e-mail list, or applies for a store credit card. In addition to the store's name on the card, it should also have the signature of the owner and the salesperson who usually takes care of the customer. Also send a small gift to the customer's home. You can base the gift on the amount of purchases made over the past year.

■ Each December send your frequent customers a personally addressed letter thanking them for their patronage, and wishing them and their families warm holiday greetings. The letter should state that a contribution is being made to (name of charity) in the name of our loyal customers. The letter should be personally signed by the store owner. The customer's salesperson should send an appropriate card.

■ After a frequent buyer makes a significant purchase, the salesperson should send a handwritten thank-you note.

■ Institute a monthly newsletter for frequent buyers. It can be similar to the one discussed on page 229 in chapter 18 regarding Internet communications. Or, it could be more focused on the frequent buyers, and their interests. Its purpose is to develop a closer relationship between the frequent buyer and the store.

Special Customer Services

Additional recognition can be given to your better customers by providing special services for them. It is another way of saying "thank you for your patronage." At the same time, you are making it easier for them to shop at your store.

■ Should the store's ratio of salespeople to customers permit it, assign a specific salesperson to each one of your frequent customers. This will probably make your customer very happy since he or she will perceive this as VIP treatment. The salesperson should, from time to time, drop a note or send an e-mail to the customer about a coming sale, a product in which he or she might be interested, a special promotion, etc. Each salesperson should get to know the preferences of his or her VIP customers in order to expedite their visits to the store. Appointments can also be set up with the customer, assuring faster and more personal service.

■ Hold special frequent buyer days or nights, running promotions, sales previews, and other events exclusively for them. The functions should be held at a time when the store is not open to the general public. Serve wine and cheese or other refreshments. Special events can include the preview of a new line, product demonstrations, the introduction of a spectacular new product, fashion shows, a reception for a noted designer or author, or even a thank-you reception for the frequent customers.

- Develop special offers for your frequent customers: a few additional percentage points off on sale merchandise, a coupon book that provides for a special discount on a different product or product category each month, discounts for shopping on different days or hours, free alterations, free delivery, etc.

- Establish an exclusive telephone number for frequent buyers to call if they have problems or want to speak to someone at the store. The phone should always be answered "Frequent Buyer's line . . ."

- If space is available in the store, set up a frequent customer lounge. Furnish a telephone so that customers can make free local calls; provide lockers for customers to check their bags while shopping in the area; serve coffee or other light refreshments; have a television set and comfortable chairs.

- Arrange discounts for your frequent customers at noncompetitive shops in the area, at local restaurants, and other establishments that might want to do business with them.

DEVELOP NEW AVENUES FOR REPEAT BUSINESS

By creating attractive new sales packages, as well as by targeting several special audiences, it is possible to build significant additional repeat business.

Automatic Gift Service

By establishing an automatic gift service, your customers will be able to provide a list of people to whom they want to send birthday, anniversary, and other gifts during the year. Give them the option of selecting the gifts at the start of the year, or set it up so that the store will contact them several weeks before each event, at which time they can decide upon the present. Ask the customers to provide a rough price range and areas of interest for each gift recipient so that you can offer suggestions when you contact them. Provide cards for the customer to sign and send with the gift. The store will handle the gift-wrapping and shipping. You should also offer this service to local companies, as well as to individual customers, during the Christmas gift-giving season.

Product-of-the-Month Club

Consider starting one or more "Product-of-the-Month Clubs," with a different item sent to members each month. The type of club and products should be based on your product lines. It might be a tie or shirt each month, a blouse or sweater, a special cake, a different wine, a three-pack of socks, a plant, etc. Take a long look at the products you sell and try to develop one or more interesting yearlong programs. This is an excellent gift-giving program; you may find that some people will want to rotate the monthly products among several different individuals. It is also a program to sell to local business firms, especially around Christmas. They may want to give a year's membership to one of their better clients.

A Gift Registry

If you already do not have a gift registry, consider setting one up. Your customers can provide key information about themselves (sizes and colors if you sell clothing; favorite wines if you own a liquor store, etc.). Thus when friends and relatives come into the store to buy gifts for them, you have all the vital information necessary to help them complete the purchase. This is also an ideal way for out-of-town friends and relatives to order gifts for the customer, especially children whose parents live in the community. Because it is a sensitive matter, it is really up to the individual to tell people about the listing. During the pre-Christmas season, however, store advertising could suggest that residents might want to check to see if people on their gift lists are registered with the store. One of the advertising themes might be, "If you are looking to buy a Christmas gift for your favorite person, check our registry, chances are we're his or her favorite store."

Special Audiences

There are a number of special audiences that retailers should seek as regular customers. For one, stores that sell "sized" products might want to set up a service for people who require nonconventional sizes. It can be done several ways: Customers register their sizes, and the store contacts them when products in their size arrive; a telephone hot line (live or taped) for customers to call for latest information on nonconventional sizes; Web site or in-store posting a current list of nonconventional sizes in stock. Through this service, the store might also try to match customers who require two sizes (a different size glove for each hand, a different size shoe for each foot). If you offer these special audience services, you will be able to get good exposure in local media and probably even in national media if you want to expand the service.

An important special audience for all retailers to reach out to is handicapped and physically challenged people. It is to your benefit to develop programs aimed at this audience so that you can make their shopping experience an easier and more pleasant one. You will earn their loyalty and their business.

Steps to take might include wider aisles so that customers in wheelchairs or using walkers can more easily maneuver through the store. Providing sales circulars and a description of the store together with a layout in braille will probably be appreciated by the blind. Deaf customers might appreciate having a salesperson who can sign. If you sell men's or women's fashions, you might offer special services for the color blind. This might include tags identifying the color of each product as well as the colors that match up to it.

Develop your program to reach this audience in conjunction with the local professional groups that represent them. They can offer advice on the steps you can take to make your store more customer friendly to their clients as well as how to best reach these potential customers. Invite them to a meeting at the store and request that they bring some of their clients so that you will get their input, too. If there is a city government agency involved with the handicapped consult with them, too.

You might also find a local foundation that might provide start-up funds to help you make your store more handicapped friendly.

If you provide the identifying color tags for color-blind customers, call it to the attention of local media. Also prepare a single-page promotional piece on the service and send copies to local ophthalmologists and optometrists so that they can give copies to their color-blind patients.

SAMPLE LETTERS TO SEND TO FREQUENT CUSTOMERS

"Missing in Action"

Dear Ms. Jones:

We miss you!

It has been three months since any frequent buyer points have been credited to your personal account, leaving you two hundred points short of the second plateau of gifts. (Mention some gifts at that plateau).

We hope that this recent inactivity in our program does not reflect any dissatisfaction on your part with our merchandise or service. If it does, please call me immediately at (telephone number) so that we can discuss the matter.

We appreciate the confidence you have shown in us through your past purchases and hope to see you back at the store in the near future.

Thank you.

                         Sincerely,

"Get Your Birthday Gift"

Dear Mr. Jones:

Happy birthday!

We hope that not only will your birthday be a happy day but also that each of the next 364 days will be equally happy, healthy, and prosperous.

As a token of our appreciation for your loyalty and continued support, we have put aside a small birthday gift for you. Next time you are in the neighborhood, please drop in so that we may give it to you.

We look forward to seeing you and wishing you a happy birthday in person.

                         Sincerely,

"A Significant Purchase"

Dear Ms. Jones:

We hope that you will be very happy with (product name) you purchased (day of week). If, for any reason, you have any questions about it, or problems, please contact me immediately. My number is 123-555-7890.

We want to thank you for shopping with us and hope you will be in to see us again soon.

Sincerely,

"Season's Greetings"

Dear Mr. and Mrs. Jones:

As we approach the holiday season, I want to take this opportunity to thank you for your business during the the past year. A store can only be successful if it has the support and loyalty of such customers as you.

We pledge that we will continue to offer quality merchandise at competitive prices and provide the professional sales services you should expect when shopping.

We would like to wish you and your loved ones a very wonderful holiday season and a healthy, happy, and prosperous New Year.

Sincerely,

"Happy New Year"

Dear Ms. Jones:

Our computer, in its new year of enthusiasm, has told us something we wanted to pass along to you.

Last year, our customers saved $1.2 million through purchases made during our seasonal sales. This is almost double the savings from the previous year! And we were able to do this without compromising the quality of our products or our services to you.

We hope that our savings to you will grow even larger during the coming year.

Thank you for your continued support!

Sincerely,

15

---■■■---

Cross Promoting and Other Ways to Extend Your Visibility

IT IS IMPORTANT for you to seek expanded exposure for your product lines and store at other locations throughout the area. A unique, carefully planned program will enable you to extend your visibility in the community and attract new customers.

CROSS PROMOTE WITH OTHER STORES

Cross promoting with noncompeting stores can be an effective technique to build additional traffic and sales. In choosing partners, select stores that appeal to the same economic segment of the population as your store. The stores may be close to you (the same block, neighborhood, or shopping mall) or some distance away.

Examples of cross-promoting "partners" might be:

- An expensive dress shop, furrier, jeweler, hair salon, florist, cosmetics store, and an upscale restaurant
- A men's clothing store, sporting goods store, shoe store, liquor store, and a hair stylist

- A children's clothing store, shoe store, toy store, bookstore, and a fast food restaurant

There should be a signed agreement among the cooperating stores covering all elements of the promotion. During its initial stages, the program should be frequently reviewed so that it can be strengthened, and problems can be eliminated, if necessary.

CROSS-PROMOTING TECHNIQUES

- Feature products from the other stores in your windows, as well as inside in a special display area. While the other retailers' merchandise should not be sold at your store, it should be used to enhance and/or accessorize your products. For example, the expensive dress shop's mannequin might also have on a stole from the furrier and accessories from the jeweler. Its wig should be set by the hair salon. Flowers or a plant from the florist should be on the table along with makeup from the cosmetics shop and a menu from the restaurant. A placard with the other stores' names, addresses, and hours of operation should always be included with the product displays.
- Give customers an "introduction card," entitling them to a special discount on their first purchase at each of the other stores. In addition, after the card has been used at all participating stores, it can then be entered into a drawing for prizes.
- From time to time, distribute discount coupons good for a thirty-day period at any of the other participating stores. This promotion is designed to spur sales during slow periods.
- Try a combination ticket, good for a rebate or special gift after purchases have been made at each of the co-promoting stores. All promotions requiring multiple store purchases should have an expiration date.
- Cross-promoting stores should also consider holding joint sales, advertising programs, and special promotions (contests, fashion shows, community events, etc.). For special promotions, you might want to hire a shuttle bus to carry customers between stores.
- A frequent buyer's program can also be organized in conjunction with other stores in the area, enabling customers to accumulate points whenever they make purchases at any of the participating stores. It could

be set up with the stores with which you are already cross promoting, an extended list of stores, or even a completely different noncompeting group of stores. A frequent buyer's program is a good technique to build new and repeat business among a target group of customers. A formal type of membership card program is probably the most effective way to conduct this multistore promotion. It could be a program that requires a purchase at each participating store in order to redeem the card for an award. The latter method can work as a "sampler," but there is no real incentive for the customer to return to any of the stores for repeat purchases.

- In establishing a joint frequent buyer's program, it is important to cost it out carefully so that each store pays for its fair share, based on the business generated. Careful records must be kept in order to determine how many points have been earned from each store so that the redemption costs per point can be charged back to the individual stores. It will probably be necessary to have an impartial accountant administer this program and/or conduct an audit for all of the participating stores.

SHORT-TERM CROSS PROMOTIONS

There are also short-term cross promotions, which you might conduct with just a single partner. A shoe store might offer a discount toward the first pair of heels at a local shoe repair shop. In turn, the shoe repair shop might give its customers a percent-off discount coupon good at the shoe store. A men's clothing store could offer a free pressing or cleaning at a local dry cleaner when a customer buys a suit. The cleaner could offer its customers a discount coupon for the clothing store. A store might tie in with a local movie theater, giving away tickets to customers for a special preview performance. That same week, the movie theater could give all ticket buyers a discount coupon good at the store.

There are other instances where you can try to get promotional exposure in other stores. If you do couponing or sell products backed by national promotional weeks or months, other stores may be happy to distribute your materials without asking for anything in return. For example, florists might offer a free rose to each patron at a nearby beauty salon along with a discount coupon toward the customer's next purchase of flowers. A restaurant might offer two meals for the price of one to customers from an upscale clothing store in the area. A fast-food outlet might distribute coupons through neighboring stores good for discounts on hot dogs purchased during "National Hot Dog Month." A sporting goods store might arrange for a men's clothing store to hold a drawing among its customers for a tennis racket. All of these so-called one-sided promotions are aimed at getting you exposure in other stores in the community with "no strings attached."

EXTENDING YOUR PRESENCE TO OTHER LOCATIONS

The objective for extending your presence to other locations in the community is to sell additional products as well as to gain exposure for, and draw new customers to, your main store.

The Mall

Those pushcarts inside malls can be rented on either a short-term or a long-term basis, with rental prices varying depending on the season. Naturally, Christmas is the high season. A downtown retailer might use a pushcart with a sampling of products as a means for introducing his or her store to mall shoppers. The products should be carefully selected to provide a good impression of your store in a limited amount of space and to entice mall visitors to want to visit your downtown location. A good deal of planning should go into a pushcart project. Your salesperson should also reflect the professionalism and knowledge of your downtown sales staff. In each package, you should include information on what can be found at your main store, your address, and directions to the store, your Web site, and perhaps an introductory coupon for a first visit.

Seasonal Stores

If you have the proper product mix, you might consider opening a store for the season at a resort area. If you sell beachwear and other summer products, it might make sense to rent space from June through Labor Day at a popular seaside area. Likewise in a skiing area from December through March, if you sell outer wear.

Motion Picture Theaters

Motion picture theaters have large lobbies, and many are seeking ways to increase their revenues. With appropriate products, a retailer might inquire about opening a counter at one or more local theaters. Appropriate products might be those related to specific motion pictures, including books and music, and memorabilia. Another possibility might be jewelry. Women are usually attracted to free-standing jewelry displays. Since a large percentage of moviegoers are coupled, there is a good chance that if the wife or girlfriend sees something she likes, her husband or boyfriend may buy it for her.

Fairs, Block Parties, and Special Events

It is a good idea to participate in promotions and events where large numbers of potential customers will be. This includes events in the neighborhood where your store is located, as well as in other parts of the city. Such events include: block parties, fairs, charitable bazaars, and fund-raising functions.

How you participate will depend on the event and what you hope to accomplish. You might set up a display and offer products for sale, as well as take orders for others. You might run a promotional booth designed to familiarize attendees with your product line and not have anything for sale. Rather, invite guests to register for your mailing list. You could give each person who signs the register an inexpensive gift imprinted with the store name (ballpoint pen, key ring, etc.), or hold an hourly drawing for prizes. In addition to a product display, you could have a "fun" skills contest. Set up a one-hole putting green, a basketball net, or ring toss game. Make it easy for people to win the small prize and qualify for a finals sweepstakes. Hold the drawing at your store, inviting all finalists to attend.

PRODUCT SHOWS OPEN TO THE PUBLIC

In many cities, there are a variety of special consumer product–oriented shows each year. They include home, kitchen and bath, auto, art, sportsmen, ski, and antique shows. If your products fit into any of the shows' categories, you might consider exhibiting and selling your products.

Before committing your store's participation, obtain as much information as possible:

- What were attendance figures for the past three years?
- What are the demographics of those who attended those shows?
- Are ticket prices too high for your target audience?
- Will the show's promoters offer discount tickets for you to pass along to your customers?
- Will they offer discount tickets through other sources?
- How much money will be spent promoting the event, and how will it be spent? Where will advertising appear?
- What other events are scheduled at the same time in the city?
- Will participation at the show disrupt the normal conduct of business at your store?
- Are products usually sold, or is it basically a show in which products are displayed and leads developed?

The answers to these questions should provide you with enough data to make a decision on whether you should participate in the show.

If you do not take exhibit space, you may still be able to participate in the show. Contact the various manufacturers whose products you carry and see if they plan to exhibit. If they do, arrange to have salespeople from your store at the booth to help visitors, and give them their business cards. Contact other exhibitors and offer to loan them any of your products, which might help complement their displays. For example, if you sell kitchenware, an appliance store may want to use your pots on the ranges they are displaying. Loan the products if you will get credit on a placard at the booth and can place your literature or business cards there.

Model Homes

If you have the appropriate products, conduct an active program of furnishing the model homes of major builders in your area. Appropriate products include: furniture and furnishings, decorative accessories, appliances, china and silverware, and anything else found in the home. Make a deal with builders to sell them, at a very good price, the products for the model home. In turn, insist that they display a placard crediting the store, along with literature and business cards. Also try to negotiate credit mentions in their real estate ads and brochures, and ask that they notify you when they sell any homes in the development. You should then send a letter congratulating the new homeowner, explaining your participation in the model home, and inviting them to visit the store and pick up a small "welcome" gift.

In return, offer the builders some in-store recognition. You might promote products being shown in the model homes with tags saying, "Featured at (name of development) model homes."

The model homes program is important since many people who are not even in the market for a house will visit them in order to get decorating ideas. Others who purchase a house in a development often try to duplicate the decor from the model home.

Empty Store Windows

A great way to get additional visibility for your store is by persuading property owners to let you display your products in the windows of vacant stores. An attractive window display in an otherwise empty store will probably make the location more appealing to a potential lessee so there is something in it for the landlord, too.

When you see a suitable vacant store, offer the owner a nominal fee for permission to place a display in the window. Explain how this attractive display will enhance the location and expedite the rental of the store. Arrange to decorate the window until the store is rented. Obviously you would select stores in locations where you want to attract new customers. But you should also select some locations near your store. This would enable you to gain additional exposure for your merchandise among people already in your immediate shopping area. All of the window displays should include a placard with the address of the store and directions on how to reach it from that location. Perhaps offer a free gift, or discount, to customers mentioning they saw the window and the "secret code number."

Attracting Tourists and Business Visitors

If you are located near major hotels and/or sell products with tourist and business visitor appeal, consider reaching out to this audience. You could promote your store and product line in the glass display cases of hotel lobbies. These display cases are very effective since they are usually strategically placed in areas of the lobby frequented by guests. Carefully plan your display so that a guest can quickly determine your product line. The store address, telephone number, and travel directions from the hotel should be on a small placard in the display case.

If the hotels provide visitors with in-room directories of local shops, try to have the information about the store included. Also, if hotels permit, try to arrange the placement of table tent cards in each guest room. You will have to provide the tent cards.

Provide the front desk and/or concierge with printed brochures about your store and product line. If your city attracts large numbers of foreign tourists, consider printing these brochures in the principal languages of the visitors. Moreover, you should have sales help who speak these languages. Visit the concierges on a regular basis to fill them in on your product line, and invite them to visit the store to familiarize themselves with what you can offer visitors. Also consider holding a reception at the store for all the concierges in the city. Both concierges and the front desk personnel are in a position to refer business to your store. So cultivate them!

Join your local Convention and Visitors' Bureau, work closely with it, and take advantage of its various visitor promotion programs. You will find that membership usually gives you an entree to the key hospitality and convention planners in the area.

Consider advertising in the various tourist publications that are distributed to visitors. Also, if one airline brings most of the visitors to your city, you may want to advertise in its in-flight publication. You should also contact the airline and see if it would be possible to develop an in-flight promotion with it. Perhaps on each incoming flight you would give away a $25 gift certificate to someone sitting in the "lucky" seat. Or perhaps special discount coupons to all arriving passengers on one flight a day. An effective promotional message to passengers would be an invitation to visit the store for a free souvenir of their trip. If people take the time to drop in for the souvenir, which could be a key chain, they may also end up making a purchase.

Airport displays can also be used to promote your store and products. However, incoming passengers usually leave an airport as quickly as possible and may not pay enough attention to your display to justify its cost.

If local sightseeing company buses carry advertising, consider purchasing space on them. If the sightseeing companies recommend shops to visitors, see if your store can be added to the list. Perhaps you can offer a small souvenir or discount to anyone visiting the store who shows a receipt from the sightseeing company.

Conventions

Conventions bring visitors to town. With the right product line, you might be able to generate business from this audience. Evaluate the potential of each convention very carefully. Select only those you are certain that your store will appeal to. You might want to take a booth and sell product, or you might want to take an ad in the convention program offering a discount for anyone who comes in with the ad. If you feel the potential is there, you might want to run a shuttle bus between the convention center and your store.

For conventions, as well as trade shows, you might want to develop a program for spouses. It might be a fashion show at the convention hall or at a nearby hotel. Try a wine tasting/shopping trip to your store, or a visit to a museum with a stop back at the store for refreshments and shopping.

Since spouse programs are expensive to sponsor, be certain they will generate sales. Focus on sponsoring programs for upscale professional groups (state medical society convention, bar association annual meeting, Young President's Club, etc.).

Free Shuttle Bus

To attract customers from different sections of the city, consider sponsoring a free shuttle bus. It could run along a regular route, picking up customers at specified stops. Or each day, it could run between a different section of the city and your store. Monday could be "Near East Side Day," Tuesday "Uptown Day," Thursday "West Yourtown Day," etc. If there is a nearby office or industrial park, you might run a lunch-hour shuttle so that workers can do some shopping during lunch.

Be certain that any bus you use has a distinctive look. It should carry your store name on the outside, perhaps with some advertising posters. Inside, advertise your specials and other products from your line. Some stores use British double-decker buses. Others paint their buses a bright color, or the store colors. Still other stores rent or purchase buses that resemble cable or trolley cars.

Since a bus represents a large investment, make certain it will pay off in additional customers and sales. Perhaps you should start off by renting a bus for special promotions and sales and see how it works out. Or you might want to use a shuttle just on weekends. If you decide to go with a bus, carefully examine the options of renting versus leasing or owning.

You may also want to consider running a shuttle bus in conjunction with some neighboring stores. While the promotional value of having an exclusive bus will decrease, you will save quite a bit of money.

Your Logo on Shopping Bags, T-shirts, and Hats

You can get ongoing exposure for your store by having its logo or name prominently displayed on a variety of items. The more attractive the design the better since more people will be willing to be a "walking billboard" for you.

Customers, especially women, like prestigious-looking shopping bags and will use them for a long time. Each time they carry the bag, they are promoting the store's name. So, put a lot of thought behind the design of your shopping bags.

T-shirts, hats, and cloth bags with your logo will also serve as "walking billboards" for the store. By developing a program to get these products into the hands of your customers, you will be gaining extended recognition for your business.

Initially consider these products as goodwill gifts to your better customers, as premiums for purchasing certain high-ticket products, or as prizes in contests. Have your staff wear them away from the store. The T-shirts draw a lot of attention when worn at beaches and parks.

It is possible that eventually you will be able to sell these products as regular merchandise.

16

---■ ■ ■---

Good Community Citizenship
Is Good Business

BY CONDUCTING AN active community outreach program, you will be able to achieve even greater visibility for your store and greatly enhance its image among customers as well as potential customers. In today's environment there is nothing as important to a business as being known as a good citizen of the community. Customers support companies who get involved.

How can a retailer get involved in the community?

- By working closely with charitable and nonprofit organizations
- Through sponsorship of events
- By sponsoring awards
- By becoming an active member and participant in the activities of one or more organizations
- By showing that your store cares

CHARITABLE AND NONPROFIT ORGANIZATIONS

Charitable and nonprofit organizations offer a variety of ways for you and your store to participate in their activities. Only you are in a position to decide the degree of involvement and with which organization(s) to become involved. Much will depend upon your marketing program, your budget, the amount of time you and your staff can devote to it, and what you hope to achieve.

Selecting the Organization(s)

There are a variety of organizations to consider working with:

- The local affiliates of the national health-related education and research organizations (American Heart Association, American Cancer Society, Multiple Sclerosis, Cerebral Palsy, AIDS, Breast Cancer, etc.)
- Local nonprofit hospitals and health-care facilities
- Local educational facilities
- Local cultural facilities
- Local nonprofit social services facilities
- Senior citizens, scouting, youth organizations, Big Brother, Big Sister, etc.
- Animal welfare and adoption centers

In selecting the organization(s) with which to get involved, make sure it meets certain criteria:

- It has an excellent reputation in the community.
- It should be nondenominational, unless your clientele is predominantly of one religion. Or become involved with several organizations that represent the major religions and nationalities in the area.
- It should have an active and aggressive group of volunteers.
- It has a good public relations and promotional support staff or capability.
- It has entree to celebrities.
- It has a good mailing list which, under certain circumstances, it will let you use.

Once you have chosen the organization(s), there are many ways in which you can work with it (them). From the menu of ideas in this chapter, a retailer might just select one or two projects. Others might devote a good part of their marketing budget to community projects.

Donate a Percentage of Receipts

Consider developing a promotion in which one or more charitable organizations receive a contribution based on your profits. It could be a one-day-a-year event billed as "Give Something Back Day," "We Care Day," or "(Name of Charity) Day," or a week-long promotion. If it is a week-long event, you could designate each day to a different charity and have that group contact its supporters to let them know that the charity will benefit if they shop your store on that day. It is an excellent way for the nonprofit organization to raise money, and an excellent way to introduce new customers to your store. To encourage these new customers to come back, you might give each one a coupon good for a discount on his or her next visit to the store. If the charitable group has access to any celebrities who might be in the city at the time, ask if an appearance at your store could be arranged as part of the fund-raising promotion. If the charity can deliver, you might set up an autograph table, or have a photographer take pictures of the celebrity with the customers. Charge a fee, giving the money to the charity.

Provide Products

Providing products to an organization is another way to gain visibility for your store and its product line. You can contribute products for charity auctions, or as door prizes for meetings and other events. If you contribute products for a charity auction, feature them in your store window in a special display promoting the auction. It is a way to get credit for something good you are doing.

People attending fund-raising luncheons and dinners are usually given a goody bag of small gifts to take away with them. If you have the appropriate product line and budget, and this is an important audience to reach, consider donating gifts for the bags: key chains, T-shirts, and other small promotional items with your logo on them. Or ask your suppliers for any overruns or samples they may want to donate.

If there is a product very much in demand and on back order with the manufacturer, you might save the last one and conduct a "sealed bid" auction with the winning bid money going to a charitable organization. Ask the charity to generate interest among its supporters. Also promote the auction in your window display and in store.

Fashion Shows and Other Special Events

Offer to produce some special event, which is appropriate to your product line, for a charitable institution with all proceeds going to the group. The event could be a fashion show, a preview of Christmas toys, an author luncheon, a lecture, a cooking demonstration, a wine or champagne tasting, etc. It could be held at the store, or at some other location. The charitable organization should have the sole responsibility for the invitations and for selling the admission tickets. It should also pay for the rental of the hall if it is held away from the store. You might even be able to sell products at the event, giving a percentage of the profits to the charity.

You might also "loan" your store to an organization for a fundraising party. Perhaps an ideal time would be a preview of your Christmas decorations, or during a "Christmas in August" promotion.

Credit Card Solicitation

If your store has its own credit card, ask local charitable organizations if you could use their mailing lists to solicit new cardholders. Offer to pay a fee to each charity for each person on its list who signs up for the card. You may also offer a bonus to the charity at the end of the first year based on the amount of sales charged on the card by its members. This should offer an incentive to the charitable organization to encourage use of your cards among its members.

The solicitation letters to potential cardholders should identify the organization that provided their names, and should explain how you will be contributing to it. Keep reminding cardholders in their monthly billing statements about the annual contribution.

Assist Organizations in Recruiting Volunteers

Help one or more charitable groups recruit volunteers. Kick off the recruiting program by announcing that your employees have pledged X-number of volunteer hours during the coming year. This will get media attention. If you advertise, consider running an ad urging local residents to become volunteers, and list the organizations that need them. Included in the ad should be information about your store's and employee's commitment to reach out and help the community. If your employees are already volunteers, mention it in the ad, and give the number of volunteer hours they have spent during the past year helping various organizations. You might even mention their names and the organizations they assisted.

As an incentive to volunteer, you might offer a one-time discount to all residents who sign up with the organization at your store during the recruiting drive.

Rewarding Volunteers

Working with one or more organizations, you can salute its volunteers in several ways. Sponsor an annual "Volunteer Appreciation" night at the store. Residents who have volunteered a significant amount of hours during the year would be invited to the party. Offer some door prizes, refreshments, entertainment, and small gifts. While you will not be selling any products that night, it is a good way to introduce these people to the store. Underwrite the cost of certificates of appreciation to be given to each volunteer. You might also underwrite the cost of a "Volunteer of the Year" award to be given to the individual selected by the organization.

An Annual Donation

If your budget permits, consider making an annual cash contribution to a charity in the name of your customers during the December holiday season. Send an end-of-the-year letter thanking your customers for their support and that you are making a contribution in their name to (name of organization) in appreciation.

Another version would be to thank your customers and ask them to name the organization to which the contribution should be sent. Tally up the responses, and figure the percentage that should be sent to each nominated organization.

Sponsor Scholarships

The establishment of a scholarship program for local high school graduates is another possible community project to undertake. You could make an initial contribution and add to it each year. You could invite both your customers and your suppliers to contribute. You might even earmark the proceeds of one or more shopping days to the program.

The awarding of the scholarships should be administered by the local school system, but you should make the actual presentation. The scholarship should carry the name of the store: "(Name of Store) Scholarship."

Encourage high school students to apply for a scholarship in your store's advertisements, in-store and in window signage; on your Web site, in bill stuffers, and other promotional materials. Also arrange to place flyers about the program on bulletin boards at high schools and youth centers. Have flyers distributed at PTA meetings.

Sponsor a Cook-off

Cook-offs are fun and a good way to raise money for charity. Such promotions are ideal for restaurants and retailers who sell food products and cooking or barbecuing equipment. However, just about any store can get good exposure for sponsoring a cook-off.

Logistically, a barbecuing competition may be the easiest to conduct. You could hold it in your parking lot or some other appropriate area in the city (a park, beach, etc.). The store would underwrite the costs, which would be nominal. Basically the store would cover prizes and promotional expenses. Have the competitors bring their own equipment and food.

Tie in with a charitable organization. The competitor entry fees, as well as spectator fees, would be donated to the charity. Get local newspaper food editors and other cooking experts to judge the event. Following the judging, the spectators would get to sample the food.

For better promotional visibility, supply all participating chefs with hats and aprons with the store or restaurant's name. Provide the winning recipes to the local food writers and invite media coverage of the event.

Sponsor Competitors in Walkathons or Bikeathons

Offer to sponsor customers or their children, who will participate in major walkathons and bikeathons, pledging X-dollar contributions for each mile walked or ridden. Set a limit on the maximum number of competitors you will sponsor so your budget doesn't get out of hand. Give each competitor whom you are backing a store T-shirt and/or hat to wear during the event. Invite all of the competitors you are sponsoring to the store a few days prior to the event for a send-off party. Invite media coverage. The charity will be happy to cooperate since this will help hype the event.

Pledge Donations Based on Sports Feats

Consider pledging a set amount of money to a local charity for every home run hit, touchdown scored, or yards gained by a local team or specific player. Keep a scoreboard in the window or in the store, showing donations made to date. Try to get the teams to flash the information on their scoreboards. If you advertise in the stadium or arena, this should not be too difficult to arrange. If you do not advertise, ask the charitable organization to try to arrange it. Also see if the organization can arrange with the team broadcasters and telecasters to announce the donations: When a home run is hit, the announcement might be, "Another (name of team) home run means Joe's Sporting Goods is donating $50 to the Ourtown Boys Club."

Library Books

A joint promotion with your customers to add books to one or more local libraries will create goodwill in the community. There are several ways this promotion can work. Get the library to provide a list of books it needs. Whenever a customer donates a book, your store can match it by donating another book from the list. Or collect contributions for the book fund, and match it dollar-for-dollar with what your customers contribute. Perhaps you can pledge to give one dollar to the local library book fund on all purchases over a certain amount (perhaps $25). If there are several libraries in the area, let the customer select the one to which the donation should be made.

MAKE A PERSONAL COMMITMENT

In addition to your store's commitment to charitable and nonprofit organizations, you, personally, should become involved with one or more groups. Active participation will enable you to get your name better known in the community as a civic leader. This will enhance your overall image, and can be a positive factor in attracting customers to your store.

Which organization(s) to support is a personal decision. Undoubtedly this decision will be influenced by your personal feelings, beliefs, and experiences.

From a business standpoint, you should become involved with at least one organization in which important business, community, and political leaders are active. This will provide you with the opportunity to develop relationships that may be helpful in the future.

SPONSORING HIGH VISIBILITY COMMUNITY EVENTS

There are many events that you could sponsor or cosponsor with other local businesses. While your store will get the most recognition and exposure as the sole sponsor of an event, it can be a very costly investment. Cosponsorship, even though it is less costly, will still enable you to get good exposure if you aggressively promote your participation in the event.

From a standpoint of logistics, it would be best to sponsor already existing events that are well-organized with the mechanics and staff for conducting them already in place.

The Easter Egg Roll

A tradition in most cities, the Easter Egg Roll or Hunt brings out young children and their families. It is a good target audience for most retailers. The value of the sponsorship is getting your name out in the community at a widely attended free event. Arrange signage throughout the area, especially at the start and finish lines and where prizes, if any, are distributed. Since the Easter Egg Roll gets good television coverage, you want to position signage so that it is in the background of all television and newspaper photo coverage. If full sponsorship is too expensive, you might just sponsor the prizes, including special merchandise prizes to the winners' parents.

Another sponsorship to consider would be the Easter Egg Hunt. Among the hidden eggs could be a few with your store's name on them, making them the big prizewinners.

Local Band Concerts

Summertime outdoor band concerts are usually popular and draw good crowds. The cost of sponsorship will depend upon whether amateur or professional musicians are playing. If you underwrite the concerts, insist that the store gets top billing: "The (store name) Summer Concert Series."

Since band concerts are community events, try to get the utility companies to promote them in their bill stuffers. Ask media to list them in their events columns. And, of course, promote them through your store windows, in-store signage, and your Web site. You might even have the band, or several of its members, playing outside your store to promote the event.

At the concert itself, if it is appropriate, have a VIP tent for elected officials, as well as your best customers.

An Annual Baby Parade

Some cities have them, others don't. Parents decorate their children's carriages, sometimes build small floats, and dress up the children for the event. A Baby Parade is an ideal event to sponsor if you sell baby or toddler products, baby foods, or maternity clothing. They usually draw very big crowds and get good media coverage. Prizes are given by age division (under six months, six months to a year, one year to eighteen months, etc.). Cutoff age should probably be about three years old. Prizes can be for the best-decorated carriage, most original float, best costume, prettiest smile, etc. The parade might be organized by, or cosponsored with a children's hospital, a chamber of commerce, an area retailers' association, or by a group of noncompeting retailers anxious to reach the baby and toddler markets and their parents.

Senior Citizen Month Event

May is Senior Citizen Month, and there are many opportunities for retailers to get involved in programs paying tribute to them. Seniors are very loyal to retailers who take an interest in them, and their children also often show their appreciation by patronizing stores that conduct programs for their parents.

Consider sponsoring or cosponsoring a one-day citywide fair during the month. Hold it at a park, armory, or other location. Ask local high schools and colleges to provide talent to entertain. Seek out talented seniors, too. Encourage each senior citizen center to display paintings and other works by artistic members. You might even have a formal senior citizen art show in conjunction with the fair.

Another opportunity would be to sponsor an awards program, honoring the city's "Senior Citizen of the Year," as well as the "Outstanding Senior Citizen" at each center. Let the seniors at each center select the honoree for the award. To add credibility, arrange to have the mayor present the awards at a City Hall ceremony.

A Halloween or Ragamuffin Parade

In cities where the annual Halloween or Ragamuffin parades are held, large crowds of spectators turn out to watch and cheer the marchers. You might want to consider sponsorship of or some type of participation in such a parade.

If you are convinced that the exposure you will receive is well worth the cost, and you have the budget, by all means sponsor the event. If you do, be certain that your name is part of the parade title. Also make certain that banners along the parade route carry your store's name.

One alternative to sponsorship is to underwrite the awards for the best floats, costumes, etc. Or you might just want to sponsor one or more floats in the parade, having your employees and their children and your customers and their children riding on it.

Amateur Play/Theater Group

You might consider underwriting a production by a well-respected local high school, college, or amateur theater company. Your sponsorship might enable the company to drop admission charges for its performances, or enable the company to take its production to hospitals, nursing homes, and other shut-ins. An ideal production to underwrite is one that has been written by a local playwright, or is an all-time classic, or a popular musical. It could also be a special production in connection with a local festival or celebration.

If you do participate, be certain that you get recognition with signage outside the theater and in the lobby. Also, an ad in the program, on the reverse side of the tickets, and editorial comment in the program should acknowledge your participation. Also request a few reserved seats to each performance. Hold a drawing for those tickets among your customers.

Another way to participate, if you have the appropriate products, is to provide the stage settings, cast costumes, hair styling, or makeup. You will get credits in the program. In addition, if what you provide for the set or cast is spectacular, some in the audience might be motivated to visit your shop. In order to promote the show and your contributions, you might feature huge photos or the props themselves in your windows. You might also ask if you could set up a table in the theater lobby to display some products or even give away samples if appropriate.

Museum Exhibit

Museums are always looking for sponsors to help underwrite special exhibitions. Some can be very expensive while others may be affordable. Contact the local museum and discuss its needs as well as yours. It may be possible to make a match between what you sell and what exhibitions it would like to stage. This match might be appealing to antique dealers, furniture stores, or even general merchandise stores. For the latter, for example, an exhibition of paintings of the Maine coast might be appealing if the store sells products from Maine. An exhibition of oil paintings of ships might interest a boat dealer, or sporting goods store. If you underwrite or cosponsor such an exhibition, be certain to negotiate a special preview showing for your customers. Also arrange for discount tickets for them if there will be an admission charge. Be certain that your store is prominently mentioned in the program, as well on museum signage and any advertising for the show. If a poster will be issued, try to get the store's name included on it. And try to get a quantity of the posters to use as door prizes at the store.

SUPPORTING LOCAL CONTESTS
AND COMPETITIONS

College and High School Competitions

There are several types of high school, junior college, and/or college competitions that might provide good sponsor opportunities. Money will be needed to cover stadium or arena rentals, as well as trophies. However, if the stadium or arena can be obtained rent-free, or admission fees will cover the rental, the expenses involved can be minimal.

A marching band competition among area high schools can be a very popular event. It should not only bring out the student bodies, but also parents and alumni, making it an ideal sponsorship for the retailer who targets this age group. It should be organized through contact with the local school board or administration. Profits from the sale of tickets should be split among the participating schools. If there are several colleges or junior colleges in the area, you might also consider a competition among them.

A high school or college cheerleader competition will also be a popular event to sponsor. You really do not need too much space, and it could be held in a high school gym. Cheerleader competitions usually attract television coverage.

Schools with ROTC often have drill teams. If there are a few in your area, you might consider sponsoring a competition among them. A gym or an armory is an ideal place to hold this event. If such a competition does not already exist, contact the high school and college ROTC units in the area. Tell them you would be willing to sponsor a drill team competition if they organized it and arranged for the site.

Volunteer Fire Department Competitions

If there are volunteer fire departments in your area, and if they have an annual competition, you might want to participate. You could, perhaps, sponsor the entire event, underwrite the awards, or just one award. Perhaps you could provide merchandise as prizes for any raffles held in connection with the event. At the very least you can devote a store window to the event, displaying the trophies to be presented as well as photographs from last year's competition.

If such a competition does not already exist, you might contact the various departments and offer to help organize one.

Planes, Boats, and Boomerangs

There are many other competitions that can be fun to sponsor. They will attract entrants, spectators, and the media. Most important, they are easy to conduct.

In a paper-airplane-flying contest, competitors make a simple paper plane and then toss it into the air. The plane that flies the farthest, or stays in the air the longest amount of time, wins. Another form of contest is to lay out the field with several different targets, each offering a special prize. The first plane to land in the center of a target wins a prize. This type of contest could be cosponsored with a local engineering college, a school of aeronautics, or the operators of a local airport.

Model boat contests can take on one of two forms: competitors exhibit the model boats they have made and are judged in their craftsmanship; or the boats sail or race in a pond or lake. A race is more interesting, will draw spectators, and is more appealing to the media. It could be arranged through a local model boat club, with the local city parks department, or even an office or industrial park that has a pond.

Boomerang-throwing contests and demonstrations are fun events, and bring out a lot of curious spectators, plus the television news cameras. After the contest and demonstration, the fans usually end up trying their hand at the Australian sport. It is an ideal sponsor opportunity for a sporting goods store, or a retailer who sells many Australian products.

The Largest Tomato, Pumpkin, Cucumber

It may be as "old as the hills" but it works! Whenever there is a competition among local gardeners for the largest tomato, pumpkin, or other vegetable, there is a lot of interest and entries. This is an ideal contest to sponsor if you sell produce or any type of food, gardening equipment, or seeds. It can be cosponsored with the state department of agriculture, or a garden or 4-H club. The competition can be held several times a year whenever the vegetable is in season. If you sponsor the event, be certain that you will be able to display the winning vegetable at your store.

Another angle might be to donate to a local charity a premium price for each pound the winning vegetable weighs. This announcement should be made when the contest is first announced.

Beauty Pageants and Other Competitions

There are usually many different pageants and competitions for titles held in a city. They may range from the local preliminaries of the "Miss

America" contest to the "Queen of the Prom" contest at a high school, from "Businessman of the Year" to "House of the Year."

Sponsorship of the local preliminaries for national and international beauty contests usually requires the payment of a franchise fee. However, you might be able to get involved by providing prizes and merchandise to the local winners. If you sell women's clothing, provide the wardrobe for the local winner. If she gets to the national finals, the exposure for your store will be greatly increased. Other merchandise award possibilities include luggage, cosmetics, bathing suits, and shoes. A beauty salon might get involved by setting the hair of the contestants.

Some of the local competitions fall into the category of beauty contests, while others honor accomplishments in business, volunteer work, etc. Sometimes the winners are selected at local pageants, and other times by business or civic organizations. There are opportunities for retailers to sponsor some of the awards. It might mean a cash contribution, providing merchandise to the winners, or providing the trophies or certificates. In some cases, a sponsoring merchant may want to have the winner appear at the store as part of a promotion. In all cases, if you are a sponsor, or are involved in the promotion, you should devote both window and in-store displays and/or signage to your role.

OTHER CIVIC PROJECTS TO SUPPORT

Community Awards

In many cities opportunities exist to sponsor awards honoring public servants as well as citizens who perform heroic deeds. If your city already has a program in place, you might get involved by offering a gift certificate to your store as one of the prizes. Or underwrite a more attractive award: a trophy or plaque instead of the certificate of appreciation. If your city does not have a program in place, you can take the initiative and sponsor one by underwriting the cost of the rewards.

Another program could be to sponsor a permanent "Honor Roll" in a central location on which the names of the honored are listed.

You could honor a police officer, fireman, civil servant, and teacher each month, as well as the outstanding one of the year in each category. Or you could sponsor heroism awards for civilians who distinguish themselves by coming to the aid of fellow citizens or law enforcement officials.

While you might participate as a sponsor of these awards, the actual selection of the winners should be by an official committee (the police selecting the officer of the month, etc.).

Donate a Horse to Your Police Department

If your police department has a mounted unit, see if your store could donate a horse to it. You would want the horse to be named after your store. Arrange a photo opportunity when you turn over the horse to the police at a ceremony in front of your store. Each year, arrange a birthday party outside of your store for the horse. Invite customers to attend and have a special treat for the horse.

Promote Voting

During voter registration and before elections, you might want to sponsor or help promote "Get Out the Vote" campaigns. You could do this through your advertising, window displays, and in-store signage, stuffers with your monthly bill mailings, and participation in citywide campaigns. One method might be to conduct a drawing for prizes among everyone of voting age who signs a pledge at the store that he or she will vote. If there is a citywide drawing for prizes among those who register to vote, consider donating gift certificates or merchandise from your store. If there is no such drawing, consider organizing one. You and your store will get great coverage in the local media.

Essay Contest

In cooperation with the local school system, you might underwrite the prizes for an essay contest among high school students. You should let the school system select the subject since it will give greater credibility to the contest.

IF A DISASTER SHOULD STRIKE

If a disaster should occur in the community, you should immediately react by offering whatever assistance you can. This could include donating your facilities as well as supplies and products. In addition, you might offer discounts to people who must replace what they lost, and even extend credit to them.

Anything you do in such a time of need will be appreciated and recognized by the community.

17

———■■■———

Marketing Your Restaurant

RUNNING A RESTAURANT is probably the most difficult form of retailing. You are not only the retailer but also the manufacturer of the end product. And your wait staff plays a more significant role than most salespeople at a conventional store. Because of so many intangibles, it is difficult to predict the success of the operation when you open its doors, and you always have hanging over your head the fact that eventually it may close.

So why is there such a high rate of failure in the restaurant industry?

■ People do not do enough research or planning before opening a restaurant. They fail to take into consideration the competition, and most important, they do not establish a point of difference between their restaurant and the competition. All too often, the new restaurant is just another restaurant in the community that is probably already saturated with that cuisine. A restaurant needs to give the diner a reason why he should visit that restaurant over Restaurant A or Restaurant B. Very few restaurateurs check census tracts in the area to get a reading on who lives there and even if there are enough potential customers to draw from the area (see chapter 4).

- Another reason is psychological. Restaurants often open in locations that previously housed a restaurant. If a person had a bad experience at the old restaurant, chances are he will be reluctant to try the new one, even with a new name, a new menu, and new management. It is psychological. On the other hand, if the person had a good experience at the old restaurant, he will go back because part of that good experience was the room and the decor. The new owner, all too often, decides to do a 180-degree turn instead of thinking how he can keep the old restaurant's diners as a base. The old customers come in and are totally turned off when they see that the wood paneled walls are now red, the natural wood floors have a blue rug covering them, the subdued lighting is now daytime bright, and the once easy-to-read menu uses catchy phrases to describe the offerings. This actually happened at a formerly busy restaurant in a mid-Atlantic state that had kept the predecessor's old name. It was out of business within three months.

- Lack of predictable food and service. People will keep returning to the same restaurant if it provides a pleasant experience and the food and service are consistently good. In larger cities, chefs come and go as do wait staff. Often as soon as a new chef arrives, he begins tweaking the menu. Customers may be coming back because they liked the original chef's menu, and as the new chef gets further away from the old menu, the regular customers may go farther away from the restaurant. Unless the new chef can attract new customers, the restaurant is going to be in trouble. Change can be dangerous if you have a large base of happy customers. However, if you want to change your menu do it gradually, perhaps eliminating the least ordered dish and replacing it with one of the new chef's specialties. Closely monitor how the new dish does; and if it works, you could gradually drop in other new dishes, still monitoring to make certain you are not losing loyal customers. Another bad omen is a transient wait staff. Diners feel more secure when they see familiar faces waiting on them each time they come to eat. Good wait staff get to know the regular customers by name and know what they like and usually order. They develop a good rapport with the diners. A rapid turnover of wait staff sends a bad signal to customers.

- Owner or chef ego. Some people go into the restaurant business for the wrong reason. They eat out a lot, see a lot of things they don't like, enjoy cooking as a hobby, always wanted to own a restaurant, and think they have all the answers for running a successful restaurant. They don't bother to listen to, or study the needs and desires of, their customers. They don't realize that it is the diner who is the most important person in that restaurant. Some chefs who open their own restaurants run into the same ego problem. They usually have their own style of cooking and are adamant about featuring it in the restaurant. They are often too hard-nosed about sticking with a menu customers are rejecting. On the other hand, chefs who are flexible and make the changes to meet the desires of their diners will succeed.

- Lack of promotion. You cannot just open a restaurant and wait for customers to show up. It needs to be promoted. The degree of promotion will vary, depending upon the number of seats, the competition, local reviews, the number of regular customers, and its perceived image in the community. An established four-star restaurant doesn't need much promotion since it will draw customers through word-of-mouth advertising and rave reviews. However, most restaurants are not reviewed by the media and those that are usually get fair to good ratings, which is not necessarily enough to fill all of the seats day after day.

- Value. What the exact formula is nobody knows, but every person has his or her own way of perceiving whether the quality and quantity of the meal is worth the price. When the value perception is lower than the bottom line on the bill, the restaurant is in trouble.

- Cleanliness. In cities where restaurant inspections are posted, violations can have a strong impact on customers. One very expensive and highly rated restaurant in the Northeast, where reservations had to be made days in advance, never reopened after being cited for a serious health violation in its ice-making machine. The owner knew people, who were paying six dollars for a drink, would never come back.

- Full utilization of the restaurant. Serving one or two meals a day without a full house may not be enough to cover expenses and make a fair profit. That's why restaurateurs have to increase the utilization of their services. Catering is a natural, and not just for lunch, dinner, and parties. Many business firms have catered breakfast meetings. In downtown areas, there is the opportunity to sell take-out coffee, rolls, and pastries to people on their way to work. There is the after-school opportunity to attract parents with youngsters; Saturday and Sunday brunches; theme events (Super Bowl, St. Patrick's Day, Friday the 13th, etc.); late-night dinners on weekends; retirement parties, promotion parties, or office showers. The list is endless. The restaurateur with a full schedule has a much better chance to survive the economic pressures of running the business.

CREATING EXCITING PROMOTIONS AND EVENTS

The success of a restaurant, like every other retail operation, is based on attracting new customers as well as keeping the old ones coming back. Not just coming back, but coming back more frequently.

While the food, service, and ambiance of the restaurant are key factors in assuring its success, creating the excitement to attract more people more frequently is what is going to make the restaurant a more viable and profitable operation. Good, solid promotions are one way to accomplish this goal.

The array of promotions available to a restaurateur is unlimited. Many are obvious and routine. Often by adding one or two minor elements, these routine promotions can become real blockbusters. While this chapter offers suggestions for giving some routine promotions pizzazz, its primary focus is to present fresh, creative ideas. In addition, many of the ideas and concepts found elsewhere throughout the book can used or easily adapted.

It is important to recognize that every promotion is not necessarily proper for every restaurant. You are going to have to take into account what is discussed in other chapters of this book, as well as your personal knowledge of the situation and your customers, before deciding which promotions will work at your location.

Home Cooking/Customer Recipe Night

The most effective promotions are those that get customers directly involved. This promotion does exactly that. Set aside a slow evening each month and make it "Customer Recipe Night." Encourage customers to submit their favorite recipes. Each month select a few to be featured that evening. Promote the event, the winners, and their recipes in the restaurant via table tents, posters, menu clip-ons, and flyers, which the winners should be encouraged to give to friends and neighbors. You may also want to advertise in the neighborhood weeklies circulated in the area where the winners live. Also send press releases and information to local media, and try to get the lifestyle pages to carry the recipes before the special evening.

In addition to being a highly promotable event, chances are that friends, neighbors, and relatives of the winners will eat at the restaurant that night, assuring you of a good turnout.

To select the recipes, try getting local food editors and/or other media personalities, including disc jockeys, to act as judges. You might also run a competition among disc jockeys, serving their winning recipes on a special "Dee Jay Night." For this one, you might have to make a donation to the winning disc jockeys' favorite charities.

Fishing Trip/Fish Fry

Another way to get customers involved would be to sponsor a fishing trip and fish dinner package. The fish caught during the day trip by the customers would be served with all the trimmings that night. If not enough fish are caught, market-purchased fish would also be served. An ideal Sunday afternoon/evening event, this type of promotion will create bonding between customers and the restaurant's management and staff. Set up the promotion with one or more local fishing boats. Set a package price for the "Fishing Trip/Fish Fry," and have a fixed price special for guests attending only the fish fry.

Local Newspaper/Magazine Recipe Night

Each month, in conjunction with a local newspaper or area magazine feature one or more of its recipes during a normally slow night, or even over a period of days. Promote through the newspaper or magazine, perhaps having the food editor and, if appropriate, the wine editor on hand to talk about the evening's menu. Ask the food editor to demonstrate how to prepare the featured recipe(s). The publication could link the event to a circulation or advertising promotion. Depending upon the prestige of the publication, this event might command a premium fixed price, allowing you to donate a portion of the gross to a local charity.

Firehouse Cook of the Month

Since firemen have such an excellent reputation for being good cooks, an interesting promotion would be to select a different local firehouse each month and invite the crew to prepare one or more of its special recipes on one of your slower nights. This has all types of customer possibilities. It might become a "Fireman's Night" event with a lot of local firemen looking at it as a chance to socialize with their fellow firefighters. It might attract a lot of people who live in the vicinity of the firehouse. It might attract elected officials as well as civic leaders. And it will probably attract regular diners who are aware of the cooking skills of firehouse chefs. This promotion will get good media coverage. A percentage of the profits should be given to the firemen's "widows fund" or a local burn center.

Visiting Chefs Program

If you have an upscale gourmet restaurant, you might try to arrange a "Visiting Chefs" exchange program in conjunction with one or more out-of-town restaurants. While your chef visits one of the other restaurants, its chef is in your kitchen. This could be a week-long or a weekend promotion. It is a highly promotable event, with local food editors interviewing the visiting chef, live cooking demonstrations, and interviews on local television. You might also be able to arrange an appearance at a mall or department store, giving you additional exposure. The visiting chef and his or her specialties should be promoted prior to the event, with advance reservations suggested. Use window signage, table tents, and flyers on a table near the exit. Have the wait staff mention it to their tables, even offering to make reservations for them. Restaurant-page advertising should also be considered.

You might also arrange one or more special sittings at a premium price during the stay. At these sittings, the chef might do a preparation demonstration and/or question-and-answer period for the diners.

Midnight Supper

One Friday or Saturday night each quarter, you might try an elaborate midnight supper, with a special menu and entertainment. Charge a premium price for this event and consider making it a black-tie affair. Serve fine wines, gourmet foods, and use elegant serving dishes (even if you have to rent them for the evening). As part of the package, you might offer pickup and drop-off limo service, have a red carpet out in front, trumpeters to greet guest arrivals, etc. Each supper could depict a theme from a different era of ancient history, with the menu and dress of the wait staff reflecting that period.

Theme Nights

On a regular basis you might run theme nights or days, featuring food and decor from different parts of the world, different eras, or different subjects of interest. Always have the wait staff dressed in appropriate costumes for the promotion. Theme nights might include "Hawaiian Luau," "Tahitian Temptation Night," "Alaskan Seafood Sunday," "Latino Night," "Gay Nineties Night," "Acapulco Appetizer Afternoon," "Outer Space Offerings," "California, Here I Come Dinner," "Caribbean Cook-out," "Carnival," etc. In some instances, you may be able to tie in these theme nights with local ethnic groups, or societies connected to the country or part of the world involved. You may also be able to, when appropriate, tie in with the consulate of the country involved. These tie-ins will give the theme nights some official standing and help draw large crowds.

Free Digital Taping of Special Events

To encourage special occasion dining and parties, use your camcorder to shoot any special events held at the restaurant free of charge, whether it be a one-table birthday party or a private, party-room event. The parties involved will appreciate this bonus, and you can be sure they will spread the word about this nice gesture.

Jazz at Noon

A popular feature at some restaurants in business districts, "Jazz at Noon" can be a crowd-pleasing weekly or monthly event featuring either professional or amateur groups. The amateur groups usually draw well, especially when they are made up of businessmen and -women, since fellow employees turn out in big numbers. It is also a good weekend brunch promotion, but you probably will have to hire a combo of professionals for that.

Lunchtime Fashion Shows

Another successful business district event is a lunchtime fashion show. Lingerie, bathing suit, men's, and women's fashion shows are usually staged in the restaurant by local retailers, or designers who look upon them as showcases for their clothing. Sometimes designers or retailers will write orders at the event. Fashion shows usually draw good-size, lunchtime crowds and profits for the restaurants. They also get good play in the media, and much of the promotion is done by the those showing the clothing.

Breakfast with . . .

An interesting approach toward developing weekend business among young families would be to hold a series of "Breakfast with . . ." events, aimed primarily for children. Among them: "Breakfast with Santa," "Breakfast with the Easter Bunny," "Breakfast with the Clowns," "Breakfast with (name) the Magician." It is a fun morning for the children and their parents and will undoubtedly introduce new faces to your restaurant.

Special Football "Widows" Afternoons

While the husband is watching the Sunday pro football games, run a women's-only event. In addition to lunch/brunch, have special events including beauty and personal improvement seminars, interesting lectures, games of chance, and other entertainment. It will have great media appeal.

A Night at the Game . . . Theater . . . Circus

From time to time put together a package that includes dinner, a ticket to a sporting or entertainment event, and postgame dessert or drink. Consider running a shuttle bus between the restaurant and the venue. Try to arrange for good seats to important games, as well as to popular events such as the theater, circus, ice show, and concerts. If you have upscale customers who are not concerned about costs, you might rent one of the special privates boxes for the sporting event. While costly, they will make a positive impression on your diners.

Such special events increase the importance of your restaurant to your customers, and enable you and your staff to show your capability as event planners.

Show-and-Tell Nights

As corny as this may sound, it can work—depending on your customers. A few times a year, invite diners to show tapes and slides of their vacations, children and /or grandchildren, or even arty stuff. It is a way to get people involved and feel as though the restaurant is an extension of the their home and life. You might limit the subject of each "Show-and-Tell" event: summer vacations, ski trips, children under three, amateur sports, humor, etc. Before running this type of event, make certain it will be a positive promotion for your restaurant and not a turnoff for your diners.

Magic Night

Young and old are fascinated by magicians. You would have to decide whether to hold a "Magic Night," or "Magic Brunch" on the weekend. You might even be able to occasionally run it as a weekday lunch for a change of pace for your business customers. In addition to a performance, the magician could also table hop, teaching customers simple hand tricks.

Celebrity Bartenders

A popular promotion for happy hour and the after-work scene, celebrity-bartender events are often done in conjunction with a non-profit organization. Celebrities could include local politicians, company presidents, athletes, radio and television personalities, company executives, newspaper columnists, and other well-known people in the community. Often they bid for the honor (with the bid money going to the charity). The celebrity's tip money and a percentage of the bar receipts also go to the charity. Another variation is for employees to nominate their boss, explaining why they consider him the "best boss in town." The winner gets to be "Bartender of the Day."

Cookbook Club

A great way for a restaurant to develop a relationship with people who like to cook, and presumably like good food, is to set up a "Cookbook Club" in conjunction with a local bookstore. Invite cookbook aficionados to meet once a month for a special meal and to discuss a newly published cookbook. The menu—or part of it—would include recipes from that particular cookbook. Arrange for a local food editor or other food expert to lead the discussion about the book. The participating bookstore might arrange a special discount price for club members to purchase each month's book. To make it an even more interesting "hands-on" evening, you might set up a committee at each meeting to plan the next event.

Twins Day

Hold an annual "Twins Day," party, inviting all twins to the restaurant for two-for-one deals on drinks and meals. You might also include a three-for-one deal for triplets. This type of event is very promotable in advance, and will probably get good media coverage. It will also build, and more pairs will show up each year. It also could lead to a more formal group, a "Twins Club," which could meet regularly at your restaurant.

Signs of the Zodiac

During the month of each sign of the zodiac, schedule a dinner or weekend lunch for adults born under that sign. Have an astrologer do a presentation about the sign and what lies ahead for people born under it. If there are too many people on hand for private readings, have a door-prize drawing for as many readings as the astrologer can do that evening or afternoon. This could be a price-fixed meal and include a copy of a book on either astrology or the particular sign of the zodiac.

Anniversary Week/Month

In order to demonstrate to your customers and community that you are running a stable, successful operation, celebrate your anniversary each year. It could be month-long or week-long and feature a whole list of special events and special pricing. It should be your way to thank your customers for their support. Give a slice of "birthday cake" to everyone who dines during the promotion, or champagne to your better customers. Small favors could also be given out. If it is a milestone (five, ten, twenty-five, etc.) anniversary, make it even more elaborate. On a few specials, cut back your prices to what they were the founding year. For a twenty-fifth anniversary, have the wait staff in that period's clothing. Get a proclamation from your city government. You may also want to use your anniversary to give something back to the community: donate books to the local library, cater a meal at one or more local senior citizens centers, or make a donation to a school's scholarship fund.

Hat, Jacket, and T-shirt Nights

If you have an informal dress policy, hat, jacket, and T-shirt nights can be fun promotions. On hat night, for example, encourage customers to wear the weirdest hats they can find and give prizes to the top three or four—same for the other nights. You might have special categories for men, women, senior citizens, teachers, etc. Get local disc jockeys involved, and have them participate as judges. This is a good TV news promotion and you might be able to have the winners appear live on early morning local news shows.

Charity Weeks/Days

A good way to attract new customers is to run a fund-raising program with a charitable organization. It could involve a meal, a day, or an entire week. The charity takes full responsibility for the promotion of the event, including a mailing to all its members and supporters about the tie-in, enclosing a courtesy card, which has to be turned in when it is used during the promotion. A percentage of the bill is donated by the restaurant to the organization.

Select charities that have a large following in the community as well as a loyal group of volunteers. Its members and supporters should be people whom you are trying to attract to the restaurant. And when they visit during the promotion, go all out in trying to make them feel welcome. To encourage the diner to return after the promotion, consider giving him or her a coupon good for a free dessert or appetizer.

After-School Specials

This is an ideal way to pick up business during the slack period between the end of lunch and the start of cocktail hour/dinner service. Parents pick up younger children from school in midafternoon and often stop off for a snack. Turn that snack into a happening at your restaurant. Set up a fixed-price, weekday afternoon event to include snack service for the parents and children with different entertainment each day. Use storytellers, cartoonists, clowns, magicians, puppeteers, balloon sculptors, etc.

New Mothers Luncheon Club

Physicians sometime organize a "New Mothers Club" among their patients. It is a support group, which meets every couple of weeks over lunch at a "baby friendly" restaurant, and gives new mothers a chance to compare notes, listen to speakers, and just socialize. It usually has a revolving membership since it is for mothers whose babies are under six months or a year old. If you have a private dining room, this might be something to look into. You could approach local physicians to see if they might organize such a group. It is a good patient relations program for the physician to sponsor.

Knights of the Round Table

"Knights of the Round Table" might be the name of a special men's club you set up that meets one night a month for dinner and to hear a speaker discuss a current topic, followed by a question-and-answer period. You might set this up in conjunction with the daily newspaper. They could provide, for example, their business editor to discuss the economy, a sportswriter to preview an upcoming sports season, another editor to discuss foreign policy, the political editor or writer to conduct a live interview with the mayor. In addition, other outside speakers could be used when the occasion arises. This should be a flat-fee event, and a moneymaker for the restaurant. A similar program can be developed for women only.

E-mail Your Order for Speedy Service

For those busy diners (or impatient ones), offer express service. If they e-mail or fax in their order and give their time of arrival, the food is guaranteed to be at their table within five or ten minutes after sitting down. If they also order a drink in advance, it will be on the table as soon as they arrive. Set this service up only for reliable regular customers to avoid no-shows.

Last-Call Specials

A good traffic builder for your last hour or so of operation would be "Last-Call Specials." You would cut prices on whatever preprepared foods you have left over (don't let the customers know they are left-overs), as well as some other dishes. In reality, you would plan ahead and feature one or two different items each day, which would reflect positively on your overall menu. You want to use this late-night promotion to attract new customers who will come back during the earlier dining hours. Another late-night feature might be to offer free seconds on some of the dishes. Your wait staff should encourage the late nighters to come back earlier sometime to see all the other great foods on the menu.

Postgame Parties

With high school and college sporting events very popular in many cities, you might consider running postgame parties. Decorate the restaurant in the team colors, have staff wearing team jerseys, let people vote for the team MVP that day. See if you can get a few cheerleaders to show up as well as athletes.

Sampling Next Day's Specials

An excellent way to build repeat business and demonstrate the versatility of your menu is to offer diners a chance to sample one of your next day's specials, or a special being offered a few days later. You might ask them if they would like to try a small sample after they finished their main course. You might include a listing of the days when the special will be served, and perhaps the recipe.

Nutritionist Night

With nutrition very much in the news, it would be advantageous to have a nutritionist serve as a consultant to the restaurant. You should have the nutritionist on hand at least one night a week to discuss the nutritional value of the meals being served that night. He or she should also circulate from table to table to answer any questions or give advice when requested. By using a nutritionist, you are enhancing the image of the restaurant since diner perception will be that nutrition is important to you in planning meals. You should also identify the nutritionist by name on the menu, followed by any degrees or accreditation the person has. You might obtain pamphlets on nutrition from government agencies and pass them along to your diners (after stamping the restaurant name on the back cover). You might be able to get the nutritionist free by letting him or her pass out business cards to diners, and also listing the nutritionist's telephone number on your menu and on your Web site.

Diet Specials/Diet Club

With the government and medical profession continually speaking out on the subject of the large number of Americans who are overweight and obese, restaurants that offer an alternative to this large group of people may fill an important niche in the community.

What can the restaurateur offer?

- Smaller portions. While your smallest steak or hamburger may be eight to ten ounces, offer a half-size portion. Offer reduced size portions on all menu items.
- Popular diet dishes. Offer dishes that conform to the recommendations of various diet authorities and associations (Weight Watchers, American Diabetes Association, the American Heart Association, etc.). In addition, offer to prepare dishes for any special medical diets any of your customers are on so long as they provide you with the recipe two days prior to coming to the restaurant. Always have skim milk available. It seems to be a problem at many restaurants. Sometimes diners are told that the chef won't permit it on the premises, others offer 2 percent milk and tell diners that it is 98 percent fat free. Skim milk is recommended by most health organizations, and there should be no excuse for not having it available. The cost is the same as for regular milk.

- Low-calorie desserts. Offer a selection of low-calorie desserts, including those approved for diabetics (sugar-free gelatin desserts available in all flavors; chocolate pudding; no sugar added, fat-free ice creams in all flavors, etc.). By offering low-calorie desserts on your daily menu, you will have a pretty good chance of extending your dessert business among customers who ordinarily pass on dessert because of its high-calorie count.

- Calorie count on all menu items. Provide approximate calorie counts on all menu items so diners can plan their meal before ordering. You might also provide other content information including fat, sodium, sugar, and carbohydrates; or indicate the items that are low-fat, low-sodium, or low-sugar.

- "Diet Club." To encourage this special diet menu, enroll diners in a "Diet Club," and have them weigh in each week. Offer a reward to anyone who eats ten meals a month at the restaurant and loses at least four to five pounds. You might offer a special prize to the person who took off the most weight in a three-month period

Some Holiday Events

Most of the ideas in earlier chapters for holiday promotions can easily be adjusted to fit the environment of a restaurant. Here are a few additional ideas:

- New Year's Eve. This should be a big night, and there is a way to celebrate it twice. Over the weekend prior to the event have a special early afternoon family New Year's Eve party so that parents and children can celebrate together. Have regular New Year's Eve decor, noisemakers, streamers and confetti, hats, and the usual midnight countdown (only this time it will probably be 3 P.M.). Another idea is to have a mock New Year's Eve celebration with all the trimmings on any evening at midnight. You might do it once a month, or just a few times a year. It all depends upon your image and the crowd you attract. There used to be a night club in San Francisco that used to celebrate New Year's Eve every evening at midnight.

- Valentine's Day is another big night for eating out. Ask the media to help you find the longest married couple in the city and make them "King and Queen Valentine." Offer a bottle of champagne to anyone who proposes that night, and have a group ceremony for married couples who want to renew their vows that night. Invite a local judge to conduct the ceremony.

- April 15. Help accountants celebrate the end of the tax season with a gala party and late-night dinner. Make it a reservation-only event for accountants, their spouses, and staffs. Try to get the local accounting society to co-promote this "End of Tax Season Gala." You can probably kick it off around ten or eleven but really go wild at midnight when tax season officially ends.

GO AFTER TOURISTS AND BUSINESS VISITORS

If you have the right location, menu, and reputation, you can attract tourists and business visitors. It will take some advertising and a lot of personal contact work. You will want to advertise in the locally published tourist guides, which are distributed at the hotels and visitors center. Offer a souvenir of some sort to any visitor who shows an out-of-state driver's license.

You should also visit the concierges of all the major hotels in the city, paying particular attention to the ones close to the restaurant. Give them copies of your menu and invite them and their spouses to be your guests for dinner. Whenever they refer people to the restaurant, send them a brief thank-you note. Also send them little gifts throughout the year. If a concierge is Irish, send him or her a small gift for St. Patrick's Day. Always send something on his or her birthday. And invite each concierge and his or her spouse back for dinner several times during the year.

Also encourage local companies and professional practices that play host to out-of-town visitors to recommend your restaurant as a place to dine. You might give the office managers at the firms special introductory cards to give their visitors, which would entitle them to a free dessert or appetizer on their first visit.

It is also important to join the local chamber of commerce and/or convention and visitors' bureau and promote your restaurant through them, especially to conventions and trade shows coming to your city. You might offer some type of welcome for these visitors: a free drink, a small discount, etc. It is also a good idea to consider advertising in the programs of the larger, more important conventions.

And finally, get to know the local sightseeing companies and guides. See what it will take to get them to recommend your restaurant to visitors. You probably will have to invite the managers and the guides and their families to come to dinner. If they sell advertising on their buses, it might be a good investment.

18

■■■

Making the Internet Work for You

IF YOU BELIEVED everything you read in the late 1990s, you could not help but be convinced that the Internet was going to dramatically change the entire retail picture during the new millennium, with the conventional retail store disappearing as everyone was going to do shopping via the keyboard of a personal computer.

It did not take very long for reality to catch up with the combined hype of the dot com entrepreneurs, the investment community, the e-commerce consultants, and the media. Yes, e-commerce was here to stay but nowhere near as significantly as we were made to believe it would. Even after a record Christmas 2002, the *New York Times* reported that after the elimination of goods that make no sense for consumers to buy online—such as gas, groceries, sofas, and appliances—online purchases accounted for only 2.5 percent of total retail industry sales for 2002. And various research firms are predicting that online sales will reach 8 to 10 percent of total retail sales by 2007. That still leaves a whopping 90 to 92 percent of the business to the conventional retailer.

That does not mean that smaller retailers should ignore the Internet. On the contrary, now is probably as good a time as ever to put your toes in the water and test e-commerce opportunities. We are not suggesting that you start thinking Amazon. Rather think small, try to learn all you can about e-commerce, and position yourself for the next step.

START AN E-MAIL PROGRAM

Start off by establishing an e-mail program between you and your customers. Create a program that your customers will find beneficial to their needs, and not the least bit annoying.

Outline the program in a brief brochure and have your salespeople hand it to customers and ask for permission for the store to send e-mails to them. Of course, get each customer's e-mail address.

Your e-mail program should include general information sent to everyone on the list, as well as specific information tailored to individual customers.

The general information would include:

- Advance information on sales and special events
- Advance information on new products or new product line arrivals
- Advance information and description of weekly specials
- Any press releases from suppliers that reflect trends or changes in style, etc.
- Any news of interest regarding the store
- Information on arrival of reordered products, which had quickly sold out

You might e-mail this general information through a monthly or biweekly newsletter, with special e-mails for any fast-breaking information you want to get into the hands of your customers immediately.

The specific information sent at appropriate times to individual customers would include:

- Personal updates on frequent buyer points—perhaps once a month
- Response to individual customer questions e-mailed to the store
- Information on specific product(s) the customer requested; informing customers when products on special order arrive
- Thank-you notes when the customer makes a special purchase

Customers should be encouraged to use e-mail to communicate with you when they have any questions; to reserve or purchase products; to make an appointment with one of the salespeople; to leave a message for a salesperson; to offer any suggestions regarding the store, products, and product lines. They should also be encouraged to critique the e-mail program as well as offer suggestions on how to improve it.

The whole idea behind e-mail is to add another level to your customer service effort and to get your customers to recognize you are operating with twenty-first-century technology. The program will work if you promptly respond to every customer e-mail the day you receive it. And it will work if you let the customer know in the initial brochure that if they prefer to call in their questions or to discuss a problem in person, they should feel free to do so; that the e-mail program is just another option your store offers to improve communications with its customers. They will appreciate that you are developing an improved communications system.

YOUR WEB SITE

Every retail establishment should have a Web site of some sort, even if it just provides your address, telephone number, hours, and driving directions. More and more stores have Web sites, and you do not want to be the odd person out among your competitors. And even if none of your competitors have Web sites, be the first in your neighborhood.

Web sites, if used properly, can add prestige to your business, be helpful in communicating with your customers, and for reaching potential customers. The key words are *used properly*.

First off, don't look in the mirror and think of yourself as the next Amazon. Rather, look at your Web site primarily as a local marketing tool to solidify your relationship with your customers, to expand your customer base by reaching out to others in the community, and as your lowest priority, to see if it attracts response from customers outside your local area.

How do you get hits on your Web site? The people who will go onto your Web site. Developing national exposure and hits can be difficult, expensive, and unnecessary for the small retailer to develop.

However, you want local hits, and those are much easier to obtain.

Give your Web address to your customers, have it in the window of your store, and feature it in your advertising, and in your flyers. It should be on business cards salespeople hand out to customers and other people they meet.

You still have to give a reason why people should go to your Web site on a regular basis, and this is where creativity comes in.

Your best customers undoubtedly will go to the site to see which products you are featuring that week. They are loyal customers, and you can probably count on them to make a weekly visit to the site, in addition to reading your e-mails.

But how do you get other customers and potential customers interested in the Web site? It is easier than you think.

Don't create a Web site that is all business. Rather, make it an entertaining and informative site that not only covers the store but offers local news and information of interest to your target audience. If women are your prime audience, perhaps run news about the activities of the women's clubs in the area, women's health information, raising children, "local woman of the week," and women's fashions. And, get the women's organizations to cooperate by giving you their news and encouraging their members to visit your site. If you target men, perhaps cover some area of sports, including high school sports. If you are targeting an eighteen to twenty-four age audience, provide news about the music they follow, reviews of newly released recordings, local appearances by musical performers, etc. You could have a Web site that features a lot of trivia, the newest additions to the local library collection, etc. It all gets down to figuring out what community information and news will help build traffic on the Web site among your target audience.

The store information you want to get onto the site should include location, hours of operation, your e-mail address, telephone number, and upcoming events. Most important, however, you want to feature the products that will have the most appeal to your target audience, including unique, exclusive, and newly arrived ones. Products that will get a person into the car and down to the store. You want the Web site to drive area people to the store.

In these still early years of the Internet, a retailer should give a great deal of thought before trying to aggressively expand the marketing of its Web site nationally. The bulk of sales right now is going to a relatively small number of big sites, and even a large percentage of big sites are not making a profit online.

Setting up a Web site with e-commerce capability is expensive.

There is a need to maintain a larger inventory so that you can promptly fill orders, the ability to quickly pack and ship them, a need to promote the site, and a lot of other problems including credit card fraud, which is costing Internet merchants more than $1 billion a year. The costs in dollars as well as man hours spent can add up.

Unless you have one or more exclusive or unique products, cater to an easy-to-reach specialized market of people, or are willing to cut your pricing to the bone, you may find it just is not cost effective to reach beyond your immediate area at this time.

It is probably best for the smaller retailer to get his or her site running and concentrate on aiming it at the local audience, gradually expanding into a wider radius around the store.

Concurrently, it is a good idea to familiarize yourself with the national players, what they are doing, and how they do it. You should, on a regular basis, visit sites large and small, including online malls. Request information on how you can participate in the malls. Attend local, regional, or even national seminars on online retailing; pay careful attention to trade magazine articles on the subject, especially success stories about smaller retailer Web sites; and study any material the retail association to which you belong has on the subject. Also go on line and seek out information on Web hosting providers, and e-commerce packages.

By broadening your knowledge of the big picture, you will then be in a position to expand your Web activity when you are ready and the market has reached the point where it is ready for you.

That doesn't mean you cannot get major exposure. You can do this as so many retailers do by offering product on e-Bay. You can also get involved through bulletin boards, e-mail discussion groups, forums, and news groups.

19

■ ■ ■

It's David Versus Goliath:
Small Retailers Take On the Chains

"WOULD YOU GO to a chain store doctor? Then why go to a chain store pharmacy?" That is the question posed in an advertisement by a family-owned pharmacy in a major East Coast city, which has taken off its kid gloves and is duking it out with the chains in its area. Its ad boasts it will meet or beat any other pharmacy's price on a prescription, accepts all insurance plans, offers free delivery, all forms of compounding, and presents a challenge: "If you fill one prescription with us, you will never want to go anywhere else. Ask your neighbors, they use us!"

The battle for survival against the chains is being fought by drugstores, pet shops, bookstores, video rental stores, and many others in cities throughout the country.

Big versus small is not a new battle. It first developed when supermarkets took on the corner grocery stores in the days following World War II. The ability of the supermarket to carry a greatly increased variety of products, because of its large space and improved refrigeration, changed the entire nature of food shopping; and a very large number of those corner grocers were forced out of business.

However, when you look at the food-shopping scene today, you find that the corner grocer has reappeared in the form of bodegas, Korean grocers, convenience stores, delis, mini marts, and gourmet food shops.

Small stores provide convenience both in location and operating hours, specialized products, and personalized service; and they enable customers to shop without enduring the long supermarket checkout lines. And for these services, customers are willing to pay premium prices.

The corner grocery has been able to make a comeback because it is filling a consumer need.

Many of the small retailers being threatened by the big chains today are taking the same approach. They have identified ways of fulfilling the needs of consumers who ordinarily would shop at chains.

There are many ways why, and how, David can conquer Goliath.

- Past performance. Small retailers who provided outstanding service for their customers do not necessarily lose them when a chain competes against them. Customer loyalty is earned and so long as the small retailer maintains the high level of service provided in the past, customers will stay with him. However, he may have to make some adjustments to surpass some of the benefits the chain brings to town.

- Innovation. Small retailers are among the most innovative men and women in the business world. The challenge of the chains offers an opportunity to put on their creative caps and make the moves to win the match. After studying every single aspect of each competitor's business (see in chapter 4), the small retailer must develop a plan that will enable them to outdo whatever benefits the competition offers its customers. While they may not be able to undercut the chains in pricing, there are value-added services they can offer their customers that will not cost hard money and can offset the price differential.

- Buying groups. Even if the small retailer participates in a buying group, he will probably still be paying more than the chains do for product, but the difference will be narrowed, giving him a better return on sales.

- Increased emphasis on customer service. Good retailers evaluate their program on an ongoing basis, always with an eye toward improving it. And they hire highly motivated, intelligent, and personable people, who like to deal with people. The small retailer who follows this tenet has a distinct edge over his big store competition.

- The owner is the store! His presence and the assistance he personally gives to customers sends a strong message that this is a locally owned business and not absentee ownership that only cares about the profits it can take out of the city. The owner must project an image of him- or herself as a strong personality who cares about his or her customers and the community and is on hand to make certain that the customer is treated fairly and receives the very best service.

- The store must clearly establish itself as locally owned. Somewhere in the store, where every customer will see it, should be some type of plaque or signage with words to the effect A LOCALLY OWNED AND OPER-ATED STORE SERVING THE NEEDS OF (NAME OF CITY) FOR MORE THAN XX YEARS.

- The store must also establish itself as a good citizen of the community through its involvement in that community and should prominently display the plaques and thank-you letters it gets as a result of these activities.

The specific steps a "threatened" retailer takes to compete against a chain will vary from store to store and should be aimed at making a "better offer" than the chains do to fulfill the needs of area consumers.

Drugstores

There is bound to be a shakeout in the number of chain drugstores in the United States. In some cities there are too many competing against one another as well as against supermarket drug departments and independents. Something has to give. How this will affect the pharmacy mix five to ten years down the pike is anyone's guess. But since pharmacies are primarily a service business, chances are very good that the independent can become the big winner because of its proven superiority in providing the counseling and service that customers want and need. The interest in alternative medicine, along with its rapidly increasing number of products, have generated an even greater need for knowledgeable pharmacists to aid customers with their product selection.

With low profit margins on prescriptions, especially those covered by insurance plans, the independent has to develop a significant nonprescription business and additional revenue-producing services to stay in business. The prescription business may bring people into the store but if a pharmacy cannot develop other business from these customers, it is in big trouble.

One pharmacist who has been successful in developing this additional business is Beverly Schaefer, the owner of Katterman's Sand Point Pharmacy in Seattle. She developed a plan of action to prove that being bigger is not a substitute for the knowledge and expertise customers want when they visit a pharmacy. And it has been responsible for an increase in volume at her pharmacy. "People seek advice and information when they shop in a drugstore, and they don't get it from reading the ingredients and claims on the label," the veteran pharmacist said. "They have questions and they want answers from a knowledgeable source." That was the thinking behind Ms. Schaefer's plan. Since 80 percent of her volume was from products whose price is determined by a third party, namely prescription plans, she decided she would concentrate on the other 20 percent of her volume, which includes the lucrative over-the-counter products about which big store employees seemed to know little.

The number of Americans who favor vitamins, herbal remedies, neutraceuticals, and other alternative forms of medicine is growing and represents an increasingly important market. Ms. Schaefer realized that customers had many questions about these wellness drugs, and wanted to discuss them with a pharmacist. She was told that it was often difficult to find a chain pharmacist who had the time or expertise to discuss them with a customer. So she positioned herself as the problem solver for her customers, an expert who could advise them on preventive medicine as well as on the multitude of nonprescription products available for everything from colds, allergies, and flu symptoms to minor pains and constipation, as well as medical equipment. Whether it is a conventional or homeopathic product, a testing device or orthopedic product, or advice on what medications to take on an African safari, Ms. Schaefer dispenses the knowledge customers urgently want and usually cannot get elsewhere.

It is this knowledgeable personal service that draws customers to Katterman's. They trust the owner and her staff and come in not only for medications but also for their immunizations, and even to have blood drawn for cholesterol, PSA, and other tests, which Washington State pharmacists can administer. The customers look upon Katterman's as their wellness center.

Katterman's Web site provides additional information on the store's products, including a section on nonprescription drugs, which customers might need for the current season, as well as its health care services, line of quality gifts, and new additions to its book section.

As for the big store competitors? It may be one of the best things that happened to Katterman's, who picks up a lot of their dissatisfied customers.

There is a variety of other things independent pharmacies are doing or can be doing to meet the competition of the chains:

- Make major renovations designed to give their place of business a fresh new look, including a modern storefront, wider aisles, improved lighting, attractive display cases, and a seating area for people who want to wait for their prescriptions, all combined to make the store more consumer friendly.

- Set up a biofeedback area where customers can get relief from various maladies by having their brain waves charted.

- Set up space so that customers can be counseled by the pharmacist in privacy.

- From time to time, hold a special "Check Your Medication" day, in which customers are encouraged to bring in both prescription and nonprescription drugs so pharmacists can check to see if taking any of them concurrently is dangerous.

- Filling veterinary prescriptions, carrying over-the-counter pet medicines, and developing an expertise in these areas so that they can be an effective adviser to pet owners.

- Offer convenience services including fax and copying services, an ATM machine, postal supplies, blood-pressure testing, and other health screenings.

- Offer expertise and products for specific needs: fertility, diabetes, HIV, newborns, respiratory ailments. By developing expertise in one or more of these areas, they are in a position of being more helpful to customers with those problems than other pharmacists and they have a strong hook for their marketing program.

- Add flavor to medications for children and pets.

- Expand in nonprescription-related areas. In some cases this expansion has been so successful that the prescription area takes up less than 5 percent of the space. One pharmacy has expanded into a three-floor mini-department store with a large toy department, its own makeup line, and a designer children's clothes department,

- Have bilingual personnel in areas where English is the second language among large groups of people in the area. In addition, have pharmacists familiarize themselves with the medications used in the appropriate foreign countries as well as the medical traditions of those countries, and try to accommodate foreign-born customers with over-the-counter products and cosmetics from the appropriate countries.

- Pharmacies in upscale areas have placed a lot of emphasis on marketing high-priced, imported nonmedicine-related products, including throat lozenges, tooth powder, lotions, toothbrushes, hairbrushes, candies, and beauty and bath products.

- Build a broader customer base by having a policy that customers must ask a pharmacist for over-the-counter products such as aspirin or Tylenol. The pharmacist generally asks the person how the product will be used, and often will recommend a more appropriate product. This technique is effective since the customer comes in contact with a pharmacist that he or she would not ordinarily see, and probably comes away very impressed with the thoroughness and professionalism of the pharmacy.

- Offer outreach programs featuring seminars and presentations on new drugs, neutraceuticals, homeopathic medication, child and teen medicine needs, veterinary medicine, and other subjects of interest. The outreach programs are usually aimed at audiences from which new customer relationships can be developed. These programs are usually held away from the store, at a location where the group normally meets, or at local community centers, church meeting halls, etc.

- Distribute a newsletter on new products and the latest news in drug research both in-store and at various out-of-store locations, including waiting rooms at doctors' offices.

- Solicit the business of companies that have medical offices on their premises; or health clubs, child-care centers, and other groups that might need health-care products.

- Some pharmacies have instituted frequent buyer programs; others offer discount cards for over-the-counter products to employees of nearby companies, or even for prescription products if the customer is not in a plan. Such cards, however, should clearly state that the discount cannot be used in connection with other discounts or prescription plans.

- Outreach programs can be aimed at doctors to make them aware of the background and expertise of the pharmacists, any health areas in which the store specializes, and any other reasons why the doctor should recommend the pharmacy, if asked. As part of this outreach program, doctors are encouraged to call the pharmacist if they have any questions about any medications.

- Many pharmacies are getting into the gift-basket business in a big way. The store will assemble custom baskets for any occasion, with any mix of products they have in stock: bath, beauty, hair care, sweets, perfumes, and colognes.

Video Rental Stores

The independent video rental retailer has to carefully monitor on-demand rentals currently available on a limited basis through some of the cable television systems. On-demand is in its infancy but has the potential of completely changing the nature of the video rental business from a retail environment to a totally online operation.

In the meantime Blockbuster draws the attention and competition from video rental stores from coast to coast. There is a broad variety of marketing techniques the small video store owner can use to attract and keep customers.

- Good service and the personal touch will go a long way to keep customers coming back to the independent video store. A frequent buyer's club or a VIP membership card program will enable a video store to track the rentals of its customers and be in a position to alert them to new releases of the type(s) of tape or DVD they usually rent. Also offer delivery and pickup service free or for a very minimal charge. If you have a frequent buyer's club or courtesy card program, reward your best customer—the person who rents the most movies during the year—with a special prize, perhaps a night out on the town. A couple of runners-up should also get some type of prizes.
- Set up an e-mail program to handle reservations, and to inform customers when the tape they reserved is available. You could use the e-mail program to also send a weekly newsletter to regular renters.
- To attract family business, offer a free children's rental with the rental of a regular tape or DVD.
- Offer nonrental services that will increase your income and attract customers. For example, transfer home videos and color slides onto DVDs. Or, if customers prefer, convert the slides onto a videotape, even adding a musical background. Provide an editing service for customers' home movies, as well as a duplicating service.
- Institute a potluck rental program, offering special discounts on any tapes rented during the last hour or half-hour before closing with the requirement that they be returned by 10 A.M. the next morning.

- Special three-hour rental rates with advanced reservations required. While the rates will be less than the conventional overnight rental, the total earned per day by a title could be considerably more.
- An after-school rental special for children's films.
- Special festivals: mystery, comedy, drama, western, war, sports, by actor or actress, by era, by director, past Academy Award winners.
- Sponsor a home movie contest for customers. Get a few local television personalities to judge the event. Arrange a screening, and make a DVD or video, and sell it with all proceeds going to a local charity.
- Tie-in promotions. Renter can order a pizza, a Coke, and a title all delivered by the same person. A local movie theater might offer its patrons a discount coupon good for a rental, while you offer your customers a discount coupon good at the movie house.
- Create a monthly package deal. A customer has to reserve a minimum of a half-dozen titles, leaving a deposit. The discount is based on the total number of videos or DVDs ordered.
- Just as bookstores promote book clubs, promote video clubs. Try organizing clubs for your customers. Ideas would be for members to review films individually and then meet to discuss them. You might be able to tie in with a local diner or inexpensive restaurant with a private dining room. Members, of course, would pay for their meals.
- Special promotions of nontheatrical films (do-it-yourself videos, diet and health-related, other instructional tapes).
- Sponsor an Academy Award contest, and perhaps a dutch treat party where customers can watch the awards on a big screen television and see how their selections fared.
- Run film trivia contests on a weekly basis. Those with the correct answers are entered in a drawing for prizes (free rentals).
- Consider special fund-raising promotions with charitable groups, churches, synagogues, schools, etc. Provide "Donation Cards" to one or more of these organizations and have them distribute the cards to its members and supporters. When the card is turned in with a rental, for which the renter pays full price, a percentage of the money will be donated to the specific organization. Such a promotion should run for anywhere from a week to a month and might only involve one organization. If it does, the PTA might be the ideal group to work with.

Bookstores

With both aggressive online and chain competition, independent book-sellers have their work cut out for them. One problem, of course, is the vast number of books an online store can offer. No local bookstore can come close to such an inventory. Price, of course, is also a major problem because of steep discounts offered online and by the chains. Still, there are people who prefer to shop at the smaller stores because of the personal service, the willingness to accommodate customers, the friendly atmosphere, the ability to browse without having to climb over the limbs of people at the chains who are sitting on the floor and reading. As with all big versus small encounters, it is usually the personal service and attention to detail by the small retailer that makes the difference between success and failure.

What can a local bookseller do to attract and keep customers?

■ Develop a frequent buyer or rewards savings card program to reward customers. Such a program enables the bookseller to track the interests and purchase patterns of individual customers. Include an e-mail newsletter as part of the program and use it to keep customers informed about new arrivals, especially books in their areas of interest.

■ Establish a reservation program for upcoming books by prominent authors. Hold a book party on publication day, inviting those who reserved copies to pick up the book and meet other fans of the author. You might arrange to have a local book reviewer or college professor conduct a discussion about the author and some of his or her past works. Serve light refreshments. This type of event brings customers together, and creates camaraderie among them, which is bound to have a positive impact on the store.

■ Develop a bulk price offer for book clubs, basing the discount on the number of books ordered. Perhaps require a minimum of eight to ten. While you may not make full profit on these books, chances are club members will return to buy other books. And, if you have the space, you might invite book clubs to meet at your store.

■ Develop an ongoing series of promotions designed to create both traffic and excitement: a cookbook promotion, featuring demonstrations by chefs from several local restaurants followed by a tasting; storytellers for a children's book promotion. For military books, run your promotion in conjunction with veterans organizations in the community and try to get them to identify any members who participated in the particular operation. For health and medical book promotions, try to get one or more local doctors to participate in an in-store seminar or even schedule health screenings. Invite customers to participate in a travel book promotion by showing their tapes or slides of trips to exotic places. For a mystery book promotion try to get a local homicide detective or crime scene investigator to make a presentation. For an animal book promotion, have a pet show at the store and/or a pet adoption day in conjunction with the local humane society. For a sports book promotion, have a local sportswriter or sportscaster relate his or her experiences covering the games. For an astrology book promotion, feature a local astrologer; and if you want to hold a fashion book promotion, try to arrange for a local dress shop to put on a fashion show.

■ Schedule a tea party one afternoon a week aimed at female customers to come in, relax, and browse.

■ One afternoon a week run an after-school special to attract parents and their children. Serve light refreshments; perhaps have a magician or storyteller; and have special pricing on specific books.

■ Feature books by local authors (even self-published ones). Set up "Meet the Author" parties, have the author speak or conduct a seminar. The fact that he or she is local means that you can expect a crowd of friends, relatives, and neighbors to be introduced to the store.

■ Use your windows to promote appropriate books during holiday seasons: love stories for Valentine's Day, books by Irish authors around St. Patrick's Day, books about presidents around Presidents' Day, baseball books at the start of the season and around the World Series, football books around the Super Bowl, books by Italian authors around Columbus Day, war books around Veterans Day. Mother's Day and Father's Day are also good times to feature appropriate windows.

■ Take into consideration the composition of the population of your area and feature promotions and events that have special significance to large segments of it: African American History Month, Hispanic Heritage Month, the national holidays of countries from which large numbers of the population come. Feature authors of, and books about, the ethnic groups and countries involved. Also arrange in-store discussions with prominent speakers from local colleges, as well as local leadership of the groups being honored. Throughout the year, keep your shelves stocked with books that appeal to these large segments of your area's population.

- Wherever possible, develop tie-in promotions with other retailers, professionals, and businesses in the community. For example, you might ask local physicians to provide a list of health-related books they recommend so that you could have them in stock. In turn you could provide the physicians with discount coupons to give to their patients when they recommend a book. The coupons would only be valid for health books. You could do the same with veterinarians for animal-care books, with nutritionists for books they recommend, and with wine and liquor stores for books on wine.

- Product extension. It is always a good idea to look for other products that have a relation to your prime business of selling books. Audio books, DVD and video tapes, and reading lamps are naturals. If you have the space, you might be able to set up a party room and rent it out for children's birthday parties, meetings, and other events. You could also set up a learning center to offer art classes, writing workshops, wine appreciation courses, and other adult education courses. And if you specialize in cookbooks, consider selling some gourmet food products, as well as food preparation appliances. You should also look into offering gift baskets. The gift basket could contain the book the customer selects to give as a present, a reading lamp, a DVD or video, and/or snack products, which you stock for use in the basket.

Pet Shops

While independent pet shops have not faced as much intense competition as drugstores, bookstores, and video stores, they still have chains out there with the ability to cut pricing because of their mass purchasing power. However, the pet industry, especially grooming, is very dependent upon a relationship between the pet owner and pet shop staff. A pet owner is only going to trust his or her pet to the shop where he or she is confident the pet will be well treated. This trust factor gives an edge to the independent.

One pet shop operator who has positioned himself to meet the challenges of the national chains is Dave Ratner. Dave is the consummate retail marketer, never missing a beat when it comes to developing a unique approach to attract customers. One year after opening a discount soda store in 1975, Ratner decided he wanted a dog, and ended up developing the highly successful four-store Springfield, Massachusetts, area chain, Dave's Soda & Pet City.

Today soda accounts for only 6 percent of his business, but it is still in the product mix and shares the store name with the principal business. It is marketing rule number one: Give your store a distinctive name that everyone will remember. How many other pet stores also sell soda?

One of the complaints animal shelters and pet activists have against pet shops is that by selling pets they discourage people from adopting shelter animals. Dave does the opposite. All of his advertising urges people who want a pet to first visit a shelter and then only come to his store if they cannot find what they want. And when he sells a pet, Dave gives the purchaser a lifetime guarantee that if for any reason they must give up the animal, the store will take it back and guarantee that it will not be turned over to a shelter.

The same marketing savvy carries over to how Dave uses television and cable. Dave buys time on the local ABC affiliate and produces his own thirty-minute show every Saturday night at 11:30 p.m. Though he is on opposite *Saturday Night Live,* he has, from time to time, gotten even better ratings. Dave's show is about pets and their needs and is shot at one of the stores, and features his employees. One reason for the latter is that viewers will recognize the employees when they come into the store, and it is the customer's brush with fame. While Dave pays for the television time, he sells advertising spots on the show, including to some of his suppliers.

Dave also advertises on cable since it is easier for him to tailor his buys. He knows his customers and knows how to approach them since cable is so segmented. Women can be reached on channels that emphasize home and gardening, and home cooking. If he is promoting reptiles, he places his spots on MTV because that's where the reptile audience can be found.

Dave has even taken a unique approach to rewarding his frequent buyers, through his "Club Dave Cards." Instead of giving a person an eleventh product after they purchase ten, Dave gives them a gift certificate with a value computed on the basis of the cumulative dollar amount, spent on ten purchases.

One thing Dave does not believe in is weekly advertising specials. Rather, using his data base he can determine the products a customer purchases and give them coupons good toward the next purchase.

Dave and his people take their show out into the community, too. They visit schools, fairs, and libraries—wherever they can reach children. They also supported a summer reading program for children by giving two free gold fish to each child who read the required number of books.

Dave's Soda & Pet City is an example of how a savvy retailer can out-market the national chains and expand from a one-store operation to a small chain of four.

20

■ ■ ■

Innovative Steps Retailers Are Taking
to Attract Customers

AMERICAN RETAILERS HAVE long been known for their ability to grow their business through innovative programs. In addition to the unique programs many have developed to compete against the chains, equally large numbers of smaller retailers have demonstrated this same creative touch in competing against their fellow small retailers.

Here's what a cross section of retailers from coast to coast are doing to grow their businesses.

■ Pat Swartley, owner of the resale/consignment shop, The Clothes Basket, in Seabrook, Texas, has developed a successful repeat business marketing method. Whenever a customer is particularly pleased with a garment selection which is his or her style or size, Pat looks up the item on her resale software program and prints out a list of other available items that the consignor brought in. Many times the customer buys all or most of the other items from that consignor. She keeps notes on which customer prefers which consignor wardrobes and calls the customer when the consignor brings in more items. She will also call a consignor to tell him or her that she has a customer who really likes his or her clothes and asks him or her to bring in more clothing. The buyer and the seller never get to know one another but they do a lot of business together through The Clothes Basket.

- Sometimes you have to market to the influencer of the end user, taking a route completely opposite of how you are reaching that end user. Buddy Roger's Music in Cincinnati, which sells musical instruments, advertises on light music stations in order to reach the parents of the schoolchildren who will be playing the instruments. They reach the students through other means since they definitely won't get them through light music stations.

- In addition to flowers, an East Coast florist sells candles, desserts, and chocolates. It makes shopping easier for someone planning a dinner party, or a romantic evening.

- The gift-basket business has expanded into just about every type of store, enabling those who offer them good incremental business. Custom made, they are a great way to get gift buyers to step up a few notches. For example, instead of buying a husband a gift-wrapped boxed shirt and tie for his birthday, a wife might be convinced to buy an appealing gift basket, adding a few pairs of socks and handkerchiefs and/or even cuff links to the shirt and tie purchase.

- Events outside the store that are designed to lure people inside the store are growing in popularity. J & R Music World in New York City offers free concerts in City Hall Park directly across the street from its store and then brings the artists into the store to autograph their recordings. Wine and liquor stores often arrange group tastings at a hall or restaurant close to the store, and offer specials to people who attend and come into the store within an hour after the tasting ends.

- Retailers all over the country are becoming matchmakers from espresso bars that keep "resumes" and pictures of singles looking for dates to laundromats with singles nights complete with wine and music. A do-it-yourself pottery shop advertises it's a great way to make friends and be creative under a headline about meeting "My New Boyfriend" at the store.

- One laundromat in New York City has gone one step further, offering an evening of comedy, with stand-up comics performing. There is no admission or cover charge. Just bring your dirty laundry.

- *Wardrobing* is a new buzz word, and boutiques are promoting their expertise in it. It is aimed at generating more dollars per sale. Instead of selling just one part of an outfit, the approach is to assemble a complete outfit for the customers.

- "We make house calls" is an approach being taken by some retailers. A Massachusetts custom tailor will travel to your home or office if you are too busy to make it to his store. Personal trainers will do the same for people too busy to get to the gym. Paint and decorating stores will often come to your house. Some barbers and hair stylists will make house calls, especially for older or bedridden people. Many shoe repair shops and dry cleaners will pick up and deliver to the home.

■ Dry cleaners have developed some original ways to service commuters. In one city, a dry cleaner has a small drop-off/pickup point at a commuter railroad station. The commuter drops his or her dry cleaning off in the morning and picks it up at night on the way home from work. In another city, commuters can drop off their clothing at a service area on one side of the highway, and pick it up at a service area on the other side of the road on the way home.

■ In the pre-World War II days, barber shops were hangouts where men exchanged gossip, discussed politics and sports, and read the daily newspaper. Barber shops are reverting to that role in some areas where there are large numbers of immigrants from the same country. The new Americans meet their old friends from abroad, read newspapers from abroad, and get haircuts and shaves from the local barber, who is also often from the same country. It practically serves as a social club.

■ The combination of stores found under the same roof is sometimes mind-boggling. Often retailers open a second unrelated store or service because their primary business is not bringing in enough money. Among these combinations are a travel agency and a laundromat; a one-hour film store and a shoeshine stand/shoe repair store; a men's barber and a shoe repair store; a real estate agency and an antiques shop; a hair salon and a lounge with a bar; and an Internet-linked café where a person can open a bank account online.

■ A tanning salon uses "Smart Cards." It keeps such information as which tanning bed the customer prefers, prior visits, and the number of minutes bought. It also notes the customer's skin type.

■ When a wine gets a rave review in a mid-Atlantic city, the liquor store posts the review in the store and in its window and offers the wine at the lowest price allowed by state law.

■ Some retailers use customers as the models in their advertising, thinking that other customers and residents of the community will pay more attention to the ads.

■ Some beauty salons and cosmetics stores will paint the faces of youngsters going out to trick or treat. There's no charge, and it is appreciated by their regular customers.

21

——■ ■ ■——

Getting Publicity Exposure
in the Local Media

EVEN IF YOU do not buy advertising time or space, you can still get exposure in your local media with an aggressive and creative publicity program. The media does not charge for publicity but you must have a good, unique story or photo opportunity in order to interest them in giving you free space or time.

You can also often gain promotional exposure in the media by providing products for various uses including media-sponsored contests.

While daily newspapers and radio and television have the greatest impact and reach the largest number of people in a city or metropolitan area, there are other media opportunities you should not overlook. This includes weekly newspapers, cable television, ethnic and foreign language media, high school and college newspapers, union publications, company house organs, college radio stations, local magazines, tourist publications, and the publications of various business, civic, religious, patriotic, and nonprofit organizations.

You may find that you have a great number of customers and potential customers reading some of these smaller publications. That is why it is important to determine the reading, listening, and viewing habits of your audience. (See chapter 4.)

ORGANIZING YOUR PUBLICITY PROGRAM

It takes time and effort to conduct a publicity program, and it is best if you can get someone who has experience in the field to help you. There are several ways to go:

Hire a Public Relations Agency

If you have the budget, hire a local public relations agency to develop and conduct your program. Agencies usually charge a monthly fee, and also bill extra for such expenses as postage, reproduction of press releases, photography, etc. Fees will vary from city to city, and are usually based on the time needed to conduct the agreed-upon program. You probably do not need a full-time person on your account unless you would want the agency to also plan and conduct your special events and community outreach programs.

It is always best to select an agency that comes highly recommended. Ask other local businessmen, business groups, and even the business editor at the local newspaper for suggestions. Some advertising agencies also offer public relations services. If you do not want to include special events and community outreach programs under your regular fee, many agencies will do that type of work on a project basis. Again the fee will vary from agency to agency and city to city.

Before hiring an agency, be certain that you become familiar with the person(s) who will work on your account. You should be confident that you will be able to get along with him or her, and that the experience level is sufficient to do an effective job for you. While knowledge of, or experience in, retail is not necessary, the person assigned to your account should have experience in the consumer products or services area, and be promotion-oriented. In addition to possessing a writing ability, he or she should be able to generate ideas and know his or her way around the local media. Ask the agency to show you samples of its work, as well as its current client list. Contact some of the firms on that list for reference purposes.

One-Person Agencies/Freelancer

There are usually one-person public relations firms and freelance help available in most major cities. You will find some very talented people among them. Some are listed in the Yellow Pages under either "Public Relations Counselors" or "Publicity Services." An advantage in using one-person agencies and freelance help is cost. Because of their lower overhead, these single practitioners can afford to charge smaller fees than larger agencies. Use the same standards in selecting a freelancer as suggested for full-size agencies, including recommendations from satisfied clients. Be sure to also look at the work he or she has done for others.

One area to watch carefully is the amount of time the individual can devote to your business. Make certain that he or she is not handling so much business that he or she won't have the time to do a professional job for you. Get a firm commitment to the number of hours that will be spent on your business. Sure signs of a problem are missed deadlines and if you have trouble arranging meetings.

You could also consider using the single practitioner to help with special events and your community outreach.

Internship Programs

A method for obtaining free public relations assistance is through internship programs at local colleges. Check to see if any such programs are available in your area. There are usually two types of internship programs: a term project for one or more students, which is usually monitored by the professor, or a project in which the student works directly for you and under your guidance and direction. It is important to remember that you are not getting an experienced professional, especially if the only public relations internship program the school has is for undergraduates. However, what the student has learned in his or her public relations courses should provide him with enough knowledge to get your store exposure in the local media.

Interns are usually not paid. However, it is often customary to give them a small stipend to cover meals and carfare.

DO-IT-YOURSELF PUBLICITY PROGRAM

If your budget does not permit the hiring of professional public relations assistance and you cannot get an intern to help, try doing it yourself or use one of your employees.

This chapter is designed to show an inexperienced person how to get publicity exposure for their store. As you will see, many of the ideas relate to promotions, sales, special events, and other programs described in previous chapters.

Step One

Your first step should be to decide which media are the most important to you. Base your decision on the results of your research as to what your customers and potential customers read, listen to, and view. *Concentrate your efforts on this media.* Contact each one and get the names of the key people to notify when you have a story. Explain when you call that you are a retailer trying to get some publicity and that you know nothing about how to do it; that from time to time, you would like to pass along ideas, and who is the person, or people, to contact. In addition to getting names, get their e-mail addresses since most people will prefer an e-mail to a telephone call. You will find that editors and broadcasters will often be sympathetic and reach out to help "amateurs." *This is your media list.* Familiarize yourself with the "pitch letters," media advisory, press releases, and fact sheets in chapter 22. You will find the formats are simple to follow. *Much of your contact work with media will be through these materials and follow-up telephone calls. Unless you or an employee has writing skills, you should probably avoid writing press releases and stick with pitch letters, media advisories, and fact sheets.* In hiring people for the store, you might try to find someone who has a flair for writing. The person could, perhaps, spend one day a week, or two hours a day, handling your publicity and community outreach program, and the rest of the time on the selling floor.

It is important not to flood media with so-called nonstories—promotions and special events that are not out of the ordinary. For example, if you are holding a "Christmas in August" promotion, invite media coverage of Santa's arrival. If you are holding a half-price sale, forget about contacting the media. There will not be any interest, and you will wear out your welcome by sending material about nonnewsworthy events. So be discreet with what you send, and don't flood media with material unless it is something unique and newsworthy. Throughout the book, you will find notations on promotions, events, and ideas that will have media appeal.

WORKING WITH RADIO STATIONS

Focus on the radio stations to which your customers and potential customers listen, as well as others that might offer large audiences and exposure opportunities. The key people to get to know at radio stations are the program director, news director, promotion director, individual show producers, and if a smaller station, the program hosts including disc jockeys.

Other than fast-breaking news, which should be phoned in to the news director or the news assignment desk, most of your initial contacts will be via e-mail unless you are advised by the station otherwise. Always include your telephone number in your e-mails in case they want to talk to you. Follow up with a telephone call a few days later. Avoid saying in your follow-up call, "I just wanted to check and see if you received my e-mail." Media people turn every color of the rainbow when they hear that so don't do it! Instead, try to offer a few more selling points about the story or idea you sent. You are a salesman so use salesmanship when talking to the media. But don't try a hard sell. If it is an idea for an interview, e-mail a note, including details on some of the subjects the person is prepared to discuss, and send the person's biography as an attachment.

Types of Exposure You Can Get
on Local Radio Stations

Radio offers you flexibility when it comes to getting exposure for your store. Within a city, there are so many different formats, different personalities with different interests, and different programs that just about any retailer can get some free exposure if he or she makes contact with the stations.

Contest Prizes

Stations with individual programs often run listener contests and need prizes to give to winners. Since the prizes are promoted on air (and sometimes in other advertising), these contests offer an excellent opportunity to get good exposure for your store and product line. Prizes you might offer would include specific products, a shopping spree with a dollar value, gift certificates or a gift-of-the-month for a three- or six-month period. If you are an advertiser on the station, you might be able to require that entries be picked up, or deposited at your store. This would help to build traffic.

Stations might give preference to advertisers, but do not let the fact that you are not an advertiser deter you from offering to provide prizes. Instead, offer to help the station promote the contest by providing window space, in-store signage, Web site exposure, and information with customer bills, and on other promotional materials. To get involved in such promotions, send an e-mail or letter to the promotion directors at the stations indicating your interest in providing prizes.

Some talk shows, as well as the pre- and post-game shows of sporting events, give gift certificates to guests who are interviewed. The value of these gifts can range from $50 to $250, depending on the show and the market. By providing gifts, your store will receive on-air mention. If you get involved in such a promotion, make certain that you get the right to approve the promotional announcements mentioning your store. You might contact the manufacturer of the product and see if it will share expenses by providing the gift at no cost, or at a reduced price.

In some cases, you will also have to pay a small promotional fee to the show's producers. You may be able to negotiate around the fee, especially if the gift is valued at the high end of the price range. If the gifts are to be given to celebrities, try to arrange for photographs to be taken of some, if not all, of the presentations. To arrange this tie-in, contact the show's producer. If he or she is not handling the arrangements for gifts, you will be put in contact with the right party.

Guest Appearances

Radio offers opportunities for guest appearances by people who have something interesting to discuss. As a retailer, you fit into that category since you are in a position to discuss trends and other subjects in which listeners will be interested. Stations with "talk radio" formats will offer the greatest opportunity, but some other stations may have some programs that might be interested in what you have to say. They include:

- General interview shows. The host has a guest and conducts the interview.
- Interview/call-in shows. After a brief interview, the telephones are open for listeners to call in questions.

- Specialized programming (business, sports, education, politics, etc.)
- Panel shows on which an expert is interviewed by more than one reporter, or where a host moderates a panel of experts in a field, discussing one or more subjects.

What are some of the subjects you, a retailer, can discuss?

- Trends in retailing.
- What's new in fall (spring, winter, summer) fashions.
- What new toys we can expect this Christmas.
- What new cooking appliances are being introduced.
- What the latest is in gourmet foods.
- What the latest popular colors are in home decorating.
- What the store of tomorrow is going to be like. (For example, you can make all types of predictions about what the retail look will be in the year 2025. It will generate a lot of interest and perhaps even controversy. You do not have to be afraid of what you predict since no one will remember what you said when the year 2025 arrives.)
- What gifts men are buying for women.
- What gifts women are buying for men.
- Trends in jewelry—is the gift gold or silver?
- How the small retailer can take on the giants.

You can also talk in depth about consumerism and product safety. With broad interest in both subjects among consumers, it is to your advantage to be a consumer advocate and spokesperson on as many shows as possible. Areas of discussion might include:

- The importance of product safety in the marketplace
- What to look for in reading labels and product instructions
- Importance of using products only as directed
- How to get additional information from a manufacturer
- What to do in an emergency
- What a store owner's responsibilities are to his or her customers (and how our store goes much further than it needs to)
- What the rights of a customer are
- What to look for in a warranty
- What the law is regarding refunds and exchanges. (If your store's policies are much more liberal, make a point of it.)

- How to get satisfaction if the retailer or the manufacturer is not responsive to your complaints

Other subjects you might discuss include:

- How to break into retail
- Careers in retail
- Your store's growth and history
- Promotional programs which will benefit local charities and non-profit organizations
- Promotional programs involving local sports teams and/or players

When appearing as a guest on radio talk shows, you should not mention your store's name in every other sentence. If you do, you will come across as being too commercial and will lose credibility among the listeners. Chances are you will never be invited back on the show by the host, and he might even cut the interview short. Instead, speak as an industry spokesman and as an expert in the field of retailing. You will gain credibility and the respect of the audience, thereby creating a positive image for your store. Of course it is acceptable to work in the store name from time to time, but be discreet in how you do it. In discussing industry trends, you might reinforce your theories with examples from the store. During a discussion on consumerism, for example, you might point out that "It has been our experience that customers at our store . . ." Your host will also mention your affiliation during the course of the broadcast.

To get on talk shows, e-mail the producer of each show and offer one or more topics you are prepared to discuss. Also let the producers know your interest and availability to appear anytime they need an expert in the area of retailing.

Disc Jockeys

Some disc jockeys develop a core of regular call-in guests. Who they are, and what they talk about usually depends on the disc jockey. This is particularly true during morning drive time. Listen to the various disc jockeys to see if there are any with whom you might relate. You might make your first move by looking for a unique, fun product to send as a gift. For example, if you sell socks, you might send one dozen green pairs for

St. Patrick's Day. Then follow up with other gifts. If you sell food, you might make it a habit to send coffee and doughnuts each day, with special treats on special occasions. Or perhaps sandwiches and other refreshments. The all-night shows are usually the most generous in acknowledging food.

Even if you do not sell a particular product, you can still send it along as a promotional gimmick. For example, on Valentine's Day, send one thousand chocolate kisses from the saleswomen at the store, and have each one sign the accompanying card. Send a special cake on the disc jockey's birthday, and point out that it was home baked for him or her. Put some unique decorations on the cake.

Another gimmick is to send "firsts' to the disc jockey: the first box of Bosc pears to arrive in the city; the first set of this year's baseball cards; the first bag of jelly beans; the first roll of Christmas wrapping paper. You can make up your own "firsts" as you go along, and the crazier the better. Disc jockeys will like it because most of them have a good sense of humor, and it gives them something to talk about. You can have a lot of fun sending these gifts, and chances are good that the disc jockey will mention the store's name on the air. If you keep sending stuff on an ongoing basis, a relationship will develop and might result in on-air appearances, with a lot of exposure for the store's name.

Send the gift so that it arrives just before the disc jockey goes on the air. If you can arrange to have someone bring it into the studio, you might even send the gift while the show is on the air. It might get a bigger play that way. In working with disc jockeys, you may be dealing with a producer or production assistant as well.

Remote Broadcasts

Some stations will, from time to time, do remote broadcasts from a store. Usually they are more receptive to doing remotes from advertisers' stores; however, there may be exceptions to the rule. If you are in an outstanding central location, you might be able to persuade a station to broadcast from your store window. The station might also agree to a remote broadcast if you would agree to run a week-long salute to the station with window and in-store displays about the on-air personalities and shows.

A significant milestone anniversary (fiftieth, one-hundredth, etc.) might also be the occasion for a remote, as would special events such as the arrival of Santa Claus for your August promotion, the in-store appearance of a famous entertainment or sports personality.

A special "Charity Day" at the store, during which part of the proceeds would go to a particular organization, might be another occasion. Work with the charitable organization in developing the promotion since it might have better contacts at the station and might be in a better position to arrange the remote broadcast.

There may be some costs you will have to absorb in connection with remote broadcasts. To arrange remotes contact the show's producer. You may also have to contact the program director.

Personality Appearances

You might arrange, for a fee, to have a disc jockey or other on-air personality appear at the store to sign autographs, pose for pictures with customers, etc. When on-air personalities make such off-the-air-appearances, they often promote them in advance on their programs. This can be an effective way to get on-air exposure and build traffic for the store at a relatively modest cost. Personal appearances should be scheduled directly with the personality.

News Programs

There is a lot of competition to get time on local radio newscasts. Even all-news stations are very selective in what gets on the air. While you will occasionally have a good news story, your best bet for getting air time will be with something unique or with a humorous slant. News story ideas appear throughout the book. Many of the subjects listed under talk shows might also fit into a news format. For example if the city legislative body is debating stronger consumer protection laws, your take on the matter could be used.

You should also send the news director at each station a telephone index card with your name, store, title, and areas of expertise that you would be willing to discuss on air. Very often, news directors have fast-breaking stories on which they want comments from different people in the field. Let them know you are available. Also provide them with your home telephone number so that they can reach you in an emergency or in case of a last-minute need after regular business hours.

WORKING WITH TELEVISION CHANNELS

While local television offers fewer opportunities to you for publicity than radio and newspapers, it is not impossible to gain exposure for your store. It is just a matter of developing appealing ideas and calling them to the attention of your local channels.

The first step is to get to know who the key people are at each television channel and how they can help you: promotion director, news director, news assignment editor, individual producers, and talent coordinators. The titles and responsibilities can vary from channel to channel.

Television channels are not as contest-oriented as radio stations but whatever promotions they conduct fall within the bailiwick of the promotion director.

The news director is responsible for the channels' news programs and overall coverage. At smaller channels, he or she may also be involved in deciding which individual stories will be covered. If the news director is the one calling those shots, he or she will be your principal contact for getting news coverage. At larger channels, there is usually a news assignment editor who presides over the news assignment desk. In that case, he or she is the one to contact.

Each locally produced news program has its own individual producer, as do many of the news segments (medical and health, business, sports, weather, etc.). The segment producers will be important to you if you have news or feature stories/ideas which fit within their particular areas of interest.

The producers of other nonnews shows are often the people to contact regarding guest appearances or special segments. At larger channels, the shows that use guests usually have a talent coordinator who arranges such guest appearances.

Types of Exposure You Can Get on Local Television

Most of the programming on television is either network or syndicated, with very little locally produced, and what is locally produced is primarily news. Your greatest opportunity for exposure on the news will be interesting feature items, material that educates the viewer about something or comments on a business story or the economy.

Since television is a visual medium, the staff at the local channel will not only evaluate your ideas for creativity and interest but also for visual appeal. So always think "visual" when developing an idea and proposing it to a channel. Your pitch to the channel should include how the story can be illustrated.

Here are some ideas about how you may be able to get local television coverage for your store:

- As an expert in your field, you can talk about product trends and demonstrate them on camera.
- If you sell women's clothing, offer to get some models to show the latest fashion lines. You can do this each season when the new lines arrive. You can also do it for jewelry, shoes, or sportswear.
- If you sell toys, arrange to have some young children test the new line of Christmas toys at the store as soon as they come in. Invite the channels to cover the event.
- Arrange to have a one-of-a-kind product, or one with a very high price tag, on display at the store and invite television coverage. It might be a $1 million necklace, a handmade dress that took five years to finish, a rare painting, some costumes worn by movie stars, or some other product that is related to what your store sells.
- Invite coverage of special events and promotions you hold. Many of the promotional ideas in this book are naturals for television coverage. Among them would be a "Christmas in August" promotion including an interview with a sweating Santa Claus; a New Year's promotion if you celebrated "New Year's Eve" every night for a week; an in-store memorabilia exhibit. Promotions with television coverage potential are noted throughout the book.
- Milestone anniversary for either the store, or the owner. The angle is the changes the store and/or retailing has gone through over the years.
- Offer yourself as an expert to make retail forecasts and to comment on any other retail topics or events: government regulations regarding retailing, consumerism, product safety, etc. Let the business news segment producer know that you are always available when they need a retailer to comment on anything. Give them your home telephone number, too, in case of late-breaking news.
- If you have appropriate products, offer to provide furnishings for the sets of any local programs. The products could range from furniture and carpeting to flowers and drapes. The product that would get

the most exposure would be fresh flowers, especially if you change the arrangements on a regular basis. The host and guests are bound to comment on them. Other products that would probably generate conversation would be art, unique lamps and shades, an odd-shaped coffee table or desk. If you are in the food business, you might consider providing refreshments for the cast, guests, and studio audience. If you provide any products, do so with the understanding you will get on-screen credits. If it is a particularly expensive item, insist on a voice-over credit.

- There may also be a chance to show new and unusual products, as well as fun and gimmicky products.
- Many of the ideas listed under the radio section are also applicable to television.
- Like radio, local television personalities can usually be booked for in-store appearances on a fee basis. You would have to negotiate the fee with the personality or his or her agent.

WORKING WITH DAILY NEWSPAPERS

Working with print media is different from radio and television in that you will be involved directly with the reporters and writers who cover your areas of interest—not intermediaries. On many occasions, when you have a story idea, you will be contacting a reporter or writer directly, rather than an editor.

Editorial responsibilities also vary more widely from newspaper to newspaper than in any other medium with which you will be dealing. That is why you should contact your local daily newspaper(s) to identify who your prime contacts should be:

- When you have a news story
- When you have a good photo idea
- When you have a business page story
- When you have an idea for a feature story
- When you have a women-oriented story

By reading your newspapers, you can identify which local columnists cover the types of stories that would logically include material about your store. Whenever you have a story or items for one of the columnists, directly contact him or her. In many newspapers, writers' e-mail addresses are placed under the article or column.

Pitching a newspaper story is very different from pitching radio or television. There are more opportunities to get exposure in a newspaper and more staff people digging up news and writing stories. As a matter of fact, stories are often written without face-to-face contact, with everything done via the telephone and fact sheets sent to the writer.

When pitching an idea, e-mail it to the writer, including enough facts to get him interested in discussing it further with you. At this time, you should prepare a fact sheet containing a good deal of the information the writer needs for the story. He would use this information, together with information he gathers from one or more interviews. You should also have brief biographies ready if you are pitching a personality piece about the owner or someone else connected with the store, such as a former professional ballet dancer who is now a salesperson, etc.

If you are promoting an upcoming event at the store, send an item about it to whoever puts together the events calendar, as well as to the city desk (or whoever is your contact there), inviting coverage.

If you have a fast-breaking story, call it in to your appropriate contact (the city desk or the business desk, depending upon the subject).

Many of the story lines discussed in the radio and television sections of this chapter will be of interest to newspapers and should be pitched to them. While they would only get a few minutes time on radio and television, they can get significant space in daily newspapers. In addition, throughout this book are promotions, special events, contests, and other ideas that newspapers may also be interested in covering.

Some stories that will appeal to newspapers:

- Anything to do with consumerism. Promote the store owner as a person who is 100 percent in favor of strong consumer laws to protect customers. The paper will love this approach, and it can draw people to the store. In addition, when such an article appears, it should be reprinted and used as a promotional piece to attract new customers.
- Trend stories. Business page editors love such stories, especially if someone is not afraid to express his opinions on what to expect ten or twenty years down the pike. No one is going to remember ten or twenty years later if what the person predicted came true, but when the predic-

tions are made, they will get good play and will be talked about. Radio and television news might even pick up on this one.

- Photo opportunities. "Christmas in August" sale with Santa wiping his brow while he stands next to a thermometer is just one example. Other photo opportunities can be found in the chapters on seasonal promotions, special events, and even sales.

Types of feature stories to pitch newspapers if you have the appropriate product lines:

- What men are buying for Valentine's Day
- Santa's coming to town with a new bag of toys
- Wives who take their husbands along to pick out outfits
- A trade-in sale that brings in all types of relics
- What to look for when reading labels, warranties, instructional booklets
- Why shop this store?
- Children rate this year's Christmas toys
- Men review the new fashions of spring (fall, winter, summer)
- What makes a good salesperson (interviews at your store)

Most newspapers publish special thematic sections during the year that offer publicity opportunities, though some require an advertisement to get a story in the section. These include Christmas gifts, new automobile models, health, summer travel, etc.

WORKING WITH OTHER MEDIA IN THE COMMUNITY

Weekly Newspapers

With smaller staffs, weeklies usually limit the number of events they cover and use more supplied press releases and photographs. By the same token, weeklies usually cover specific areas, and if your store in not within the area, chances are you won't get any material in the paper unless it involves someone who lives in its circulation zone. For example, if you run a contest and someone from the zone is the winner, a smaller weekly would run something. If one of your employees is promoted and lives in the area, it would run that, too. It might also run fashion news, new product stories, an unusual seasonal photo, or pet picture.

However, if the weekly does cover the area where your store is located, it might run some of the press releases you send to them, especially if you also advertise in the paper. Among the items it might run are:

- Advance stories on special events and promotions
- Photos of area residents at the store during such an event, if you can provide names
- Stories on community outreach programs and events undertaken by the store
- Profiles of the owner, manager, or an outstanding salesperson—especially if he or she also lives within the circulation area
- Picture and story of local customer cashing in frequent buyer's club points for expensive gift
- Local person named "Customer of the Month"
- Picture of local resident with a celebrity at the store

Ethnic Newspapers

Concentrate on those publications appealing to significant numbers of current as well as potential customers.

There is one important point to remember. Ethnic publications will usually be interested only in news and features that involve the ethnic group they cover. This usually limits what you can get in the publication. The stories with appeal will be personality pieces about the owner, manager, or salesperson of the year if any are members of the appropriate ethnic group; customers of the ethnic group who win store contests, serve on its advisory committee, are named "Customer of the Month," or model at the store's fashion show; a salesperson who is honored for distinguished service; special in-store exhibits in conjunction with Martin Luther King Day, African American History Month, and National Hispanic Heritage Month.

Some of the story ideas mentioned earlier in this chapter can be used for ethnic publications as long as they involve a member of the respective group.

Foreign Language Newspapers

If there are significant numbers of foreign language-speaking residents in your community, chances are there will be newspapers published for them. These publications may offer good publicity opportunities for a retailer. You should be interested in those newspapers read by your target audience.

Foreign language publications, like ethnic publications, will only be interested in stories with a relationship to their readers. The list of stories will be similar to those included under Ethnic Newspapers; however, there are additional topics and angles in which foreign language newspapers would have an interest:

- Foreign language assistance offered to customers at the store
- Products sold at the store that are manufactured in the country where its readers originated
- Shopping visit to the store by a large tour group from the country
- Service offered by the store to handle the shipping of purchases to the country
- Any promotions or special events honoring the country, or one of its citizens
- Interview with the store owner or manager upon his or her return from a visit to the country comparing retailing here and in the country visited

Cable Television Systems

Cable offers limited publicity opportunities since network programming occupies most of the cable systems' channels; however, there are exceptions. In some cities there are local all-news channels that include news, entertainment, business, and lifestyle programming. They use guests on some of the programming and cover special events. If such a channel exists in your area, contact it and find out how you might work with them. They would probably be interested in many of the ideas proposed for radio and television earlier in this chapter, as well as many of the promotional ideas discussed throughout the book.

You should also contact any local sports channels in the area that give merchandise to guests who appear on any of its programming. You might be able to trade merchandise for promotional recognition.

And contact the cable system manager(s) to explore other opportunities, including the possibility of providing merchandise for prizes in any contests it runs.

Local Magazines

Many cities have local magazines. Some cover the local business scene, while others are consumer-oriented. Circulation of both types is usually upscale with the "movers and shakers" of the community among the readers.

Editorial contents vary from magazine to magazine so you need to determine how you and your store will fit into the picture. Most of the consumer-oriented city magazines have some type of shopping column with some going for offbeat merchandise. If you have products that fit into the style of the publication, it is probably a good idea to send a picture of the product to the shopping editor. If they like what they see, they will ask to borrow the product and have a professional photograph it for the magazine. For the Christmas gift season, most run a special section on gifts. Try to get in on that issue. Magazines work months in advance on the Christmas issue so don't be surprised if its deadline is in June or July. At some point, invite the shopping editor to visit the store and have lunch with the owner.

If the magazine has an events section, and the store has a good event coming up, send the information to it. Again, you might have to send it weeks in advance to make the issue closest to the event.

Some local magazines run profile stories on successful and/or unique businesses and their owners. Try selling them on doing a story on you and your store if it fits the description. Some of the ideas previously mentioned in this chapter can also be applied to these local magazines, including comments on trends and consumerism.

Also get to know the staff at any local business magazines, and invite the appropriate editor(s) to visit the store. Encourage them to contact you anytime they need background information about retailing, or about business in general. Outline to them some of the story ideas mentioned in this chapter as well as appropriate ones mentioned elsewhere in the book.

If these publications run reader promotion contests and need prizes for winners, see if you can trade off product for advertising and/or editorial space.

Tourist Publications

Tourist publications usually contain listings of stores, entertainment, tourist facilities, museums, and other tourist destinations. They normally only list those stores that advertise in the publication.

However, even if you do not advertise, you should send tourist publications material about your special sales, exhibits, promotions, new and unique products, as well as a description of the store and its product lines. Chances are, however, their response will be a call from an advertising salesman.

High School Newspapers

If your merchandise appeals to high school students, try to get some publicity in the local high school newspapers. It is not the easiest thing to do. Your stories should be informative, and aimed at helping the students.

First develop an idea, and then contact the editor to ask him or her to consider assigning a reporter to write it. Types of stories a high school newspaper would run:

- Your announcement of an internship program for high school seniors
- An interview with a recent graduate who started in the stock room and is now a salesperson at the store
- An interview with the store owner who discusses what a teen shopper should look for when shopping for clothes
- An interview with the owner on careers in retailing
- The announcement of the sponsorship of a scholarship or student award
- The sponsorship of an essay and/or art contest
- The announcement of special discounts for students with perfect attendance

You could also offer products for student auctions, raffles, or other school contests and even underwrite a student activity, theatrical production, or senior class night.

College Newspapers

Like high school newspapers, college papers are tough to crack. However, if college students are among your target audience, you have to try to reach them through this medium.

Most of the ideas suggested for the high school newspapers may also be used for college publications. The only exception would be the discount for perfect attendance.

Additional ideas for the college newspaper might include announcing a special "College Night" at the store one evening a month, with refreshments and special discounts; underwriting a lecture series on retailing; underwriting the newspaper's annual writing awards contest; underwriting an annual award for the college student who did the most to assist the community.

College Radio Stations

If any of the local colleges have their own student-run radio station and college students are among your target-audience, show interest in it. Offer the store owner as a program guest to discuss careers in retailing, suggest remotes from the store when you are having an interesting special event or "College Night," provide information on fads, new products and other items on-air personalities can talk about. See additional ideas in the paragraphs on High School and College Newspapers. If the station sponsors listener contests, offer gift certificates to your store as prizes.

Union Newspapers and Magazines

If union membership is high in your area, it is important to get publicity in the various union publications. You need to develop angles to which unions and union members can react.

First off, the store must be unionized since it is doubtful that a union publication would run a story involving a nonunion place of business.

Stories taking a strong proconsumer stand, telling readers what their rights are when shopping, and what to do when they have a problem with a retailer would probably interest a union publication. So would a strong prounion stand: The store will only sell union-made products; the store boycotts products from countries where labor is exploited, etc.

When a union member wins a prize in one of your contests, take a picture at the store and send it to his or her union's publication; take a picture of a union member's child with Santa and do the same. If you offer special benefits to union members (a discount by showing union membership card, special credit program for union members while on strike, etc.), send releases to the union publications.

22

■ ■ ■

Samples of Materials to Send to Media to Get Publicity

THIS ENTIRE CHAPTER contains samples of material to send to media to generate publicity for your store.

Pitch Letter

As the name implies, the letter pitches a story idea or a guest appearance. The preferred way to send pitch letters is by e-mail. The pitch should be as brief as possible. You want to convince an editor or a producer that you have a good story. Give a quick summary of the idea, what an interview subject can discuss, and how it is unique. Often a fact sheet or media advisory is sent along with a pitch letter.

Media Advisory

Sometimes called an assignment memo, a media advisory contains important information decision makers would need to decide whether or not to send someone to cover an event. A media advisory tells what the event is, where it will be held, and when and who the participants will be. It either directly or indirectly provides various story and picture possibilities.

Fact Sheet

Fact sheets provide outlines of important details that can be used by media to prepare a story, to prepare for an interview, or to use as talking points on radio and television.

Press Release

Press releases are stories sent to media for possible use. For your purpose, press releases will contain information about coming promotions, special events, sales, and other activities. You might also send some press releases regarding accomplishments that reflect favorably on the image of the store. Press releases are often rewritten before being used by the media and sometimes lead to a more comprehensive staff-written story about the store. It is important to understand that not all press releases you send will be used. So don't get discouraged, it happens even to the best professional publicists.

General Letter

Samples of several letters or e-mails you should consider sending to media indicating a desire to become a regular source for news, to express interest in providing prizes for media contests, and to provide gifts to guests on radio and television programs.

To give you an idea of what a family of materials for a specific event will look like, the first four samples will be a pitch e-mail, a media advisory, a fact sheet, and a press release for a "Witches Brew Recipe Contest."

PITCH LETTER/E-MAIL TO LOCAL MEDIA TO COVER IN-STORE EVENT

The annual "Witches Brew Recipe Contest" finals will be held at Smith's Kitchen Products Store, Saturday, October 27, at 10 A.M. We hope you will be able to cover. Seven recipes have been selected for the finals to be judged by two witches and one warlock, along with Mary Ames of Ames Cooking School. Samples of the seven finalists' brews will be available to everyone who attends the taste-off.

The person who submits the winning recipe will receive a one-week, all-expenses-paid trip for two to Salem, Massachusetts. The runners-up will receive a one-year's supply of brooms. All seven will receive $100 worth of kitchenware from Smith's.

Smith's will have Halloween decorations in its windows and throughout the store, including a 250-pound pumpkin, thought to be the largest grown in the area.

A media advisory with additional facts on the event is attached. For additional information, please call 234-555-8901. Hope you will be able to cover.

MEDIA ADVISORY TO SEND TO ENCOURAGE COVERAGE OF AN EVENT

MEDIA ADVISORY

"WITCHES BREW RECIPE CONTEST" FINALS SET FOR OCTOBER 27

The fourth annual "Witches Brew Recipe Contest" finals will be held at 10 A.M. Saturday, October 27, at Smith's Kitchen Products Store.

The Event:	Seven finalists have been selected and their recipes will be judged during a taste-off
The Judges:	Two witches, one warlock, and Mary Ames of the Ames Cooking School
The Time:	10 A.M.
The Date:	Saturday, October 27
The Place:	Smith's Kitchen Products Store
	1234 Main Street (Corner of Oak Avenue)

Photo Opportunities

- Witches and Warlock judges will be in costumes
- Finalists' brews will be available for sampling by all customers
- Store and windows will be decorated for Halloween
- On display at the store will be a 250-pound pumpkin, said to be the largest grown in the area
- Presentation of prizes: Winner gets one-week, all-expenses-paid trip for two to Salem, Massachusetts, presentation to be made by a "certified witch"

- Runners-up will receive one year's supply of brooms. All seven finalists will receive $100 worth of kitchenware from Smith's

For further information, contact Arnold Smith, 234-555-8901

SAMPLE FACT SHEET

FACT SHEET

FOURTH ANNUAL "WITCHES BREW RECIPE CONTEST" FINALS

- For the fourth consecutive year, Smith's Kitchen Products Store is sponsoring a "Witches Brew Recipe Contest" in conjunction with Halloween.
- The finals will be held at Smith's Saturday, October 27, starting at 10 A.M.
- From September 1 to October 12, area residents were invited to enter the contest by submitting their original recipes for a "Witches Brew." There were no restrictions for entering the contest.
- On the closing date, 1,276 entries had been received. That was 129 more than last year, and 764 more than the first year of the contest.
- Preliminary testing and judging of the recipes was done by Mary Ames and her staff at the Ames Cooking School.
- Seven finalists were selected. They are: Sarah King, 444 East Oak Street; Arthur Goldler, 309 Stir Drive; Susan Major, 1 West 101st Street; Dorian Scali, 9 East Jefferson Avenue; Bea Wiser, 2203 Central Avenue; Janice Lightlee, 410 West Avenue; and Robert Leonard, 16 Rush Street.
- The finalists will prepare their brews the morning of October 27 at Smith's. Judging will begin at 10 A.M.
- The judges will be Mary Ames, two witches, and one warlock. The witches are Dame Ellen Mae and Flying Florence. The warlock goes by the name of Exzee. All three claim they were born in Transylvania.
- The winner will receive a one-week, all-expenses-paid trip for two to Salem, Massachusetts. The six runners-up will receive one year's supply of brooms. All seven finalists will also receive $100 worth of kitchenware from Smith's.

- Following the judging, the brews concocted by all seven will be available for sampling. The seven recipes will also be distributed.
- The public is invited.
- Smith's Kitchen Products Store sells a complete line of kitchenware and food products. It also owns the Ames Cooking School and provides free cooking lessons to customers who purchase a minimum of $500 worth of products a year.

For further information, contact Arnold Smith, 234-555-8901

SAMPLE PRESS RELEASE

FOR IMMEDIATE RELEASE

Contact: Arnold Smith
234-555-8901

TWO WITCHES AND ONE WARLOCK TO JUDGE ANNUAL "WITCHES BREW RECIPE CONTEST"

The fourth annual "Witches Brew Recipe Contest" finals will be held Saturday, October 27, at Smith's Kitchen Products Store, 1234 Main Street. The judging will begin at 10 A.M.

Two witches, Dame Ellen Mae and Flying Florence, and one warlock, Exzee, will join Mary Ames of the Ames Cooking School in judging the concoctions of the seven finalists. The public is invited to attend and will be able to sample all seven brews.

The entrant whose brew is judged the best will win a one-week, all-expenses-paid trip for two to Salem, Massachusetts. Runners-up will receive a one-year's supply of brooms. All seven will also receive $100 worth of kitchenware from Smith's.

The seven finalists are Sarah Kling, 444 East Oak Street; Arthur Goldler, 309 Stir Drive; Susan Major, 1 West 101st Street; Dorian Scali, 9 East Jefferson Avenue; Bea Wiser, 2203 Central Avenue; Janice Lightlee, 410 West Avenue; and Robert Leonard, 16 Rush Street.

NOTE: The format for a press release includes the following:

- Always use your company name and address at the top of the first page.
- Always indicate a release date, or "For Immediate Release."
- Always list a contact, along with telephone number where the person can be reached. That is the person for media to call if there are any questions. The contact must be knowledgeable and have your authorization to speak to any callers.
- The headline should tell, in a few words, what the story is all about. The headline on the release is not the headline that will appear in print. Newspapers write their own headlines.
- The first paragraph is the lead, and should tell the story as quickly as possible. It usually provides the basic facts: Who, What, When, Where, Why.
- The rest of the story is body text, where you present in greater detail the facts to back up the information in the lead.

PITCH LETTER/E-MAIL TO SEND TO MEDIA TO ARRANGE INTERVIEW WITH STORE OWNER

"Too many Americans spend too much money for unnecessary automobile repairs."

That's not a statement by Ralph Nader. It is by John Burns, owner of Burns Automotive and Repairs on 2343 Central Avenue. The 35-year old Burns, whose dealership sells more than 200 cars annually and services and repairs more than 3,000 cars a year, estimates that more than 20 percent of automotive repairs are unnecessary, or can be easily done by the car owner.

We thought you might like to have John appear on your program to discuss (for newspapers, substitute: to interview for a story on) the subject of unnecessary automotive repairs. Coming from someone in the business, it is bound to attract significant listener (for television use: viewer) interest.

Specific subjects John will be prepared to discuss include:

- How to determine if a repair is really necessary
- How to find out if you are being ripped off on the pricing for replacement parts
- Ten simple adjustments and repairs anyone can do and save $250 in the process

Along with this letter, I am sending John's biography, and a complete list of subjects he can discuss.

If you need additional information, please call me at 666-555-8888. NOTE: This format can be used for letters/e-mails sent to arrange newspaper, radio, or television interviews. If possible, start off with a dramatic opening line, which the recipients would not expect coming from a retailer.

PITCH LETTER/E-MAIL TO SEND TO TELEVISION PRODUCERS TO DEMONSTRATE NEW PRODUCTS ON SHOW

Christmas may be ten weeks away but Smith Toys has received its first shipment of Christmas toys.

There are a lot of exciting new toys being introduced this year:

- A singing country & western doll
- Night vision goggles similar to those used by the military
- A 100,000-piece jigsaw puzzle
- A remote-controlled talking robot
- A remote-controlled flying eagle

Arnold Smith, the owner of Smith toys would welcome the opportunity to appear on *This Day in Thistown,* along with the children of three customers, aged 5 to 7 to demonstrate the newest of the new Christmas toys.

It should make an interesting and informative segment for your viewers.

I am enclosing a fact sheet, which describes these new toys and games in greater detail.

I will call in three to four days to see if there is any interest on your part.

Many thanks for your consideration.

Arnold Smith
666-555-8888

NOTE: This letter can very easily be edited and used to pitch a newspaper story.

PITCH LETTER/E-MAIL TO ATTEMPT
TO ARRANGE A LIVE REMOTE

When was the last time you had a robot do the weather on the five o'clock news?

As a matter of fact, when did a robot ever do the weather at your station, or any other one in the area?

"Charley the Robot" is going to be at Olson's all day Friday, April 17, as part of our annual Spring promotion.

We thought it would be a pleasant change of pace for your viewers if Charley helped Bill Smith deliver his forecast that evening live from our store. Charley is quite a talker.

As part of our Spring promotion, we have two possible settings for the forecast: an April showers display of colorful umbrellas and rain slickers, or a May flowers display with a garden scene and live tulips.

We hope that you will be able to bring the weather center to our store on April 17.

John Olson
666-555-8888

LETTER TO MEDIA TO MAKE THEM AWARE
OF YOUR AVAILABILITY AS A SOURCE
OF INFORMATION

For the past 25 years, I have been involved in retail in Thistown as the owner of Larry's Women's Fashions. I have also served for four terms as president of the local merchants' association.

During this quarter century in retail, I have gained considerable expertise in several areas that might be of interest to you.

I would be very pleased to assist you in providing information anytime you may need material in the following areas:

- Women's Fashions. Our store has an excellent reputation among the fashion-conscious women of the community. We attend both the Paris and New York shows each year and can provide you with updates after each show. We also have an extensive collection of pictures of fashions from the past fifty years.

- The Changing Scene at Retail. We are active in several national retail organizations, as well as their local chapters, attend their conventions, and are up-to-date on what is going on in retail today, and what to expect in the future.
- Retail in Thistown. Having been president of the local merchants' association, I am very familiar with the problems local retailers face: taxes, fees, petty crime, zoning regulations, etc. Also the opportunities: good economic development, loyal, local customer base, absence of the big discount chains, good traffic control, and parking facilities in the downtown area.

You can call us anytime for information on any of these subjects or in any other areas in which you need input. Along with this letter, I am enclosing cards with both my home and business telephone numbers. You can call evenings and weekends, if necessary.

Hope we can be of help to you in the future.

LETTER TO RADIO AND TELEVISION PROMOTION DIRECTORS OFFERING TO PROVIDE PRIZES FOR CONTESTS

We have always enjoyed your station's listener (viewer for television) promotions, and have even entered a few of them ourselves.

While we have never been winners, we were wondering if we could do the next best thing: provide the prizes for the winners in your next contest?

Not only are we willing to provide the prizes but we will also assist you by promoting the contest in our Main Street windows, on our in-store signage, and in a mailing to our customers.

I will call you in a few days to see if we can get together and discuss this possible participation.

I look forward to talking to you.

LETTER TO RADIO AND TELEVISION PROGRAMS THAT GIVE GIFTS TO GUESTS

Guests are such an important part of your show that we feel they deserve nothing but the best when it comes to the gifts they receive for appearing.

That's why we would very much like to provide the gifts you give to your guests.

As you may know, we have been in business for over thirty-five years at the same location and have developed an excellent reputation for the fine quality of the merchandise in our store.

We would be willing to provide specific gifts, or even gift certificates. As part of our participation with your program, we will promote the show at our store.

I will call you next week to see if we can arrange this tie-in.

AND DON'T FORGET YOUR SUPPLIER PRESS RELEASES

As part of their marketing program, manufacturers often prepare press releases about their products, and send them to retailers for local use. By filling in a few spaces, you have a good localized press release to send to media.

If your suppliers send such material to you, be sure to use it. If they do not, ask that you be put on the mailing list to receive them. If need be, contact the public relations departments of your supplier companies and let them know you want to work with them.

23

—■■■—

Using Advertising and Other Paid Services to Promote Your Store

PUBLICITY ENABLES YOU to gain exposure in media without paying for the time and space. It will help you develop a positive image for the store, and will attract people to shop. However, you exercise very little control over how, when, or where your message appears because it is entirely up to the editors and broadcasters to make that decision. You are at their mercy.

The only guaranteed way of delivering the message you want delivered when you want it delivered to your customers and potential customers is through advertising and other paid marketing vehicles.

This chapter is designed to familiarize you with these paid outlets, and suggest various options you might exercise for organizing your advertising program

ORGANIZING YOUR ADVERTISING PROGRAM

The amount of money you plan to spend on advertising will generally determine how you should organize your program. If you have a very modest budget and can only afford a minimal effort, you would go in one direction. On the other hand, if you are willing to commit a substantial amount of money to a program, you may not have any alternative but to hire an advertising agency.

Before deciding on how to organize your effort, it is important that you realize how many different components comprise the planning and execution phases of an ongoing advertising program.

A few elements are:

- Planning a strategy that dovetails with your marketing and business plan
- Evaluating the available media and selecting from those that will provide the most effective and cost-efficient ways to reach your target audience
- Writing copy
- Designing layouts and preparing the artwork
- Taping and recording
- Buying time and space
- Production

Your Budget

The first step you should take is to allocate funds for your advertising budget. Only you know the costs of doing business and how much you can afford to spend on advertising. On the average, a retailer usually spends somewhere around 3 percent of gross sales. You should check with the national association that covers your field of retailing. Most associations have statistical data on advertising expenditures of member stores.

An Advertising Plan

No matter what the size of your budget, it is always a good idea to have an advertising plan. It serves as the blueprint for your program. It states your objectives, the budget, your media plan, creative approach, etc. A lot of the research you gathered (see chapter 4) will be included in the plan, too.

There are several ways to develop the plan. If you use an advertising agency, it will usually develop the plan for you. If not, contact the business schools at local universities to see if they have internships or team projects. If they do, see if you can arrange for your advertising plan to be developed as part of a team project, or by an intern. Other possibilities are to hire a marketing professor, a freelancer, or someone working at an advertising agency who wants to moonlight. Ask friends or fellow retailers for recommendations or place an advertisement in the classified section of the newspaper.

Conducting the Program

Because there are so many different elements in an advertising program, it will be virtually impossible to handle it all by yourself. The only exception might be if your entire program consists of Yellow Pages advertising, a few direct mail letters to customers, and/or a limited number of radio spots. In this case, Yellow Pages salespersons will usually help write your ad; some radio stations will do likewise; and you might be able to write your own direct mail letters.

The options for conducting the program include:

- Hiring an advertising agency. It is usually best to use a local agency, or one no more than fifty miles away. Ask for recommendations from friends, other business firms, and the local chamber of commerce. A helpful directory, which lists advertising agencies, staffs, and clients, is the *Standard Directory of Advertising Agencies.* It can usually be found at public and business libraries.

- Hiring an advertising manager. If you are spending a considerable amount of money, you might hire someone to coordinate and oversee the work of your agency, or to set up your own operation. This does not have to be a full-time job for the individual. He or she could be a semi-retired advertising executive who spends a day or two a week working for you, or a person who also has other responsibilities in the store.

- Using freelance help. Freelancers may be individuals moonlighting from their regular advertising jobs, or men and women who freelance full time. Call the advertising departments of local business firms for recommendations. Or, you can place an advertisement in the local newspaper. It is important that when you use freelance artists or writers that their work be supervised and that they be given direction. That is why it would be to your advantage to have some type of advertising manager overseeing the entire program.

Other Support

Look for support for your program from vendors and manufacturers. Check with your suppliers and determine what, if any, cooperative advertising programs and vendor support they offer. Most daily newspaper advertising departments can help you determine this information. Also see if the manufacturers have advertising slicks and other materials they will furnish free of charge. Check with local media to see what extras they might offer. Will they offer assistance in preparing ads? Do they offer free or low-cost audio- or videotaping facilities? Will they provide an announcer to do audio spots at no cost? Do they have any other special support programs? Do they offer research reports on the local population and its purchasing habits?

DELIVERING YOUR MESSAGE

There are about two dozen different types of paid outlets, which you can use to deliver your message. They range from newspapers, radio, cable, and network television to bus shelters, the Internet, and high school publications.

What do they offer?

Daily Newspapers

About 54 percent of adults read a newspaper on an average weekday, and more than 64 percent read one on an average Sunday. To obtain a newspaper, a person has to buy it and is obviously making an investment. As with all media advertising, whether or not the person sees your ad is another question. Dailies normally have an image of credibility among their readers and wide acceptance in the community. A daily newspaper offers a great deal of flexibility to the advertiser. You can pick the day of the week you want to run your ad; you can vary its size; and you can place the ad in the sections of the paper where you think you can best reach your audience. Moreover, you do not have a long lead time. You can quickly schedule an ad if the need suddenly arises. If you see that a competitor has drastically cut prices on a product, you can quickly prepare and run an ad meeting him or her head on, or even beating the price. Another benefit is that since today's newspaper is old tomorrow, readers can cut out and save your ad or coupons. They have a reminder of what to shop for, something they do not get from radio or television. If the newspaper has area sections, you can limit your message to the people you want to reach and greatly reduce your cost-per-thousand circulation. On the other hand, if you are in a very large city and there is only one edition, you may be paying for a lot of wasted circulation. When reading a newspaper, people usually do not get up to go to the bathroom or refrigerator when they get to an advertisement, something they may do when a commercial appears on television. Besides, even if they go to the bathroom when they reach your ad, it is still there on the same page when they return to the sofa. On the other hand, there is a lot of "clutter" in a newspaper. Since about 60 percent of the newspaper is advertising, readers may flip through pages of ads to get to the stories. There is no guarantee they will read your ad.

Weekly Newspapers

Since weekly newspapers usually cover a specific section of a city, they enable a retailer to carefully target the advertising to the audience he or she wants to reach.

There are several differences between weeklies and daily newspapers. While some weeklies are purchased, others are given away free of charge. The person picking up a free paper may not be as committed to it as he or she would be if a purchase was required. On the other hand, if it is the only weekly in that section of the city and does a good job, it could have as loyal and dedicated a readership as a paid circulation weekly. Unlike daily newspapers, some weeklies may not have their circulation verified by a recognized circulation auditing agency. You should ask your local weeklies how you can verify their circulation. Another difference is that, while you can vary the size of your ad, you don't have the flexibility of picking the day you want it to be published, and you have a longer lead deadline. Readers may also have a tendency to keep the paper for a longer period of time, and because of that, be reluctant to clip out an ad or coupon.

A very positive factor is that many readers look upon their weekly newspaper as their prime source for news about their neighbors and neighborhood. As a result, they probably read it more carefully than they do their daily newspaper. This could mean they become more aware of the ads and pay closer attention to them, especially since they, too, are from local merchants. Ask your local weekly newspapers to provide you with any research studies they have done on their readership patterns.

Radio

Radio is the only medium that can easily be with you all of the time. You can hear it at home, in the car, at work, on the beach, and even when walking down the street. With more than fifteen different formats (though all may not be available in every community), it offers you flexibility to target your audience based on the music (or talk) it prefers. It is a strong medium with younger demographics. Industry reports indicate that the average adult eighteen years and older spends three hours a day listening to radio.

Radio is probably the least expensive medium when it comes to production time and costs. A simple commercial may be read by an announcer, or taped (sometimes at the station). Even an elaborate radio spot will cost less than the production of a print ad, or a television commercial. Copy changes can be made very quickly, enabling you to react instantly on events that might have an impact on your store (snowy weather sale, arrival of a popular product, which had been on back order, etc.). A good catchy spot will attract listeners' attention and through repeated airings will leave an indelible impression on their minds.

A negative is that the listener does not have a permanent record of what is said during a spot and could forget sale items and other important information. Outside the home and office, chances are the listener cannot or will not take notes. Another negative is that if you only have a limited schedule with the station, a listener may miss your message because he or she wasn't tuned in when it ran.

Since radio audiences become attached to on-air personalities, many become highly credible spokespersons for advertisers. If your spots run on a program hosted by such a personality, it would be to your advantage to have him or her read them live.

Television

The medium with which people spend the most time each day is television. It is also the medium that enables you to reach the largest number of people at any one time. A television commercial can be very powerful and convey a strong message about your store, your products, and your image.

On the negative side, a good television spot is expensive to produce and may be beyond the reach of the average small retailer. With a limited budget, you would have to decide whether the production costs of a television commercial could be more effectively used to buy time or space in another medium. However, there may be ways to reduce production costs. Your suppliers may have spots about their products, which can be localized with your store's name. You might be able to get university students studying advertising or television production to shoot spots for you as part of a class project. Your local channels may also have ideas, or offer low-cost production facilities to get your business. Local cable systems also usually have facilities for shooting spots.

Cable

With so much highly specialized programming, cable enables you to target specific segments of the population through local spots on the networks that appeal to them. Over 60 percent of cable viewers have fifty-four or more choices. And if there are multiple cable providers in your area, you can also target your audience geographically. Cable viewing by affluent households is greater than broadcast TV, and penetration ratings and total cable viewership are growing consistently.

Since cable offers relatively low advertising rates, you can buy a considerable amount of time and achieve high ad repetition. However, ad clutter is a problem. So is satellite TV since homes that receive their cable programming via satellite do not receive the local commercials.

In examining cable, be certain to get as much local viewing data as possible. It is important to develop statistics on what percent of local cable viewers receive it via satellite. It could be very high in some areas. Also look into locally generated news shows and other programming as a possible advertising medium.

Magazines

There are three types of magazines you might consider: the locally published general city magazines, local business magazines, and the local/regional editions of national magazines.

Locally published city magazines usually have an upscale readership, and are favored as an advertising medium by restaurants and entertainment facilities as well as upscale boutiques and other retail establishments. They project a very high quality image, which will rub off on your store if you are an advertiser. Moreover, these city magazines are usually found in the waiting rooms of doctors, dentists, and attorneys, as well as other businesses, which results in extended visibility for your ad. In addition, home subscribers usually keep them for a period of time.

The local/regional editions of national magazines enable you to rub shoulders with the large national advertisers. It is good image building for your store to be included in a regional edition. You can then feature the ad on easels with the tag line "As Seen in *XXXXX*." Customers will be impressed.

But there are drawbacks as well. Costs can be high, especially if you draw the bulk of your customers from a small concentrated area of the city where the publication has good penetration, but which only represents a small percentage of its circulation. In this case, you will be paying a premium price for the circulation you want. On the other hand, the extended reach of the advertising may enable you to broaden the areas from where you will draw customers. Before making an advertising commitment, ask for a zip code breakdown of its subscribers.

If you have a limited budget, you must determine the value of going into one of these magazines on an infrequent basis. Are you getting maximum value when you combine space costs with ad preparation and production costs? You might be able to reach the same audience more efficiently, for example, with direct mail.

There is one exception. The Christmas gift-giving issues of the local city magazines are usually very well read and used as a shopping guide by their readers. It may be worth a one-shot effort.

Ethnic Publications

If large numbers of your customers belong to an ethnic group, or you are trying to reach out to a group, you should study its local publications as a possible advertising medium.

Ask for media kits to determine if the readership is the audience you are trying to attract to the store, as well as the audience that you already serve. As with all media you have under consideration, determine if the publication projects the same quality image that you want your advertising to project.

Another factor to weigh is whether or not you are already reaching your target audience through your general media advertising. If the answer is yes, you must determine if the additional advertising will reinforce your other message with this group, or if it is of no value. Ask for an audited circulation statement before placing any advertising.

Ethnic publications may fit in the same category as weekly newspapers in that they, too, may be more thoroughly read than dailies. This would have to be determined by reading any research reports they produce.

There may be other factors that will influence your decision to advertise.

Foreign Language Publications

If you have large numbers of foreign-born men and women who are your customers, as well as others you would like to attract, determine if they read any foreign language newspapers. If they do, look into the possibility of advertising in one or more. Your advertising might not be on a regular schedule, but it might be good politics to advertise in issues around the holiday season, around the country's national anniversary day, etc.

Your advertising should be in the language of the newspaper, and you should consider asking the advertising staff of the newspaper to translate it for you. You should also have the translation checked by at least two other sources to make certain it is correct.

Tourist Publications

If one of your goals is to attract visitors to the city to your store, you should examine the various tourist publications distributed to visitors at hotels, airports, restaurants, and convention centers. You should also consider advertising in the programs of the various trade shows, which bring out-of-town visitors to the city. Since these are giveaways, it may be impossible to get an audited circulation report. What you should do is check the various hotel front desks and other places where the magazines are supposed to be distributed in order to make certain that they are actually available. Do this several times over a few months' period. Visitors do use these guides for selecting entertainment and dining facilities, as well as sightseeing. How often they use these guides for shopping recommendations is something you should check out. Call other advertisers and ask them if they are satisfied with the response to their advertisements. Also ask the publisher for any research he or she might have on the subject.

Advertising in these guides will probably only be successful for you if you are located in the areas where tourists stay or visit, or if you are offering a unique product or product line or exceptionally good pricing on well-known products (watches, etc.). It may be a good idea to offer a discount in your ad if the tourist brings it to the store. This would enable you to pinpoint its effectiveness.

Other Publications

There are probably dozens of other types of publications in your area where you might consider placing an ad from time to time. They can include high school, college, union, and military publications, as well as those published by fraternal, religious, business, civic, veterans, patriotic, senior citizens, and nonprofit organizations. There may also be programs of balls and fund-raising banquets, and theater programs. The list is endless.

You will probably want to consider a regular schedule only if you see a group as a source of important customers. For example, if your product line is aimed at teenagers, you might advertise in high school and/or college publications. You will probably find the costs for this advertising quite low. If you offer special pricing for senior citizens, you may want to run ads in their publications, especially around May, which is Senior Citizen Month.

In other publications, you may want to run advertising in conjunction with special promotions aimed at the groups. If you run a Veterans Day promotion, you may want to take out small space ads in the veterans' organizations' newsletters "saluting" the veterans on their day, and announcing the promotion. You will probably get good response from advertising in these newsletters because the membership appreciates this type of acknowledgment.

Theater-program advertising can be an effective buy for restaurants in the area where the theaters are located, as well as if theater patrons are part of your target audience.

Internet

Internet advertising might be beneficial for calling attention to your Web site or just your store name. If you do such advertising you should consider the Web sites of local media, as well as any city sites in which listings are available. The negative is that many Internet users tune out such advertising or block them out with software designed for that purpose.

Like the entire e-commerce picture, Internet advertising should be closely followed to see in what direction it is heading.

Yellow Pages

At one time the Yellow Pages were one of the most important local publications for the retailer. However, right now their effectiveness is questionable. Everybody is getting into the act and in some cities it is not unusual to find three or more companies publishing their own editions and distributing them door to door. Which one the consumer keeps and refers to is unknown so you are taking a very big gamble by placing an ad in any single edition. And it probably isn't worth the money to advertise in all of them in a multibook area. Besides, you already have a listing in the Yellow Pages. You might want to evaluate online directories.

Other negatives of multibook Yellow Pages are that if you do buy an ad in one it can only be changed once a year, and you are lumped together on the same page as your competitors.

A possible positive use for restaurants would be to consider running a page ad with their menu. However, you still have the problem of which book to go into, and you cannot change the menu ad for a year.

Shelter Advertising

Bus shelter advertising continues to grow. While buses stop at these shelters, their passengers are just one audience reached. Motorists and pedestrians are also targets for the advertising. You will probably want any bus shelter advertising you do to be within a two- to three-mile radius of your store, especially if it is within the area from which you draw most of your customers. You should also consider using the shelters of the bus routes that lead to your store.

Telephone Side Panels

Similar in concept to shelter advertising, these back-lit panels are on outdoor telephone kiosks in heavily traveled areas. They are easily visible to both pedestrians and motorists. They offer excellent creative opportunities. You might buy into kiosks on the streets surrounding your store, offering directions on how to reach it. "Turn right on Rush Street and walk 30 feet to our front door." "Walk two blocks north and turn left," etc.

Parking Meters

This is one of the latest areas to place advertising. Since the space is small, all you can get on it is your store name and perhaps a line of copy. You would want meters in the vicinity of your place of business.

Transit

Airport and bus terminals, railroad stations, bus and train interiors, side and rear panels on buses, and taxi roofs are other locations that might fill your advertising needs. Factors to consider include the traffic patterns of your customers and potential customers, the visibility you will receive in the community, and the cost effectiveness.

Airport advertising would only be effective if you are courting tourists, or your customer base consists of many frequent travelers. Bus terminal and railroad station advertising would also only be effective if your customers use these facilities.

Exterior and interior bus advertising and interior train advertising can be effective if you can target it for those routes and lines that customers would take to reach your store. An advantage of exterior bus advertising is that it is highly visible to both motorists and pedestrians. Motorists stuck in traffic behind or alongside a bus can never forget the advertising on its exterior.

Outdoor

Effective for communicating simple ideas and for reinforcing and reminding consumers of advertising messages communicated through other media, outdoor advertising is a cost-efficient buy and can usually be strategically located on routes leading to your store.

There are, however, several negatives. You must determine if outdoor advertising will be effective in reaching your audience. It is possible that billboards may never come within view of your customers or target audience, especially if they and the store are located within a city's borders. If your billboard is off a fast-moving highway, motorists will not have much time to read more than one strong message, and it has to be a simple one at that. Another negative can be public opinion. There are groups of people and even entire communities who have been fighting to eliminate billboards. If there is active opposition to billboard advertising in your community, you should study the situation before coming to a decision to use them.

Stadium, Aerial, and Other Outdoor Advertising

There are several other ways to advertise your message out of doors: at sports stadiums, using outdoor balloons and airplanes, your own trucks and vehicles, and even bumper stickers.

Sports stadiums, as well as indoor arena advertising can be an exceptionally good buy if your advertising is strategically located so that it will be picked up during television coverage of games. Near the scoreboard is always a good location. Ask the stadium marketing people for game videotapes so that you can study the camera angles. Same with hockey and basketball: study game tapes before making an indoor arena buy.

Aerial advertising also attracts attention and is effective in areas where it can be used. Since September 11, 2001, there have been restrictions placed on such flyovers at certain locations including sports stadiums. Before agreeing to any contract, insist on a map of the flight pattern and use it to evaluate whether it would be an effective buy.

Any vehicles you have, especially those of your service force if you have one, should carry store signage that projects a positive image of your business. They are a moving advertisement for your store as they drive through the community.

You might also develop a unique and attractive bumper sticker and give it to your customers. If it is unique and not very commercial, many will probably use it. An example: if you sell baby clothing, a "Baby on Board" sticker with a small size store logo.

Flyers and Bulletin Board Posters

Both flyers and bulletin board posters can serve an important function in your marketing mix.

Bulletin board posters can be used to support any special sales and promotions you conduct throughout the year, which are aimed at segments of the population. For example, if you run special sales for senior citizens, send posters to each senior citizen center and organization for their bulletin boards. Do the same with veterans' organizations if you run a Veterans Day promotion. You can also send bulletin board posters to business firms, apartment houses, fraternal organizations, and military bases in the vicinity of the store when you are running special events or general sales.

Flyers can be used many ways, depending upon your type of store. You could have someone distributing them in the streets around the store (if it is legal in the community, and you do not feel it will reflect negatively on the image of the store). You could also distribute them in bulk at apartment complexes, business firms, under doors (again if it does not compromise your image). It is also possible to arrange to have flyers inserted and distributed in local newspapers. If you check with your daily newspaper(s), they can tell you if it's possible to insert them by distribution zone.

Direct Mail

A very effective technique for targeting specific groups by location, interests, product use, and even demographics, direct mail offers you great flexibility in presenting your message.

The disadvantages include relatively high cost per contact, a low response rate, and its image. Too many people regard it as junk mail, and it is said that as much as half is thrown away without being opened. However, if your store has a good image and reputation in the community, chances are a higher percentage of people will open the mail it receives from your store.

Because of cost, ideally you should rely on a Web site and e-mail to keep your customers informed about sales, special events, and other information you would communicate through direct mail.

Since you cannot send e-mail to people who do not request it, it makes it more difficult to reach potential customers directly unless you use the mails. You might want to try some small, carefully targeted mailings to see if they bring in new customers. Your mailing should include an appealing offer, perhaps $10 off on the first purchase of $50 or more.

A less expensive way to participate in a direct-mail campaign is to go into a group mailing where expenses are shared. There might be marketing groups within the community who arrange such mailings. There is also a national firm, Valpak, which operates in over two hundred cities in the United States. It breaks its mailings into groupings of approximately ten thousand homes by carrier routes. By grouping retailers together, it can produce a mailing for a retailer for around $400. This not only includes the mailing but also the design, layout, and printing of the mailing insertion. If you cannot find the nearest Valpak office, go to their Web site **www.valpak.com.**

Coffee Sleeve Advertising

The newest advertising medium is on coffee sleeves, which slip over the paper take-out cups so drinkers do not burn themselves. It is a good way to literally get your message into the hands of potential customers. Brite Vision Media sells the advertising space and places the sleeves at locations where paper cups are used. Its Web site is **www.britevision.com.**

THERE ARE SO MANY OTHER WAYS

There are countless other ways for gaining exposure. They include messages on your postage meter, attractive shopping bags, in-store PA-system announcements, and advertising messages on the plastic bags newspapers sometimes use for home delivery.

Let your imagination run away with itself.

THE MOST EFFECTIVE ADVERTISING

The most effective advertising is also the least expensive. It is word-of-mouth advertising, with the words coming from the mouths of satisfied customers. This book contains the ideas and techniques aimed at making your customers happy and satisfied with all aspects of their shopping experience. We hope you have initiated, or will, some of the ideas and techniques so that you, too, can be the beneficiary of this priceless word-of-mouth advertising.

24

■ ■ ■

Need Help?

THERE IS PLENTY of help available to the small retailer, both on-line and through direct contact.

We suggest you start off by going to the Small Business Administration (SBA) home page at **www.sba.gov.** You will not only find descriptions of the many programs available, as well as the listings of its network of Small Business Development Centers, Small Business Information Centers, and SCORE (Service Corps of Retired Executives) offices. They provide a wide variety of information and guidance free of charge.

■ The Small Business Development Center program is a cooperative effort of the private sector; the educational community; and federal, state, and local governments. They provide management and technical assistance.

■ SCORE, a nonprofit association dedicated to entrepreneur education and the formation, growth, and success of small businesses nationwide, is a resource partner with SBA. Many retired retailers volunteer their time and have been extremely helpful, to the extent of even visiting the locations of the retailers they counsel. This service is also free of charge. You might also visit SCORE's Web site **www.score.org.**

■ The Small Business Information Centers provide a one-stop location where current and future small business owners can receive assistance and advice. The centers combine the latest computer technology, hardware and software, an extensive small business reference library of books and publications, and current management videotapes to help people plan their business, expand an existing business, or venture into new business areas.

Also log on to the Small Business Development Center National Information Clearing House **www.sbdcnet.utsa.edu.** It offers a wealth of information and has links to other Web sites as well as trade magazines and associations.

The New York Public Library Small Business Resource Center also has a wealth of information. Its Web site is **www2.nypl.org/smallbiz.**

Other Web sites have been provided throughout the book. We strongly suggest that you go online and search "retail marketing," "retail research," "small business," and "retail associations."

Chase's Calendar of Events is a good reference book to use to learn more about the holidays celebrated by just about every religion, as well as the national holidays of all the countries of the world. It also has information about thousands of "off-the-wall" events, some of which, depending on your customers and store, might be something to consider if you want to try an offbeat promotion. Many libraries have the book. It not, it is available from Contemporary Books, Two Prudential Plaza, Suite 1200, Chicago, IL 60601–6790.

Index

questionnaire for, 44–47
telephone interview, 48–49
Welcome Back party, 124
Frequent Buyer's Program, 37,
173–81
Frequent customers. *See*
Customer reward
programs
Front door
appearance/design, 74–75
host at, 76

Games of chance, ideas for,
148–50
Gift baskets, 247
Gift certificates, 11, 100, 178
Gift registry, 182
Gift service, 181
Gift wrapping, 64
Giveaways
illustration competition
calendar, 153–54
logo on, 195
promotional, 91, 94, 97, 99,
103, 104–5, 107
sales calendar, 144–45
Graduation month,
promotion, 101–2
Grandparents Day sale, 143

Halloween events, 107, 153
Handicrafts exhibit, 127–28
Happy Hour sales, 133–34
Health screenings, 129
High school newspapers, 267
Hiring, sales personnel, 56–57
Hispanic Heritage Month,
promotion, 105
Hispanics, growth of
population, 16–17
Holiday promotions, 88–110
African American History
month, 93
Armed Forces Day, 101
Chinese New Year, 92
Christmas, 109–10
Christmas in August (CIA),
103–4
Cinco de Mayo, 99
Columbus Day, 105–6
Easter, 98–99
Elvis Presley's birthday, 91
ethnic/religious sensitivity,
110
graduation month, 101–2
Halloween, 107
Hispanic Heritage Month,
105

Independence Day, 102–3
information (*Chase's
Calendar of Events*), 296
Labor Day, 104–5
Mardi Gras, 95
Martin Luther King, Jr. Day,
92
Mother's Day/Father's Day,
100
New Year, 90–91
Presidents' Day, 94–95
by restaurants, 226–27
St. Patrick's Day, 95–97
scope of promotion, 89
special shopping nights, 123
Super Bowl, 92
Thanksgiving, 108–9
Valentine's Day, 93–94
Veterans Day, 107–8
Winter Festival, 97–98
Hospital gift shops, 19
Hot line, for customers, 65
House calls, 247–48
Husbands' corner, 65

Immigration, trends, 16–17
In-store food service, 20–21
Incentive program, for sales
personnel, 60–61
Independence Day, promotion,
102–3
Independent research firms, as
information source, 30
Interior of store, 75–76
display tips, 75–77
movement control, 76
promotions, space
requirements, 85–86
promotions and decorations,
89
signs in, 77–78
International Music Products
Association, 14
International products,
promotion of, 96, 106,
124–25
Internet
e-mail program, 229–30, 290
online sales, growth of, 18
Web site for business,
230–32, 290
Internship programs, 251
Interviews, telephone
interview, 36–37, 47–49

Kmart, 21
Kosher food, 20
Kwanzaa, promotion, 109

Labor Day, promotion, 104–5
Late Night Sale, 137
Leap year sale, 140
Library
as information source, 29
special events, 128–29
Lighting, in store, 76
Literature rack, 79–80
Live entertainment. *See*
Performers
Liven It Up program, 11
Location
convenience of, 54–55
expanding to other
locations, 189–90
Logo, on clothing items,
195
Lost customers. *See* Former
customers
Lottery sale, 137
Lounge/sitting area, 65, 79
Low-pricing approach, 54

Magazines
coverage, 266
paid advertising, 286–87
Magicians, 117, 220
Main Street Program, 11–12
Mardi Gras, promotion, 95
Markdowns. *See* Sales
Marketing strategy
convenient location, 54–55
goal of, 51
pricing policy, 53–54
product line, 52–53
and research, 22–50
sales force, 55–61
Martin Luther King, Jr. Day,
promotion, 92
Media
cable TV, 265–66
community media, 263–67
fact sheet, 271, 273–74
frequent buyer's program
promotion, 178–79
general letter, 277–79
holiday promotions, 91, 95,
105
initial contact, 252
live performances, 119
magazines, local, 266,
286–87
media advisory, 270, 272
newspapers, 261–65, 267–69,
283–84, 287–88
pitch letter to, 262, 270,
271–72, 275–77
press release, 271, 274–75